Queering
the
Gothic

~

MANCHESTER
1824

Manchester University Press

Queering the Gothic

∼

EDITED BY

William Hughes and Andrew Smith

MANCHESTER UNIVERSITY PRESS

MANCHESTER AND NEW YORK

distributed in the United States exclusively by Palgrave Macmillan

Copyright © Manchester University Press 2009

While copyright in the volume as a whole is vested in Manchester University Press, copyright in individual chapters belongs to their respective authors, and no chapter may be reproduced wholly or in part without the express permission in writing of both author and publisher.

Published by Manchester University Press
Oxford Road, Manchester M13 9NR, UK
and Room 400, 175 Fifth Avenue, New York, NY 10010, USA
www.manchesteruniversitypress.co.uk

Distributed in the United States exclusively by
Palgrave Macmillan, 175 Fifth Avenue,
New York, NY 10010, USA

Distributed in Canada exclusively by
UBC Press, University of British Columbia, 2029 West Mall,
Vancouver, BC, Canada V6T 1Z2

British Library Cataloguing-in-Publication Data is available

Library of Congress Cataloging-in-Publication Data is available

ISBN 978 0 7190 8643 4 paperback

First published by Manchester University Press in hardback 2009

This paperback edition first published 2011

The publisher has no responsibility for the persistence or accuracy of URLs for any external or third-party internet websites referred to in this book, and does not guarantee that any content on such websites is, or will remain, accurate or appropriate.

Printed by Lightning Source

FOR VIC SAGE

Contents

	Acknowledgements	page ix
	Notes on contributors	xi
1	Introduction: Queering the Gothic *William Hughes* and *Andrew Smith*	1
2	'Love in a convent': or, Gothic and the perverse father of queer enjoyment *Dale Townshend*	11
3	'Do you share my madness?': *Frankenstein*'s queer Gothic *Mair Rigby*	36
4	Daniel Deronda's Jewish panic *Royce Mahawatte*	55
5	'That mighty love which maddens one to crime': medicine masculinity, same-sex desire and the Gothic in *Teleny* *Diane Mason*	73
6	Gothic landscapes, imperial collapse and the queering of Adela Quested in E. M. Forster's *A Passage to India* *Ardel Thomas*	89
7	Antonia White's *Frost in May*: Gothic mansions, ghosts and particular friendships *Paulina Palmer*	105
8	Devouring desires: lesbian Gothic horror *Gina Wisker*	123
9	'The taste of blood meant the end of aloneness': vampires and gay men in Poppy Z. Brite's *Lost Souls* *William Hughes*	142
10	Michael Jackson's queer funk *Steven Bruhm*	158
11	Death, art, and bodies: queering the queer Gothic in Will Self's *Dorian* *Andrew Smith*	177
	Index	193

Acknowledgements

We would like to express our gratitude to everyone who supported this project and commented upon various parts of it. We would like to acknowledge the support and encouragement of our colleagues at Bath Spa University and the University of Glamorgan, and in particular would like to thank Professor Jeff Wallace and Dr Bryony Randall for their comments on sections of the manuscript. We would also like to thank the anonymous readers at Manchester University Press for their helpful advice and Matthew Frost, senior commissioning editor at the Press, for his continued enthusiasm for the project.

Finally, we would also like to thank Felicity Hidderley and Joanne Benson for their tolerance and support throughout the editing of this project.

William Hughes and Andrew Smith

Notes on contributors

Steven Bruhm is Robert and Ruth Lumsden Professor of English at the University of Western Ontario, London, Canada. He is the author of *Gothic Bodies: The Politics of Pain in Romantic Fiction* (1994) and *Reflecting Narcissus: A Queer Aesthetic* (2000), as well as authoring numerous articles on Gothicism and queerness. He is co-editor, with Natasha Hurley, of *Curiouser: On the Queerness of Children* (2004), and is currently at work on a project entitled 'Only the Dead Can Dance: Choreographies of Mortality'.

William Hughes is Professor of Gothic Studies at Bath Spa University. He is the author of *Beyond Dracula: Bram Stoker's Fiction and Its Cultural Context* (2000) and, with Richard Dalby, the co-compiler of *Bram Stoker: A Bibliography* (2004). He is editor of *Gothic Studies*, the refereed journal of the International Gothic Association and, with Andrew Smith, has co-edited *Bram Stoker: History, Psychoanalysis and the Gothic* (1998); *Empire and the Gothic: The Politics of Genre* (2003) and *Fictions of Unease: The Gothic from Otranto to The X-Files* (with Andrew Smith and Diane Mason, 2002).

Royce Mahawatte holds degrees from the universities of London, Oxford and East Anglia. He is an Associate Lecturer in the Department of Cultural and Historical Studies at the University of the Arts, London, and is preparing a monograph on George Eliot and the Gothic.

Diane Mason is a freelance writer and occasional lecturer in English Literature at Bath Spa University, where she researched her PhD on Victorian fiction and medical culture. She is the author of *The Secret Vice: Masturbation in Victorian Fiction and Medical Culture* (Manchester University Press, 2008) and co-editor of *Fictions of Unease: The Gothic from Otranto to The X-Files* (2002). She has recently co-edited a new scholarly edition of *Dracula* (2007) and has contributed articles to journals including *Gothic Studies* and *Women's Writing*.

Paulina Palmer was, before retiring, senior lecturer in the English Department at Warwick University and taught on the Women's Studies MA. She now teaches part-time for the Gender Studies MA at Birkbeck, University of London.

NOTES ON CONTRIBUTORS

Her publications include: *Contemporary Women's Fiction: Narrative Practice and Feminist Theory* (1989); *Contemporary Lesbian Writing: Dreams, Desire, Difference* (1993); and *Lesbian Gothic: Transgressive Fictions* (1999). She is currently working on a book entitled *The Queer Uncanny*.

Mair Rigby is an Associate Tutor in English Literature at Cardiff University. Her PhD thesis explored the extent to which queer theory and Gothic fiction can be considered mutually illuminating fields of academic inquiry, focusing particularly on Mary Shelley and her novel *Frankenstein*. She has published an essay on John Polidori in *Romanticism on the Net* and has an essay discussing female desire in *Frankenstein* forthcoming in an edited collection.

Andrew Smith is Professor of English Studies at the University of Glamorgan where he is Co-Director of the Research Centre for Literature, Arts and Science (RCLAS). He is the author of the *Edinburgh Critical Guide to Gothic Literature* (2007); *Victorian Demons: Medicine, Masculinity and the Gothic at the Fin de Siècle* (2004) and *Gothic Radicalism: Literature, Philosophy and Psychoanalysis in the Nineteenth Century* (2000). He has co-edited eight volumes of essays. He is the co-series editor of *Gothic Literary Studies*, and *Gothic Authors: Critical Revisions*, published by the University of Wales Press.

Ardel Thomas is currently the Chair of Lesbian, Gay, Bisexual, and Transgender Studies at the City College of San Francisco. She received her PhD in Modern Thought and Literature from Stanford University with a concentration in nineteenth century queer Gothic horror. Her publications include *Writing for Real: A Handbook for Writers in Community Service* (2003) co-authored with Carolyn Ross. She has published widely on the Gothic and is currently writing a book on queer Victorian Gothic horror for the University of Wales Press.

Dale Townshend is a Lecturer in English Studies at the University of Stirling, where he teaches on the MLitt in The Gothic Imagination. His publications include *The Orders of Gothic: Foucault, Lacan, and the Subject of Gothic Writing, 1764-1820* (2007); *Gothic: Critical Concepts in Literary and Cultural Studies* (2004), co-edited with Fred Botting, and *Gothic Shakespeares* (2008), co-edited with John Drakakis. He is currently at work on a project on suicide in Romantic-era writing.

Gina Wisker is a Professor and Head of the Centre for Teaching and Learning at Brighton University. She has published widely on pedagogic issues and literary topics. Her most recent books include *Key Concepts in Postcolonial Fiction* (2007); *The Postgraduate Research Handbook* (second edition, 2007); *Horror Fiction* (2005); and *Postcolonial and African American Women's Writing* (2000). She is the editor of *Dissections: The Journal of Contemporary Horror*.

1

Introduction:
Queering the Gothic

∼

William Hughes and Andrew Smith

Gothic has, in a sense, always been 'queer'. The genre, until comparatively recently, has been characteristically perceived in criticism as being poised astride the uneasy cultural boundary that separates the acceptable and familiar from the troubling and different.[1] Gothic is, in this respect, a compromise, a balance between the conflicting tastes and aspirations of orthodoxy and heterodoxy. On the one hand, Gothic has both maintained and displayed many of the stylistic and structural devices associated with the non-Gothic literatures which have preceded and accompanied it from the mid eighteenth century to the present. On the other, these possibly superficial appropriations tend to mobilise unpalatable if not actually taboo issues – such as sexual deviance, arbitrary power, miscegenation and apostasy – even where a fearful publishing industry demands that these troubling things should be contained by the eventual triumph of a familiar morality. In consequence, the genre frequently espouses a characteristically conservative morality, and frequently a conventional and rather public heterosexuality. Yet, even as it appears to function as a curious bastion of acceptable behaviours, the inconsistency of Gothic proclaims a brittleness of definition which is imperfectly concealed by plot and characterisation.

For all its superficial resemblance to more mainstream literary modes, Gothic historically appears to lack the commitment to absolute definitions of identity and substance that arguably characterise such mainstream literatures. Even where conventional moralities and identities are proclaimed as ultimately triumphant in a Gothic text, the very fact that they have been challenged signifies that they have been interrogated and, if their boundaries have been tested, then they have equally been contemplated.[2] The questionable moment, however brief, hints of pleasures still unrealised or unavailable but now known. Known and experienced, even vicariously, they become now a temptation, now an alternative. They trouble the mind, expand its capability to look beyond the obvious and immediate. To condemn Gothic for its perceived 'bad taste' is, in essence, to condemn it for acknowledging those very alternatives to monolithic orthodoxy. The endurance of 'taste' will always be compromised by the presence of 'bad taste'. To be queer in Gothic terms is, in a sense, to know both, seemingly to adhere to one and yet to desire (even in the form of vicarious enjoyment) the other. It is to juxtapose the familiar and the unfamiliar, the rational and the supernatural, the past and the present, the acceptable and the condemnable. Gothic is dangerous, as a morally pernicious literature, not for the conclusions it reaches but for the unease encountered in the fictional progress towards denouement. The tempting 'queerness' that Gothic presents is thus that of assimilation to the alternative, acceptance of the valid claims of heterodoxies that might be, variously, cultural, theological, political or, indeed, sexual.

There is, of course, a literal queerness – in the popular, sexual, sense of that term – about many of the authors conventionally regarded as being central to the development of Gothic. The documented same-sex affiliations of Horace Walpole and many of his successors from William Beckford to Oscar Wilde, and from Jewelle Gomez to the anthologist of lesbian vampire narratives, Pam Keesey, cannot be denied. Similarly, contemporary Gothic writers, such as Anne Rice and Poppy Z. Brite, irrespective of their stated sexual orientation, have successfully established a literary presence in recent gay consciousness.[3] In criticism, also, apparently heterosexual authors from earlier periods – most notably Bram Stoker – have become scripted as closet or repressed homosexuals.[4] Caution must be employed here, however. Any undue stress on the production of Gothic by gay and lesbian authors, whether their sexuality be closet or public, would serve to negate the contribution of those participants in the genre who, to all intents and purposes, parallel a heterosexual narrative with a heterosexual lifestyle. Gothic is not, and has never been, an exclusively homosexual genre. Its queerness, therefore, is more than a matter of encoded sexual preferences and identities.

The queer Gothic, it may be argued, is predicated upon something more pervasive and, at times, more elusive than sexual identity. It is more, even, than the campness with which Gothic is so frequently – and so glibly

– associated in criticism. However, that camp quality which proclaims, often self-consciously and even humorously, both an awareness of difference and an expression of the power to mock, surprise and shock, may well be a key to the more elusive queerness of the genre.

To be queer, when taken outside of the sexual connotations of that term, is to be different. The essence of that difference is vested not merely in terms of how one (or of how one's work) is perceived by an avowedly non-queer world but also in how the queer self (or the queer text) relates to the very expression of queerness. Queerness, in this sense, is a quality which may be said to inflect a sense of difference not confined simply to sexual behaviour but which may equally inform a systematic stylistic deviance from perceived norms in personal style or artistic preference. Horace Walpole's relationship to the Enlightenment politics and architecture of his day, for example, is, by this definition, as queer as Oscar Wilde's self-imposed aesthetic distance from the hearty masculinity of the late Victorian age of empire and industry. One might consider, too, that Poppy Z. Brite's self-conscious adoption of Gothic tropes in her long and short fiction is a form of performance that parallels her own self-confessed status as a sexual polygamist and onstage exhibitionist.[5] Brite's fiction consistently focuses its gaze upon outsiders and social misfits who, if they find it at all, gain solace only in the company of other heteronormative outcasts; Brite herself is an outsider, her provocatively fragmentary biography suggests, even when she is in the company of lovers.[6] Even when her lovers are heterosexual, Brite herself is somehow queer, and with a queerness that far exceeds the specific homosexual content that has seen her work applauded by an aware gay readership.[7]

Queer is, in this respect, a matter of both setting oneself aside (personally or artistically) as different, and of reflecting upon that process by a textuality that may lie at any point between camp parody and confrontational acerbity. Queer, like Gothic (and, for Brite, like Goth also), is both performance and style, and the very nature of this process means that it will exist in a tense space between referential association with the normative and absolute separation from its morals and aesthetics. To be queer is to be different, yet it is also to be unavoidably associated with the non-queer, the normative which, though it implicitly represses through the mechanisms of conformist culture, may yet serve as the catalyst to liberation. The two states exist in reciprocal tension. If the queer is to be regarded as the abjected demon of the non-queer, then the reverse may also apply. In queer terms, one may be – horror of horrors – a closet heterosexual, and one's literary queerness may be subsumed within a conformist conception of genre and expression. One may compromise, or may have to compromise: to be queer is to be poised always upon the threshold of the non-queer.

Bearing this in mind, Susan Stryker's highly personal 1998 definition of the relationship between a queer sexuality and a broader and more pervasive heteronormative queerness may be seen as highly relevant to the Gothic's own exemplification of unorthodox or transgressive identities and practices. For Stryker, to be queer is to be different but not necessarily to be isolated. The sexual queer is, in fact, but one of many parallel identities in an underworld of heterodoxies. Prefacing the 1998 'Transgender Issue' of *GLQ: A Journal of Lesbian and Gay Studies*, she writes:

> I named myself queer in 1990. In doing so, I felt I could complete the statement 'I am a —' for the first time in my life without adding any caveats. The term allowed me to align myself with other antiheteronormative identities and socio-political formations without erasing the specificity of my sense of self or the practices I engaged in to perform myself for others. By becoming queer first, I found that I could then become transsexual in a way I had not previously considered.[8]

Queer is, in this sense, community – and, if it has a sexual origin as a theoretical or critical term, then that origin has in a sense provided a vehicle through which difference of all kinds might conveniently be mobilised. The queer thing about Gothic is that it refuses to be exclusively queer in the sexual sense, and the queerness of Gothic is such that its main function is to demonstrate the relationship between the marginal and the mainstream, between reciprocal states of queerness and non-queerness.

The queer *in* Gothic is thus, in this respect, fundamental to the whole cultural project that *is* Gothic. Its presence not merely acknowledges but also codifies difference. It further exemplifies how that heterodox state, though defined by orthodoxy, may persist successfully (for a time at least) when fictionalised as being subject to its own rules and conventions. Hence, the queer may be said to effectively deconstruct the very standards by which its own 'deviance' is reckoned and quantified. If the queer state may persist successfully, even if only for a short disruptive period, then it retains the potential to construct itself as a viable alternative to all that is not-queer. Though not structured from its outset as integral to the broad, revisionist 'queer project', with its aggressive queering of intellectual history as envisaged by Donald E. Hall, the queer content of Gothic none the less establishes the same type of involuntary 'broad alliances' between queer and non-queer identities: thus, 'we find telling traces of the "abnormal" even among "normal" (canonical, heterosexual) philosophers and theorists' and 'the credibility of the very concept "normality" is thereby rendered highly questionable'.[9] The very presence of the queer makes the assigning of Absolutes, in fiction as much as in criticism, a futile act.

If feminist criticism and its descendants in gender studies have, as Susan Gubar suggests, 'lost their political urgency and become "established" in a really clichéd ivory-tower way',[10] and if Gothic, too, has moved from the margins to the mainstream of academe, then the conjunction of the two represents both a necessary step and a vital opportunity for criticism.[11] Though Gothic has historically been queer, the recognition of the breadth and the critical implications of that term have come to critical awareness painfully late. A reconsideration of the queerness of Gothic will push the genre, in critical terms at least, once more away from the comfortable centre and back towards the uneasy margins of transgression and experimentation – a place where it undoubtedly belongs.

In '"Love in a convent": or, Gothic and the perverse father of queer enjoyment', Dale Townshend (Chapter 2) provides a queer reading of such early Gothic romances as William Beckford's *Vathek* (1786), Matthew Gregory Lewis's *The Monk* (1796) and Charles Maturin's *Melmoth the Wanderer* (1820). Taking his theoretical cue from Michel Foucault's discursive history of perversion and Jacques Lacan's account of perversion as *père-version*, Townshend argues that the queerness of early Gothic writing resides as much in its historical positioning as it does in the constructions of paternity to which it gives form. Through an account of Foucault's later turn towards ethics, Townshend's chapter concludes with a focus upon the easily overlooked ethical dimensions to the queerness of the masculine Gothic mode.

In recent years there has been a steady proliferation of academic publications addressing the extent to which *Frankenstein* (1831) can be read as a tale of dangerous queer sexuality. In particular, the work of queer theorists, such as Eve Kosofsky Sedgwick, has led scholars working within the fields of both Gothic and Queer Studies to read this text as one that is particularly concerned with desire between men.[12] Building upon this critical trend, Mair Rigby in '"Do you share my madness?": *Frankenstein*'s queer Gothic' (Chapter 3) develops the question of *Frankenstein*'s engagement with sexual rhetoric in the early nineteenth century in order to explore further some of the ways in which the signifying practices of queerness are written into the language and, therefore, the signifying practices of Gothic fiction. Taking a broadly Foucauldian approach, Rigby proposes that many of the conventions, signs, codes, linguistic figures, narrative devices and rhetorical tropes that have come to be recognisable to readers as 'Gothic' can be recognised also as signifying 'queer'. Moreover, Gothic fiction still has much to reveal about sexual discourse and, in this respect, *Frankenstein* is a productive text for discussing how the genre can illustrate modern western culture's tendency to produce the possibility of sexual nonconformity as a kind of Gothic horror story.

In 'Daniel Deronda's Jewish panic', Royce Mahawatte (Chapter 4), develops the issue of cultural visibility by suggesting that George Eliot seemingly flouts Gothic conventions by explicitly, in *Daniel Deronda* (1876), representing the relationship between Daniel and Mordecai as an intimate one. Mahawatte argues that Eliot links such a human drama to the apparently political drama of Zionism, so creating a layering of agendas in which homosexuality is granted a possible place of concealment, which both allows and prevents a queer reading of the narrative. Mahawatte suggests that this layering of sexual and political agendas is drawn from the Victorian Gothic, and this way of looking at the nineteenth-century Gothic enables a reading strategy which revises Eve Kosofsky Sedgwick's claim that homosexuality is only metaphorically present in the form. Mahawatte thus provides an innovative reading of how camp and the Gothic are combined in Eliot's work.

Diane Mason, in '"That mighty love which maddens one to crime": medicine, masculinity, same-sex desire and the Gothic in *Teleny*' (Chapter 5), examines how *Teleny, or The Reverse of the Medal* (1893) can be related to a variety of nineteenth-century medical contexts concerning 'perversion'. Mason further reveals how the novel's apparently medicalised representation of homosexual erotic love contains some strikingly Gothic elements through reference to Eric, Count Stenbock's short story 'The True Story of a Vampire' and George Du Maurier's *Trilby*, both published in 1894. The chapter not only discloses the heavily medicalised nature of much nineteenth-century pornographic writing but also frames a critical revision of the links between culture, gender, sexualities and the history of medicine, and illustrates how Gothic 'horrors' concerning homosexuality and perversion are generated within such contexts.

In 'Gothic landscapes, imperial collapse, and the queering of Adela Quested in E. M. Forster's *A Passage to India*' Ardel Thomas (Chapter 6) explores how Forster's 1924 novel develops images of queer identities

INTRODUCTION

through debates about identity and race which are familiar from the Gothic. Thomas examines how the courtroom drama of the novel focuses on the monstrous possibility of miscegenation (an Indian accused of raping an Englishwoman). However, this fictional trial becomes, Thomas argues, entangled in questions of sexuality as race and queer sexuality and queer sexualities with racial possibilities become aligned. Through a close reading of the respective roles of Adela Quested and Mrs Moore, Thomas argues that both become associated with a sexual and racial monstrosity through which Forster develops a typically Gothic ambivalence about racial and sexual identities. Thomas's chapter reveals how reading Gothically opens up Forster's novel for a new evaluation of its account of identity politics.

Paulina Palmer, in 'Antonia White's *Frost in May*: Gothic mansions, ghosts and particular friendships' (Chapter 7), argues that White's *Frost in May* (1933) can be contextualised to the concept of the 'lesbian Gothic' which helpfully illuminates White's representation of adolescent female subjectivity and sexuality. The 'lesbian Gothic' also conditions her depiction of the role that fantasy, in the sense of both her characters' flights of imagination and their experiments in creative writing and dramatic performance, plays in their psychological formation and development. Although the word 'lesbian' does not appear in the novel, same-sex desire is represented indirectly through sensuous descriptions of the female body and intertextual allusions to other erotic texts. Lesbian attachments, though recognised as potentially subversive, are none the less depicted as easily contained by the heterosexual status quo. Palmer explores how such images are developed through a Gothic ambiance which can be examined through the queer perspectives of Judith Butler and Eve Kosofsky Sedgwick.[13]

In 'Devouring desires: lesbian Gothic horror' Gina Wisker (Chapter 8) explores how women writers have used werewolves and vampires in order to explore 'transgressive' sexualities such as lesbianism. She argues that these representations are imaginatively liberating and carnivalesque because such shape-shifting disrupts notions of the unified 'self'. Wisker makes reference to writings by Tem, Rice, Brite, Califia and Forrest. The principal focus of her article is on 'Wilding' (1992) by Melanie Tem which explores the dangers of coming out to one's family using the formulae of fairytale and legend, while undercutting romantic fictions.

In '"The taste of blood meant the end of aloneness": vampires and gay men in Poppy Z. Brite's *Lost Souls*' William Hughes (Chapter 9), considers how the vampire has become an ambivalent emblem of gay sexuality in late twentieth-century Gothic fiction. Noting first the rather muted and implicit sexuality represented, in particular, by *Interview with the Vampire* (1976), the chapter moves to consider the more explicit and visceral erotic practices depicted throughout Poppy Z. Brite's *Lost Souls* (1992). *Lost Souls*, Hughes argues, represents a significant departure from the association between vampirism and a diseased degeneracy popularised by Bram Stoker's *Dracula* (1897), its imitators and its subsequent adaptations. In place of the vision of the vampire as a deficient, debased and Othered human, *Lost Souls* constructs a parallel community, simultaneously gay and vampiric, subject to its own forms of social and physiological evolution. Difficulties – for both vampires and gay men – perceptibly arise when one transcends the boundaries of same-sex/same-species community. The central message of *Lost Souls*, it might be argued, is vested in the novel's epilogue, with its reassertion of a golden age of exclusive and supportive community, existing within the world of mortals and straight sexuality but not necessarily committed to it.

In 'Michael Jackson's queer funk', Steven Bruhm (Chapter 10), considers how Michael Jackson's use of the Gothic in *Thriller* (1983) and *Ghosts* (1997) queers the temporality of childhood. By placing the medieval *danse macabre* at the heart of these two videos, Jackson figures childhood (his own in *Thriller*, that of his alleged child 'victims' in *Ghosts*) within the queer temporalities of the death drive. Exploiting this parallel between the medieval *danse* and the Freudian *fort–da*, Bruhm reads Jackson's choreography as an allegory of the ego's undoing, an allegory that radically critiques normative investments in linear psychosexual development. Bruhm aligns this critique with Lee Edelman's theory of the *sinthom*osexual to read the ways Jackson's bodily pulsions figure queerness's disintegration of the Child as a category of the normative.[14] This chapter makes an innovative and important contribution to the understanding of the Gothic and queer theory in non-text-based media.

Andrew Smith, in 'Death, art and Bodies: queering the queer Gothic in Will Self's *Dorian*' (Chapter 11), explores how Will Self's *Dorian* (2002) engages with issues of theatricality that become associated in the novel with a camp version of the postmodern. Smith argues that Self associates postmodern art with a metaphorics of emptiness that become linked to representations of death and the AIDS crisis of the 1980s. Smith's chapter explores how Self's strangely humanist reading of camp misreads theatricality as a sign of emptiness which turns in on itself so

INTRODUCTION

that 'humanity' becomes the source of horror because it is unable to generate the types of meanings that humanism searches for. Smith argues that the novel implicitly indicates how close the Gothic imagination and a humanist metaphysic had become by the 1990s and, obliquely, how queer theories of subjectivity (indebted to Wilde) enable the kind of transcendence that Self cannot affect. Ultimately *Dorian* develops an ideological reading of the queer Gothic which makes it complicit with the various heteronormative structures of power that it ostensibly opposes. The chapter therefore contributes to scholarship on Wilde, queer theory and the contemporary Gothic.

The chapters in this volume have all been specially commissioned. The breadth of texts and approaches illustrates the rich critical complexity which is involved in reading texts through queer theories. It is hoped that this volume will help to stimulate further discussion of how reading the Gothic in this way provides new insights into what queer really means.

NOTES

1 See, for example, Robert Kiely, *The Romantic Novel in England* (Cambridge, MA: Harvard University Press, 1972), p. 41; Richard Davenport-Hines, *Gothic: Four Hundred Years of Excess, Horror, Evil and Ruin* (London: Fourth Estate, 1998), p. 11.
2 Cf. Maggie Kilgour, *The Rise of the Gothic Novel* (London: Routledge, 1995), pp. 5, 8.
3 Davenport-Hines, *Gothic*, pp. 358, 360.
4 See Talia Schaffer, '"A Wilde Desire Took Me": The Homoerotic History of *Dracula*', *ELH*, 61 (1994), 381–425.
5 Davenport-Hines, *Gothic*, p. 359.
6 See Caitlin R. Kiernan, '... And in Closing (For Now)', in Poppy Z. Brite, *Self-Made Man* (London: Orion, 1998), pp. 173–80 at p. 179; Poppy Z. Brite, *Drawing Blood* (London: Penguin, 1993), p. i.
7 Brite's first two novels, *Lost Souls* and *Drawing Blood*, were short-listed for the Lambda Literary Award for Gay Men's Science Fiction/Fantasy in 1992 and 1993 respectively.
8 Susan Stryker, 'The Transgender Issue: An Introduction', *GLQ: A Journal of Lesbian and Gay Studies*, 4/2 (1998), 145–58 at p. 151.
9 Donald E. Hall, *Queer Theories* (Basingstoke: Palgrave, 2003), p. 56.
10 Quoted in ibid., p. 79.
11 For a survey of the changing position of Gothic in academia see William Hughes, 'Gothic Criticism: A Survey, 1764–2004' in Anna Powell and Andrew Smith (eds), *Teaching the Gothic* (Basingstoke: Palgrave, 2006), pp. 10–28, *passim*.

12 See Eve Kosofsky Sedgwick's *Between Men: English Literature and Male Homosocial Desire* (New York: Columbia University Press, 1985). Her *Epistemology of the Closet* (London: Harvester Wheatsheaf, 1991) has also made a significant contribution to queer readings of literature, and her *The Coherence of Gothic Conventions* (London and New York: Methuen, [c.1980] 1986) to an understanding of the Gothic. Other important contributions include Terry Castle's *The Female Thermometer: Eighteenth-Century Culture and the Invention of the Uncanny* (Oxford: Oxford University Press, 1995) and her *The Apparitional Lesbian: Female Homosexuality and Modern Culture* (New York, Columbia University Pres, 1993). Other important studies include Paulina Palmer's *Lesbian Gothic: Transgressive Fictions* (London: Cassell, 1999), George E, Haggerty's *Queer Gothic* (Urbana and Chicago, University of Illinois Press, 2006) and Max Fincher's *Queering Gothic in the Romantic Age* (Basingstoke: Palgrave, 2007).
13 See Judith Butler's 'Imitation and Gender Insubordination', in Diana Fuss (ed.), *Inside/Out: Lesbian Theories, Gay Theories* (London, Routledge, 1991), pp. 13-31.
14 Lee Edelman, *No Future: Queer Theory and the Death Drive* (Durham, NC: Duke University Press, 2004).

2

'Love in a convent': or, Gothic and the perverse father of queer enjoyment

Dale Townshend

If contemporary popular culture is anything to go by, the Gothic is more in need of a straightening out than a queering up. Perverse though this statement may seem, one need only survey some of the many popular-cultural appropriations of a few classic Gothic fictions in order to make the point clear. Mary Shelley's *Frankenstein* (1818) was readily camped up in Jim Sharman's filmic adaptation of Richard O'Brien's *The Rocky Horror Picture Show* in 1975. From book and stage play, through popular West End musical, to staggering box-office success, Victor Frankenstein's aversion for his monstrous progeny was transformed in the hands of Tim Curry's sweet transvestite into an account of the lipsticked creator's queer love for his creature – a bronzed, deliberately anachronistic 1950s beefcake complete with dumb-bells and posing shorts. As if this work of queering was not enough, Bill Condon's film *Gods and Monsters* (1998) has more recently returned, through the intertexts of Shelley's myth and its queer filmic reincarnations in James Whale's *Frankenstein* (1931) and *Bride of Frankenstein* (1935), to examine the complex interchange between divinity and monstrosity, queer attraction and repulsion in the relationship between an older Whale, the gracious and sophisticated British film director, and his horticultural rent boy, a young, sexually ambiguous all-American gardener.

Bram Stoker's *Dracula* (1897), the other seminal Gothic fiction of the nineteenth century, has met with a similar fate. Here too, it is the countless filmic adaptations of this powerful late-Victorian myth that have amplified the play of queer desires between, say, the Count and a jejune Jonathan Harker, or between the three infernal sisters and Lucy Westenra. The suave advances of Bela Lugosi in Tod Browning's classic *Dracula* (1931) would play themselves out in the more self-consciously queer filmic contexts of *Fright Night* (Dir. Tom Holland, USA, 1985) and *Razor Blade Smile* (Dir. Jake West, UK, 1998), more daringly in the gay pornographic fantasies of *Love Bites* (Dir. Kewin Glover, USA, 1988) or *The Vampire of Budapest* (Dir. Kristen Bjorn, USA, 1995), and most notoriously in the vampings of the saturnine Marquis de Suede [*sic*] in Roger Earl's *Gayracula* (USA, 1983). If these examples of queer appropriation of the Gothic seem all too narrowly 'gay', one need only recall the tradition of lesbian vampire films – their male heterosexual audience notwithstanding – in their various interpretations not only of *Dracula* but, more directly, of Sheridan Le Fanu's 'Carmilla' of 1872, from *Dracula's Daughter* by Lambert Hillyer (USA,1936), to Gabrielle Beaumont's *Carmilla* (USA, 1990).

The queer monstrosities so meticulously dissected in Jonathan Demme's *The Silence of the Lambs* (1991), or by David Mamet and Ridley Scott in their compelling sequel *Hannibal* (2001), are only two examples of what Michael William Saunders and Harry M. Benshoff have identified as cinema's long-term exploitation of the monstrous queer.[1] Of course, film is not the only cultural medium through which the work of Gothic queering has been achieved: Michael Rowe and Thomas S. Roche's collection *Brothers of the Night: Gay Vampire Stories* (1997) and Pam Keesey's *Dark Angels: Lesbian Vampire Stories* (1995) have relocated the queer vampire firmly within the genre of the gay short story, while Anne Rice in *Interview with the Vampire* (1976) would lend to the homoeroticism of Lestat's interaction with his victim Louis a form of timeless, historically transcendent support. From the queer terrors of Shirley Jackson's *The Haunting of Hill House* (1959), through what Steven Bruhm has taken to be the spine-chilling queerness of some of Stephen King's popular fictions, to more recent postmodern Gothic fictions such as Will Self's *Dorian* (2002), the task of queering the Gothic has already been achieved.[2] Either that, or it was never necessary in the first place.

Perversely, then, we might say that, with respect to the Gothic and criticism's queer query, there is nothing new under the sun: old news, always-already begun, perhaps altogether unnecessary. But this chapter is perverse in another way too, especially in its claim that, for all its apparent queerness, Gothic writing, from the time of its inception towards the end of the eighteenth century, is tightly bound up within the heteronormative, even 'heterosexist' ideals attendant upon the romance form. Admittedly, this is not exclusively so: Coleridge's 'Christabel' (1798, 1816), for one, had manipulated the structures of literary romance to decidedly queer effect in its account of the ambiguous emotional and sexual affections between Geraldine and Christabel herself, while the countless responses, parodies and rewritings that the poem occasioned would variously eradicate, intensify or reformulate the romance's queer desirings. More recently, postmodern appropriations of the formal features of Gothic romance by, say, Angela Carter in *The Passion of the New Eve* (1977) or Jeanette Winterson in *Sexing the Cherry* (1989) would recuperate its ambulatory, wildly phantasmatic turns as a vehicle for lesbian-feminist love, desire and sexual politics.[3] But still, this does not disguise the fact that, in by far the majority of cases, heterosexual marriage, in which hero and heroine are united to one another in a monogamous, peculiarly asexual emotional bond, appears to be the teleological goal to which most early Gothic fictions aspired. To effect a happy marriage between its sentimentally betrothed hero and heroine, we might say, became the *raison d'être* of many an eighteenth-century Gothic romancer.

Ann Radcliffe's Gothic fictions are entirely representative in this respect. In Radcliffe's earlier work, the machinery of literary romance is brought into play in the staging of the various frustrations, delays and prohibitions to which a particularly modern, decidedly bourgeois conception of marriage – that is, marriage for the sake of sentiment, or what *The Mysteries of Udolpho* (1794) terms 'conjugal felicity' rather than financial prestige and political advantage – is subjected over time.[4] In *A Sicilian Romance* (1790), the numerous obstacles to the love between Julia and the sentimental hero Hippolitus are eventually overcome, and the narrative will draw to a close only once the nuptials between the two sisters and their respective male suitors have been assured. In *The Romance of the Forest* (1791) too, Theodore and Adeline will, despite the odds, eventually be joined to one another through matrimonial bonds based almost entirely upon considerations of romantic love and mutual sentimental attraction. Although, as Rictor Norton has argued, Radcliffe's later romances such as *The Mysteries of Udolpho* and *The Italian* (1797) are not without a range of teasing, heavily encoded references to same-sex female desire, the closure of both fictions is achieved only once Emily and Valancourt, Ellena and Vivaldi, respectively, have committed themselves to one another through the legal and emotional bonds of the heterosexual marital relation.[5] Consequently, it is fair to argue, along with Robert Miles and Ann Williams, that Gothic romance is an important cultural agent in the deployment of modern sexuality as mapped out by

Michel Foucault in his *The History of Sexuality: An Introduction* (1976).[6] Consistent with the broader discursive shifts of late eighteenth-century European culture, Gothic systematically replaces the older system of feudal alliance, including primogeniture and the patrilineal transmission of inherited property and wealth, with the discourse of *scientia sexualis*, the modern bourgeois construction of romantic marital relations.

To this discursive endeavour, the role of the father is crucial. If matrimony in late eighteenth-century Gothic already discloses the relations between romance and some of the definitive features of modern western patriarchal society, these bonds will be further enhanced by the figure of the father that is invariably invoked as a symbolic authority to preside over the consolidation of the marital bonds at the narrative's termination. The ending of Radcliffe's *The Italian* is entirely characteristic: although the Marchese di Vivaldi had initially been strongly opposed to his son's marriage, he is eventually recuperated as a sound, utterly reformed paternal presence to preside over the nuptials of the younger generation at the narrative's close. Throughout eighteenth-century Gothic, similar examples abound: fathers who, for much of the narrative, had been variously lost, absent, feckless or lacking, are either transformed, reformed, rediscovered or entirely replaced by sound paternal authorities who eventually preside over the legal and sentimental consolidation of romantic marital arrangements. While the staple ingredients of most Gothic narratives seriously call the authority of the father into dispute – consider the scenes of incestuous sexuality in Walpole's *The Mysterious Mother* (1768), or the opposition to the dictates of parental duty consistently staged in Radcliffe's *A Sicilian Romance* – the paternal function, albeit substantially modified and reconfigured, is eventually invoked as a means of reimposing a compromised sense of cultural order, stability and coherence. In this sense, it is apposite to claim that Gothic writing often consists of the transgression of the *nom-du-père*, the father in all his legislative, law-administering symbolic functions, but only in order to assert the importance and inviolability of what Lacanian psychoanalysis has designated as the Name-of-the-Father or paternal metaphor.[7]

How perverse it is, then, to situate alongside the heteronormative ideals of fictions such as *The Mysteries of Udolpho* and *Clermont* (1768) those romances, often associated with the male tradition in 1790s Gothic, in which the desires of the father are subjected to a range of queer representations. Certainly, William Beckford's *Vathek* (1786) and Matthew Gregory Lewis's *The Monk* (1796) phantasmatically throw into relief effete fathers who no longer officiate as imperious symbolic authorities, but who embark rather upon a programme of perverse, queer desiring with passionate abandon.

Vathek presents a particularly salient case in point: many contemporary readers were certain of nothing if not the extent to which the author's notorious queer proclivities received in this tale a form of embarrassing disclosure. Such, at least, were the impressions of Mrs Hester Lynch Thrale Piozzi who, in her in her *Thraliana: The Diary of Mrs Hester Lynch Thrale* (1791), noted that 'Mr Beckford's *favourite Propensity* is all along visible I think; particularly in the luscious Descriptions given of Gulchenrouz'.[8] Lest her readers were unsure as to what, precisely, the author's strange predilections might be, Mrs Thrale continued to spell out in no uncertain terms some of the names implicated in the queer scandal in which Beckford was implicated two years before the publication of *Vathek*. Lord Loughborough had spread a scandalous rumour concerning Beckford's compromising relations with the adolescent William Courtenay while Beckford and his wife were staying with the Courtenay family at Powderham in 1784. 'What a World it is!!!!', exclaims Hester Thrale. And what a queer, queer world is *Vathek* indeed: the Giaour demands as a libation the blood of 'the most beautiful sons of thy vizirs and great men' for, as Carathis acutely observes, 'There is nothing so delicious, in his estimation, as the heart of a delicate boy palpitating with the first tumults of love'.[9] Although the Caliph figures for the most part as a heterosexual polygamist, he also betrays a queer attraction to the Giaour during the latter's incarnation as the Indian merchant: 'In the transports of his joy, Vathek leaped upon the neck of the frightful Indian, and kissed his horrid mouth and hollow cheeks, as though they had been the coral lips and lilies and roses of his most beautiful wives' (163). The timely intervention of Vathek's phallic mother alone is capable of interrupting this queer embrace. Eventually subjecting its main protagonist to interminable punishment in the infernal regions of Eblis, the didactic ending of Beckford's romance – 'Such was, and such should be, the punishment of unrestrained passions and atrocious deeds!' (254) – warns of the consequences of having transgressed the father's moral authority.

For all its need to conserve the paternal function, Gothic romance, from the originating moment of Walpole's *The Castle of Otranto* (1764) onwards, had simultaneously demonstrated a lurid fascination with the enjoyments of the perverse father, a ghastly phantasmatic inversion of the paternal function who, unlike the examples of sound paternity offered up by Clara Reeve's Old English Baron, Radcliffe's St Aubert, the reformed Marchese di Vivaldi or Roche's Clermont, wilfully embark upon a path of perverse enjoyment: Manfred's incestuous enjoyment of his intended daughter-in-law in *The Castle of Otranto*, Beckford's Caliph's programme of unrestrained enjoyment, Father Schedoni's illegal, adulterous enjoyment of his brother's wealth, wife and family in Radcliffe's *The Italian*.[10]

Indeed, as the case of Father Ambrosio's attraction to the Rosario/Matilda figure in Lewis's *The Monk* so clearly illustrates, the perversity of the Gothic father's enjoyment frequently resides in its avowedly queer predilections. Perhaps unsurprisingly, chapbook renditions and retellings of Ambrosio's perverse desire often threw its queerness into graphic, sensationalist relief. In the anonymous and undated *Father Innocent, Abbot of the Capuchins; Or, The Crimes of Cloisters*, for instance, the interaction between the Abbot, Father Innocent, and Philario, the Rosario/Matilda figure, is highly erotically charged:

> The abbot gave him [Philario] his blessing, and as the eager youth started from the ground, he pressed the abbot's hand to his lips, and quitted the apartment. Soon after the priest descended to vespers, much surprised at the mystery of the youth's behaviour.[11]

Later, yet still prior to the disclosure of Philario's female name and identity, the young novice will kiss Father Innocent on the mouth and, in a gesture of love and devotion, strew flowers around his cell. Still, it has to be said that, on the surface of things, the fantasy of paternal perversion in *The Monk*, as in Walpole's *The Mysterious Mother*, appears to be constituted more in relation to the incestuous sexual act than any overtly queer, homoerotic desires. In *The Monk*, Father Ambrosio eventually rapes his sister Antonia, while Walpole's Father Benedict wilfully sediments the doubly incestuous marriage between the hero Edmund and his sister-turned-daughter. Yet even here, what often accompanies the trope of the father's incestuous perversion in Gothic is an unmistakable (though also decidedly inchoate) sense of homoerotic desire, the spectre of same-sex love and attraction that signifies its otherwise invisible presence through the graphic horrors of the heterosexual incestuous relation.

That incest in Gothic is often conflated with homoerotic desire is a point that has been argued by Eve Kosofsky Sedgwick,[12] George E. Haggerty[13] and Robert Miles.[14] Certainly in *The Monk*, the fantasy of incestuous enjoyment is never far away from the homoerotic perversions of the father, especially in those portions of the narrative which detail

Ambrosio's erotic dealings with the androgynous Rosario/Matilda figure. Ambrosio's initial attraction to Rosario/Matilda, as well as the consummation of their affair following Matilda's revelation of her female identity, is irrevocably incestuous, particularly given that their relationship is defined by, and suspended within, the range of familial relationships – sister, son, father, mother and so on – set in place by the practices of the Catholic Church. But this quasi-incestuous bond graphically assumes some rather queer, homoerotic dimensions when Matilda, even following the disclosure of her feminine self, is persistently named and signified by Ambrosio and the other monks in residence at the monastery in and through the masculine pronoun. In the following exchange between the ailing Monk and the nurturing Matilda, Ambrosio implores one whom he at this point knows to be a woman to forget her feminine nature and continue to exist with him in masculine bond of fraternity or brotherhood:

> 'Then live for me, Matilda, for me and gratitude!' – [He caught her hand, and pressed it rapturously to his lips.] – 'Remember our late conversations; I now consent to every thing; Remember in what lively colours you described the union of souls; Be it ours to realize those ideas. Let us forget the distinctions of sex, despise the world's prejudices, and only consider each other as Brother and Friend. Live then, Matilda! Oh! live for me!'[15]

Ambrosio's invoking of the asexuality of brotherly affection at this point does nothing to eradicate from their relationship the pulses of urgent erotic attraction. On the contrary, the monk's sexual desire for the temptress only increases once the symbolic brotherly relations between them have been consolidated. Paradoxically, in fact, Matilda's masculinity appears to increase exponentially following her disclosure of her female identity:

> She assumed a sort of courage and manliness in her manners and discourse but ill calculated to please him. She spoke no longer to insinuate, but command: He found himself unable to cope with her in argument, and was unwillingly obliged to confess the superiority of her judgment. Every moment convinced him of the astonishing powers of her mind. (232)

In so far as it involves the physical union between two who are ostensibly brothers, their sexual intercourse is as incestuous as it is queer: 'father' seduces 'son' as 'brother' seduces 'brother'.

A similar sense plays itself out in the 'Tale of the Spaniard' Alonzo di Monçada in Charles Maturin's *Melmoth the Wanderer* (1820). Alonzo is

∼ 17

relating to John Melmoth, in painstaking detail, the story of his escape from the monastery into which he had been coerced by his parents. While Alonzo and his accomplice, the parricide, are concealed in an underground vault, the latter recites a story of transvestism, cross-dressing and queer male desire that directly replays Lewis's account of Ambrosio's interactions with the Rosario/Matilda figure in *The Monk*. Like the affection that grows between the Father and the son Rosario, Maturin's parricide takes voyeuristic pleasure in the friendly affections that circulate between two fellow clerics, a monk and a male novice:

> Some time after, a young novice entered the convent. From the moment he did so, a change the most striking took place in the young monk. He and the novice became inseparable companions – there was something suspicious in that. My eyes were on the watch in a moment. Eyes are particularly sharpened in discovering misery when they can hope to aggravate it.[16]

As innocuous as the interaction between them might initially seem, it is not long before the parricide's suspicions are aroused. The requisite, somewhat 'hygienic' forms of brotherly love between them are patently in danger of assuming certain romantic and erotic proportions:

> The attachment between the young monk and the novice went on. They were for ever in the garden together – they inhaled the odours of the flowers – they cultivated the same cluster of carnations – they entwined themselves as they walked together – when they were in the choir, their voices were like mixed incense. Friendship is often carried to excess in conventual life, but this friendship was too like love. (205)

In a scene in the cloistered garden that directly recalls Ambrosio being bitten by a serpent in *The Monk*, the parricide's suspicions are confirmed: the novice's deft movements when her finger is cut by a peach-knife betray her true feminine identity. Enraged but also curiously titillated by this discovery, the voyeuristic parricide relates his suspicions to the Superior, who, in bursting into the room of the couple, discovers there a scene of heterosexual passion, the 'wretched husband and wife ... locked in each other's arms' (207). Although the disclosure of the novice's femininity seeks, as in Lewis, to dismantle the queer attractions between the monk and the novice that had been generated during the time when the cross-dressing novice had maintained her male disguise, it remains difficult to divorce the Superior's responses to this strange sight of 'love in a convent' (207) from the tale's initial concerns with homoerotic desiring. In fact, as Maturin's tale suggests, the Superior, given the context of an all-male clerical establishment, may well have been altogether less horrified by a spectacle of queer sexual activity between two of its brothers than by either heterosexual intercourse or bestiality respectively: as the parricide claims,

> He was a man (of course from his conventual feelings) who had no more idea of the intercourse between the sexes, than between two beings of a different species. The scene that he beheld could not have revolted him more, than if he had seen the horrible loves of the baboons and the Hottentot women, at the Cape of Good Hope. (207)

For all its unravelling of the scene of queer transvestism, heterosexuality in 'The Spaniard's Tale', like heterosexual incest between a brother and a sister in *The Monk*, presents hardly a less horrific alternative.

For every Gothic male who is commanding of respect and worthy of emulation, there exists a perverse, frequently queer version. For every Clermont a Vathek, for every St Aubert an Ambrosio. Theoretically, the logic behind this strange cultural inversion is easy to see, particularly if one makes explanatory recourse to Freud's mythologising of perversity and the paternal function in *Totem and Taboo*, and, beyond that, to the particular inflections Freud's myth would receive in the later psychoanalytic gestures of Jacques Lacan and Slavoj Žižek. As Freud's story goes, Darwin's primal horde was originally governed by a tyrannous father, a perverse paternal figure who lorded a dreadful form of authority over his sons, monopolising the sexual enjoyment of all the tribe's women for himself. As the object of their hatred, he was also, as the original father of the tribe, the much loved and admired object of the sons' identifications. Dissatisfied with their father's unfair advantage over themselves, the sons of the primal horde conspired against the father, killing him and devouring him. However, even following his murder, the father of the primal horde continued to exert an ambivalent power over the brothers, strangely returning through the feelings of guilt and remorse that their act of patricide had engendered within them. As Freud notes, 'the dead father became stronger than the living one had been'.[17]

In his early *Écrits*, Jacques Lacan alludes to the numerous points of correspondence between his notion of the Name-of-the-Father and Freud's paternal mythology in *Totem and Taboo*. Linked within the Lacanian schema with the paternal function of symbolic Law, the Name-of-the-Father is the particular agent and embodiment of cultural or symbolic law that has manifested itself in and through language since the beginning of time, demanding that the subject cede his incestuous desire for the mother and identify with the paternal position.[18] Yet if the return of the murdered father of the primal horde in the form of the paternal metaphor represents a certain recuperation of the paternal function, Lacan and Žižek argue that the spectre of paternal perversity also persists in haunting all the sons and brothers, intricately linked, as they are, by the networks of difference and symbolic exchange. However, unlike Freud who, in *Totem and Taboo*, had attributed to the tyrannous father of Darwin's primal horde a certain ontological existence, Žižek argues that he has no existence outside of the workings of fantasy.[19] According to this phantasmatic scenario, we lack enjoyment because he, the perverse father, has stolen it.[20] But since, for Lacan, *jouissance* is always already impossible to the symbolic subject – there is no subject in possession of the real substance of loss and symbolic exile – the perverse father of enjoyment has no ontological existence outside of the neurotic constructions of the fantasy. As Žižek puts it, 'The point is rather to acknowledge that part of enjoyment is lost from the very beginning, that it is immanently impossible, and not concentrated "somewhere else", in the place from which the agent of prohibition speaks'.[21] The father of enjoyment and the symbolic Name-of-the-Father figure as inverted mirror images of one another, each defining itself in and through its perceived differences from the other.

Žižek foregrounds the paternal metaphor's negative reliance upon the fantasy of the paternal perversion by elaborating upon some of the implications of Lacan's conceptualisation of perversion as *père-version*. The perverse father of enjoyment is a phantasmatic or mythological 'version' of the father, the *père*, created by the symbolic Name-of-the-Father in an attempt at accounting for the remoteness of *jouissance* to the symbolic subject. Thus,

> Lacan prefers to write *perversion* as *père-version*, i.e., the version of the father. Far from acting only as symbolic agent, restraining pre-Oedipal, 'polymorphous perversity', subjugating it to the genital law, the 'version of', or turn toward, the father is the most radical perversion of all.[22]

However, in Freud's *Totem and Taboo*, the perverse father initially presiding over the terror-stricken sons of the primal horde demonstrated a voraciously heterosexual appetite – it was largely his sexual monopolisation of all the tribe's women that pre-empted the act of patricide in the first place. The reconfiguration of the laws of marriage encompassed by Foucault's discursive shift from ancient alliance to modern sexuality necessitates, in late eighteenth-century Gothic, the phantasmatic construction of the perverse father of particularly queer rather than heterosexual enjoyments. Against this spectre of queer paternal perversity, the paternal metaphor presiding over the celebration of modern, bourgeois marriages at the romance's end will be incited to deploy itself, expounding the virtues of monogamous, reproductive heterosexual romance against the polygamous perversity of the queer Gothic father. Against his risible, often Catholic example, we construct our heterosexual, conjugal, monogamous British Protestant selves, and, if our cultural enjoyment of these marriages is in any way lacking, it is because he, this queer perverse father, has stolen it.

The father's queer perversity in Gothic romance is borne out by a number of other historical and theoretical considerations too. In his *Seminar I: Freud's Papers on Technique, 1953–1954*, Lacan, in a highly evocative turn of phrase, established an important link between perversion and a desire that dare not speak its name:

> What is perversion? It is not simply an aberration in relation to social criteria, an anomaly contrary to good morals, although this register is not absent, nor is it an atypicality according to natural criteria ... It is something else in its very structure.
>
> A certain number of perverse inclinations have not without reason been said to arise out of a desire which dare not speak its name. Perversion in fact is to be placed at the limit of the register of recognition, and that is what fixes it, stigmatises it as such.[23]

Firstly, perversion is defined for Lacan as an aberration in relation to certain received social criteria. Secondly, perversion marks a departure from what are deemed to be a range of natural laws and social standards. Thirdly, and perhaps most importantly, perversion is intimately related to a desire that dare not articulate itself, be it in terms either of the difference it poses to the symbolic order of language or of its disavowal, rejection and repression by the workings of the subject's imaginary consciousness.

Although it is fair to argue that Lacan at this point does not specifically wish to import into his discussion of perversion a consideration of homosexual desire, the conditions he lays out for both the definition and ontological existence of perversion seem particularly suited to a reading of the queer inflections assumed by the perverse versions of the father in the writings of Walpole, Beckford and Lewis. Almost certainly, Lacan's invocation of a perversion 'which dare not speak its name' is a deliberate allusion to Lord Alfred Douglas's encoding of homosexual relations in his poem 'Two Loves' (1894). Through this, Lacan's discussion of perversion becomes inextricably linked to considerations of homosexuality as the archetypal perversion from the outset – as Judith Feher-Gurewich has argued, the theorist does little to shift the relations between perversion and homosexuality rather conservatively set up by Freud in *Three Essays on the Theory of Sexuality* (1905).[24]

But this reference to Wilde's Lord Douglas is important in another way, since it serves to locate Lacan's discussion of perversion within a particular moment in the sexual discursive history of the West – namely the initiation and consolidation of the modern homosexual identity by such figures as Wilde, Bosie and others in the last two decades of the nineteenth century. In other words, through Lacan's invocation of Bosie's famous line, perversity becomes tied specifically to the late nineteenth-century figure of the modern homosexual, a discursive category that postdates the queer fathers of Gothic romance by almost a century. For, as Foucault in *The History of Sexuality* is keen to stress, the category of the homosexual is only a relatively recent discursive invention in the history of western sexual discourse: 'Westphal's famous article of 1870 on "contrary sexual sensations"', he provocatively argues, 'can stand as its date of birth'.[25] As one particular manifestation of the pervasive 'implantation of the perverse' within nineteenth-century culture, the discursive construction of the homosexual occurred not against but rather *within* the interest of modern bio-power, or as yet another instance in which the discourse of *scientia sexualis*, in seeking to extend the range and scope of its applications, permissively constructed an ever-broadening range of perverse alternatives to the procreative heterosexuality of the Malthusian couple. Again, its implications for power are easy to see: much like the dynamic in which the spectre of the queer father in Gothic sustains the fantasies of heteronormative romance, the homosexual identities that appear in their more modern but by no means less horrific forms in the later Gothic productions of Stoker, Wilde, Stevenson and others encode more the encroachment of modern bio-power than any revolutionary sexual politics. Although Foucault, in these historicising gestures, does not wish to foreclose upon the existence of homoerotic activity prior to the late nineteenth-century formalisation of a homosexual identity – the second and third volumes in *The History of Sexuality* notably present rigorous genealogical accounts of ancient Roman and Greco-Roman homoerotic activity – he does sound a notion of warning to the critical rediscovery of an anachronistic 'homosexual' identity in the eighteenth-century writings of Walpole, Beckford and Lewis. Queerness, however, presents itself here as a less anachronistic alternative: the 'queerness' of the perverse Gothic father resides in the fact that his cultural representations significantly precede the discursive invention of the modern homosexual. The queerness of early Gothic writing, we might say, is partly the result of its historical provenance.

Jeffrey Weeks's various supplements to Foucault's sexual historiography afford greater insight into some of the historical conditions that pertained to the cultural representation of queerness at the end of the eighteenth century.[26] Following Foucault, Weeks maintains that homoerotic activity in Britain at this time lacked a specific definition and sense of legal and administrative identity particular to itself, but fell instead, together with other sexual aberrations such as incest, bestiality and necrophilia, under the general category of 'sodomy'. In fact, in the published legal account of 1760 ramblingly entitled *The Trial of Richard Branson, for an Attempt to commit Sodomy, on the Body of James Fassett, one of the Scholars belonging to God's-Gift College, in Dulwich. Tried at the General Quarter Session of the Peace, Held at St Margaret's-Hill, in the Borough of Southwark*, buggery – signifying the act of anal penetration – figured as one particular form of sexual immorality within the broader category of 'sodomitical crime'.[27] While, for Wilde and Bosie at the end of the nineteenth century, homosexuality might well have been the desire that 'dared not speak its name', for writers of Gothic romance a hundred years earlier the articulation of a definite homosexual identity was an historical impossibility.

However, existing side-by-side with a number of other sexual perversions within the general portmanteau category of sodomy, homoerotic desire ambivalently suggested to the eighteenth-century mind a number of affinities with incest, affinities, as argued, such as those exemplified in Lewis's *The Monk*. An attack on sodomy in the *Gentleman's Magazine* of May 1752 employed terms that were suited to the condemnation of incest and buggery alike, especially since both were perceived as constituting spectacular outrages against the categories of God, nature and the law:

> No rank, no condition, no consideration whatsoever should tempt any man to conceal such a design, such an outrage intended against God, nature and law. With as much reason may any man conceal an attempt to murder, as an attempt of Buggery.[28]

Like incestuous sexuality, homoerotic activity challenged the cherished distinctions of cultural existence with a threatening lack of differentiation, not least of them the differences between the two sexes. Both incest and homoerotic couplings constituted forms of erotic activity that were procreatively unfeasible, flagrantly non-reproductive manifestations of desires that each in their own ways threatened the Utilitarian principles slowly accreting around the productive monogamy of the heterosexual couple. As early as 1689, *A Short Treatise on these Heads, viz. Of the Sins of Sodom* had set in place an identification between sodomy, indolence and gross forms of unprofitability.[29] Both incest and sodomy were markers of what *A View of the Town: In an Epistle to a Friend in the Country. A Satire* (1735) referred to as 'unnat'ral lust', and, as the Reverend Dr Allen, amongst others, in his 1756 sermon *The Destruction of SODOM improved, as a warning to GREAT BRITAIN* noted, both posed a threat to the work of British nation-building.[30] It is no wonder, then, that contemporary Gothic writers display, like Lewis, a preoccupation with the proximities between queer and incestuous desires – in the Halls of Eblis section towards the end of Beckford's *Vathek*, the two princes who had long nurtured a queer romantic attachment to one another are pictured alongside the incestuous coupling of Kalilah and his twin sister:

> The two princes who were friends, and, till that moment, had preserved their attachment, shrunk back, gnashing their teeth with mutual and unchangeable hatred. Kalilah and his sister made reciprocal gestures of imprecation; all testified their horror for each other by the most ghastly convulsions, and screams that could not be smothered. (254)

Same-sex lovers, committers of incest and various other sodomites are meted out their punishments in Beckford's Orientalist version of hell. Achieving cultural representation in eighteenth-century Gothic in a number of displaced and sublimated forms, intimations of queer desire haunt the figure of incest as it had scandalously featured in the fictions by a number of male writers.

Significantly, queer desire in *The Monk* and *Melmoth the Wanderer* figures as an exclusively Catholic phenomenon, a form of perversion that, for all its unproductivity, breeds wildly and profusely within the confines of the all-male Abbey or monastery. Indeed, as Haggerty has recently argued, Gothic fiction's incessant queering of Catholicism in works such as Lewis's *The Monk*, Roche's *The Children of the Abbey* (1796) and W. H. Ireland's *The Abbess* (1799) is of such cultural significance as to suggest that Catholicism plays 'a more active role in the history of sexuality than has previously been acknowledged'.[31] In queering Catholicism, as in other respects, Gothic writing appears to be particularly inflected with the discursive climate of its historical moment, for fantasies of homoerotic sexual activity between either male or female members of apparently celibate Catholic communities had played a considerable role in British Protestantism's abjection of the Catholic Other throughout the seventeenth and eighteenth centuries.

A few years after the formal consolidation of Protestant supremacy in Britain following the Glorious Revolution of 1688, a series of morning lectures was delivered in Southwark, London, by a range of eminent Protestant ministers. In 1779, almost one hundred years later, printed transcripts of these sermons were compiled, edited and published in Edinburgh under the title *An Antidote Against Popery: Or, The Principal Errors of the Church of Rome Detected and Confuted*. In Sermon XIX in the collection, one Mr Tho. Vincent ambitiously undertook the task of demonstrating that 'The popish doctrine, which forbiddeth to marry, is a devilish and wicked doctrine'.[32] The object of his attack on the clerical celibacy is particularly Catholic: popes, bishops, priests, deacons and virgin nuns variously feature in his condemnation of clerical celibacy. In fact, upon the basis of its criteria for entry into a monastery or convent alone, Catholicism, Mr Vincent argues, perceives marriage and conjugal relations as sins far surpassing in gravity and magnitude the transgressions of both sodomy and extra-marital fornication – the writer seems disappointed but also largely unsurprised to discover that, while a sodomite may legitimately enter into the Catholic priesthood, this would ironically not be an option for a married person. Thus, he boldly concludes, 'I shall do the Papists no wrong in saying, that they account it a greater crime for ecclesiastical persons to marry, than for them to commit fornication or sodomy' (145). Through rhetorical recourse to a number of spurious rhetorical syllogisms, Mr Vincent was eventually able to conclude that the enforced celibacy of the priest, by dint of the sheer unnaturalness of this requirement alone, would inevitably lead to the cleric's indulgence in sodomy: 'This popish doctrine doth lead unto much lewdness and villany [*sic*], namely, unto fornication, adultery, incest, Sodomy, murder, and the like lewd practices, which have been the product of this prohibition to marry' (154).

This line of argument, in fact, reads much like a paraphrase of Ambrosio's experience in *The Monk* – wholly unable to maintain his pious public appearance, Lewis's Ambrosio violates his vows of celibacy in order to indulge in sodomy with Rosario, fornication with Matilda and incest with Antonia. In Mr Vincent's estimation, the marriage of the clergy and the exercising of conjugal rights is by far a more favourable alternative to the illicit sexual acts into which sexual deprivation is likely to force the celibate monk: 'in such a case it is the express command of God that such persons should marry for the quenching of those burning lusts, and the preventing of that filthy and abominable sin of fornication' (152). The writer of this sermon places the blame squarely upon the shoulders of the Catholic Church: sexual desire is, at once, natural and God-given, and any attempt at tampering with its course will only ever result in the perversions of sodomy, incest and fornication. As the publication of 1766 entitled *The Fruit-Shop, A Tale; or, a Companion to St James's Street* put it,

> In popish convents, as well as nunneries abroad, how many are the diseases attendant on celibacy; all of which there is but one way of curing: and that nature points out to every member of society, however savage; to which the more civilized give a sanction by laws.[33]

From this work of elaborate cultural fantasy, Catholic communities of celibate women were not immune: Robert Samber's English translations of *Venus in the Cloister; or, the Nun in her Smock* (1725) provided a titillating transcription of a dialogue between a female novice named Agnes and an older, more experienced nun, Sister Angelica, intent upon seducing her.

As Gothic writing itself attests, the body of the Catholic was sexualised throughout the eighteenth century in decidedly queer ways. And if the queerness of fictions such as *The Monk* and *Melmoth the Wanderer* resides partly in the devices of cross-dressing and gendered disguise, Mr Vincent's diatribe in *An Antidote Against Popery* does not end without an almost identical account of transvestism and secret sexual rendezvous within the all-male confines of a monastery:

> I shall add but two instances more, of two famous women, one a pope; and the other a popess: The woman-pope was pope Joan, who succeeded Leo IV. Sat in the Papacy two years and six months, supposed to be a man, until at length being with child, she fell in labour in the midst of a solemn procession, whereby her sex and lewdness were discovered together. (478)

This inflammatory piece of anti-Catholic discourse is anything but an isolated incident – the links between sodomy and Catholicism had played themselves out in such notorious eighteenth-century legal cases as the trial of Gabriel Lawrence for sodomy in 1726, and later, with the publication of *Reasons for the Growth of Sodomy, in England* in 1749.[34]

'LOVE IN A CONVENT'

Queerness in early Gothic writing, it quickly becomes clear, presents neither a permanent, durable nor sustainable model of sexual desiring. As in a Shakespearean comedy, it exists fleetingly in the transvestite embraces and affections of a monkish couple which, upon the surface of things, scandalously appears to consist of two males, but which, upon the disclosure of the truth, is eventually revealed to be a mistaken form of forbidden heterosexuality: Ambrosio and Matilda underpin the initial queerness of the Ambrosio/Rosario scenario, while, in *Melmoth the Wanderer*, the parricide and the Superior of the convent burst in upon the secret lovers in order to discover beneath the appearance of homoerotic affection a male monk's love for a female novice. In both cases, queerness is a spectral mirage that is upheld and underpinned by a clandestine form of illicit heterosexuality, and, in both instances, it is a spectre that is rapidly dispelled by the disrobing of the monkish cross-dresser in the romance's formal imperative towards truth. In a fiction such as *Vathek*, the queer desirings of the Caliph, the Giaour and the two young princes receive their just ends in the punitive mechanisms of the Halls of Eblis; in a number of other contexts, it is almost entirely elided by, and conflated with, the monstrosities of heterosexual incest.

Although, in Clara Tuite's estimation, there remains something positive about Gothic writing's tendency to represent ineffable forms of queer desire through displaced forms of monstrous heterosexuality – in *The Monk*, she argues, 'The figure of masculine homoeroticism is clearly legible ... but is spared the graphic, sensational portrayal that heterosexual sex undergoes' – this does deny queerness a voice of its own.[35] Elsewhere, the spectre of the queer Gothic father serves as a necessary phantasmatic supplement to the deployment of modern sexuality, with the heteronormative impulses of the modern romance being incited to effect and consolidate an impressive range of conjugal relations as a perceived antidote to the horror, terror and chaos that paternal perversion had occasioned. To say the least, queerness in early Gothic is consistently bound up in the problems of negative representation.

The complexity at stake here, though, was that, while Gothic writers, almost without exception, would recoil in horror from the queerness that their texts entertained, most, often to the point of social notoriety, were of a queer disposition themselves. As Eve Kosofsky Sedgwick in her pioneering study *Between Men: English Literature and Male Homosocial Desire* (1985) has argued, three of the Gothic's original architects were, at least in today's terms, homosexual: 'Beckford notoriously, Lewis probably,

Walpole iffily' (92-3). Subsequent attempts at queering the Gothic through the work of authorial biography has reached similar conclusions: recent work by Rictor Norton, Timothy Mowl's *Horace Walpole: The Great Outsider* (1998) and *William Beckford: Composing for Mozart* (1998) are only a few cases in point. The apparent split that this biographical endeavour introduces between the Gothic writer's patently queer identity and the largely negative portrayals that queerness receives in the fiction have prompted critics to resolve what they take to be the fundamental 'ambivalences' at stake in the queerness of Gothic at the end of the eighteenth century. Brian Fothergill's study *Beckford of Fonthill* (1979), for instance, has attributed the ambivalences of queer attraction and repulsion in Beckford's romance to the mind of a pleasure-seeking sensualist wracked with an overwhelming sense of Calvinist guilt.[36] Jerrold E. Hogle has identified similarly ambiguous relations to homoerotic desire in *The Monk* and *The Castle of Otranto*, identifying in both texts a process of encoding and disavowal, tracing and erasing, as if avoiding at all costs a definite sense of 'coming out'.[37] Since Lewis, in Haggerty's estimation, was of these three authors the most public in terms of his queer persona, it is not surprising that *The Monk* provides for Haggerty a clear illustration of the tensions between homosexual self-fashioning and homophobic censure, sexual expression and fearful silencing at the end of the eighteenth century.[38] In each case, queer textual slippage and undecidability is traced back to certain tensions within the authorial psyche itself.

But there is another way of perceiving these ambivalences. For all their negative portrayals, their moralistic censorings and their stagings of conservative recoil, these queer moments within the otherwise heteronormative structures of fictional romance are of ethical value, articulating for both their authors, their readers and their historical moment alike the ethical possibilities for a mode of queer desiring that remains uncolonised by the power-saturated distributions of modernity's sexual discourses. This is so in a number of respects. While the queerness of the Catholic priest, abbot, monk or novice in Gothic writing continues to maintain its psychoanalytic relations to the trope of *père-version*, the perverse version of the father, it mobilises and represents the ethical possibilities for a mode of queer desiring that has not been entirely disciplined, channelled and Oedipalised by the Name-of-the-Father and its attendant range of cultural norms and laws. Žižek's defence of Lacanian psychoanalysis against the terms of Deleuze and Guattari's critique in *Anti-Oedipus: Capitalism and Schizophrenia* (1972) is pertinent here: what

Deleuze and Guattari fail to take into account is that the most powerful anti-Oedipus is Oedipus itself, the Oedipal Name-of-the-Father which only exists and functions as such in relation to the non-Oedipal spectre of father of perverse enjoyment.[39]

In Gothic terms, the disciplined and regulated forms of heteronormative desire set in place by the turns of fictional romance rely substantially upon the alternative ethical modes of desiring articulated by the spectre of the father's queer perversion. In other words, there exists at the limit of law and the paternal metaphor in Gothic writing the phantasm of queer perversion that resists the prohibitive, heteronormalising gestures of the paternal metaphor even as it is defined in relation to them. Perversion, moreover, represents for Lacan the substance of ethical action *par excellence*, be it the perversion of the Sadean libertine adopted as the template for ethical action in Lacan's essay 'Kant with Sade' (1963) or the perverse recalcitrance of Antigone in Sophocles' tragedy who, perhaps like Beckford's Vathek, will neither relinquish nor refuse her desire. Certainly, Lacan's earlier reflections on perversion in the first Seminar outlined above do not pass without at least a gestural reference to the ethical possibilities at stake in the trope of cultural perversion: 'Perversion', Lacan ends by saying, 'is an experience which allows one to enter more deeply into what one might call, in the full sense, the human passion' (221). This is no small thing in the work of a theorist devoted to recuperating precisely that – the passion and desire of the subject that exists always at the limit of symbolic and imaginary forms of objectification. And surely, if there is one thing which Gothic's most memorable villains from Faust to Frankenstein, Vathek to Ambrosio and Melmoth and beyond have come to understand, it is the meaning of human passion in all its depth, its scope and its intensity. For all queer theory's aversion to what it has often taken to be the 'unremittingly heteronormative' effects of the psychoanalytic paradigm,[40] Lacanian theory is useful in opening up the Gothic's queer perversions to its ethical possibilities.

If this seems a dangerously ahistorical approach, Foucault's reading of the sexual practices of late eighteenth-century culture locates these aspects of Lacan's ethical paradigm within a range of specific historical conditions. Foucault's celebrated account of the birth of the modern homosexual in *The History of Sexuality, Volume I*, for instance, nostalgically encodes the eighteenth-century portmanteau category of sodomy as a favourable alternative to the nineteenth century's meticulous preoccupations with the homosexual, the exact nature of his identity and the precise turns his perversion might take: 'The sodomite had been a temporary aberration; the homosexual was now a species' (43). Formulated in a phrase, and identified or 'betrayed' in even the subtlest of gestures and poses, the sexual practice of the modern homosexual came to determine the most intimate nature of his identity. Here again, the eighteenth century's disregard for the particular human *subject* of the sodomitical act seems, for Foucault, to have constituted historically a far less problematic mode:

> As defined by the ancient civil or canonical codes, sodomy was a category of forbidden acts; their perpetrator was nothing more than the juridical subject of them. The nineteenth-century homosexual became a personage, a past, a case history, and a childhood, in addition to being a type of life, a life form, and a morphology, with an indiscreet anatomy and possibly a mysterious physiology. (43)

The extension and intensification of modern bio-power in the course of the nineteenth century required the eighteenth-century category of sodomy to be subdivided, internally ordered or systematically carved up, with the range of aberrant sexual practices it contained each given its own name, identity, aetiology and attendant discursive anchorage. It was at this point, of course, that perversity was rendered complicit in the permissive and productive interventions of modern bio-power. The modern homosexual was one of the results of this process, and, although this marked a triumph for modern power, this was not achieved in human terms without an increased and prolonged subjection.

Gothic romance, though, by dint of its historical provenance alone, confronts the discursive constrictions of modern homosexuality with the breadth and discursive indistinction of the eighteenth-century sodomite. Opening up, via transvestism, the field of sexual desire to the forces of theatricality, performance and play, Gothic queerness, much like the work of queer theory itself, resists and disrupts the restrictive nineteenth-century distinctions between the heterosexual and the homosexual through a foregrounding of desires that are anchored permanently in neither one nor the other. Ambrosio loves and desires the male Rosario only later to be stirred to even greater erotic heights by a female Matilda, Virgin Mary or Antonia, perhaps much the same way in which William Beckford, with his harem of young boys, simultaneously enjoyed a long-standing marriage. The queer fathers of Gothic writing are nothing if not polymorphously perverse: as Vathek's sensory excesses, or the scopophilic visual delights of Ambrosio, so clearly attest, their desires resist the confines and limitations of phallic support and enactment, while their attractions to both male and female open up the body to a greater array of possible pleasures. Remaining unbound by the fixities of the modern homosexual identity, these queer fathers embark upon a desire-fuelled path of identification and re-identification, a making and an unmaking of the desiring self that brings to mind the figure of the Baudelairean dandy which, together with a Kantian emphasis upon reason, lies at the heart of Foucault's conceptualisation of the ethical subject in the later essay 'What Is Enlightenment?' (1978).

Uncannily, the queerness of Gothic romance also presents itself as the ideal point of articulation for the contemporary queer-theoretical endeavour for, if, as so many queer theorists have argued, queerness defies and unsettles the orthodoxies of fixed sexual identities, the Gothic had articulated a similar defiance through its preoccupations with paternal perversion from *The Castle of Otranto* onwards. If, in Moe Meyer's phrasing, queer theory represents 'an ontological challenge to dominant labelling philosophies', this is a challenge that had already been issued in the queer father's slippery resistance to sexual ontological consistency in Gothic romance of the late eighteenth century.[41] Indeed, Meyer's useful account of the contemporary queer-theoretical endeavour may well stand in place of an account of paternal queerness as it figures in the writings of Beckford and Lewis – both discourses seem to signal 'an ontological challenge that displaces bourgeois notions of the Self as unique, abiding, and continuous while substituting instead a concept of the Self as performative, improvisational, discontinuous, and processually constituted by repetitive and stylized acts'.[42]

It is at this point, too, that queer theory stakes out its difference from the work of gay liberation, being based, as it is, upon the politics of sexual identity. As Tim Dean elaborates, 'Whereas gay liberation had placed its trust in identity politics, queer activism entail[s] a critique of identity and an acknowledgement that different social groups [can] transcend their identity-based particularisms in the interest of resisting heteronormative society'.[43] Queer is to gay what deconstruction is to western metaphysics. While gay opposes straight, queer, perhaps more ambitiously, sets about resisting and disrupting the social discourses that regulate sex, gender and sexual practice. It is in all these senses that, as Judith Feher-Gurewich has argued, queer theory is, in itself, perverse in the extreme.[44] By contrast, though, those solitary queer figures who stalk the pages of Victorian Gothic fictions in closer historical proximity to the discursive birth of the homosexual – Dorian in Wilde, Dr Jekyll in Stevenson – seem particularly limited and sexually circumscribed, tied and subjected, as it all too often turns out, to a self-conscious sense of what constitutes a particularly homosexual way of being. Lacking in the movement and sexual fluidity of their eighteenth-century forebears, their desire can be directed only towards one gendered object at a time. It is no coincidence, then, that, in place of the sexual versatility of subjects such as Ambrosio and Vathek, Dorian Gray and Dr Jekyll are forced to make recourse to their Gothic doubles, substituting for the permissive terrains of eighteenth-century queer desiring the restricting structures of the homosexual doppelgänger and its public heterosexual other. Queer becomes homosexual as perversion becomes nineteenth-century inversion: imprisonment in the Gothic dungeons of the eighteenth-century Gothic romance has been transformed into the numerous forms of increased subjection attendant upon the structures of modern sexual binaries. Within such a state of affairs, horrific doubling, in fiction as in life, seems the only likely option.

Against modernity's sexual nightmare, the queerness of Gothic romance here, too, functions as an entirely ethical alternative, and one much closer in spirit to the same-sex romantic and erotic practices which Foucault had unearthed in ancient Greek and Greco-Roman cultures in *The Use of Pleasure* (1984) and *The Care of the Self* (1984), the second and third volumes of *The History of Sexuality*. Though by no means without their own difficulties – both cultures articulated certain anxieties concerning, for example, the power dynamics of activity and passivity and the importance of eventual marriage – the homoerotic practices of the ancient world constitute, for Foucault in these later studies, an ethical alternative to the category of the homosexual enshrined by the modern discourse of *scientia sexualis* in the West, a category which a queer Foucault himself, for one, consistently resisted.

NOTES

1 See Harry M. Benshoff, *Monsters in the Closet: Homosexuality and the Horror Film* (Manchester: Manchester University Press, 1997); Michael William Saunders, *Imps of the Perverse: Gay Monsters in Film* (New York: Praeger, 1998).
2 Steven Bruhm, 'On Stephen King's Phallus; Or The Postmodern Gothic', *Narrative*, 4/1 (1996), 55–73.
3 See Patricia Duncker, 'Queer Gothic: Angela Carter and the Lost Narratives of Sexual Subversion', *Critical Survey*, 8/1 (1996), 58–65.

4 Ann Radcliffe, *The Mysteries of Udolpho* (1794), ed. Bonamy Dobrée (Oxford: Oxford University Press, 1968), p. 2. All subsequent references are to this edition, and are given in parentheses in the text.
5 See Rictor Norton, *The Mistress of Udolpho: The Life of Ann Radcliffe* (London: Leicester University Press, 1999), pp. 137–51.
6 Robert Miles, *Gothic Writing 1750–1820: A Genealogy* (London: Routledge, 1993), p. 15. See, too, Anne Williams's *Art of Darkness: A Poetics of Gothic* (Chicago: University of Chicago Press, 1995).
7 See Fred Botting, 'Aftergothic: Consumption, Machines, and Black Holes', in Jerrold E. Hogle (ed.), *The Cambridge Companion to Gothic Fiction* (Cambridge: Cambridge University Press, 2002), pp. 277–300.
8 Rictor Norton, *Gothic Readings: The First Wave, 1764–1840* (London: Leicester University Press, 2000), p. 340.
9 William Beckford, *Vathek* (1786), in *Three Gothic Novels*, ed. Peter Fairclough (Harmondsworth: Penguin, 1968), pp. 151–255 at pp. 170, 232–3. All subsequent references are to this edition, and are given in parentheses in the text.
10 For an elaboration upon paternal perversion in the Gothic see the discussion in chapter 5 of my *The Orders of Gothic: Foucault, Lacan, and the Subject of Gothic Writing, 1764–1820* (New York: AMS Press, 2007).
11 Anon., *Father Innocent, Abbot of the Capuchins; or, The Crimes of Cloisters* (West Smithfield: Printed for Tegg and Castleman, at the Eccentric Book Warehouse, n.d.), p. 15.
12 Eve Kosofsky Sedgwick, *Between Men: English Literature and Male Homosocial Desire* (New York: Columbia University Press, 1993), p. 91. All subsequent references are to this edition, and are given in parentheses in the text.
13 George E. Haggerty, 'Literature and Homosexuality in the Late Eighteenth Century: Walpole, Beckford, and Lewis', *Studies in the Novel*, 18/4 (Winter 1986), 341–52 at p. 239.
14 Robert Miles, 'Ann Radcliffe and Matthew Lewis', in David Punter (ed.), *A Companion to the Gothic* (Oxford: Blackwell, 2001), pp. 41–57 at p. 52.
15 Matthew Gregory Lewis, *The Monk: A Romance* (1796), ed. Howard Anderson (Oxford: Oxford University Press, 1973), p. 89. All subsequent references are to this edition, and are given in parentheses in the text.
16 Charles Maturin, *Melmoth the Wanderer*, ed. Douglas Grant (Oxford: Oxford University Press, 1989), p. 205. All subsequent references are to this edition, and are given in parentheses in the text.
17 Sigmund Freud, *Totem and Taboo: Some Points of Agreement between the Mental Lives of Savages and Neurotics*, trans. James Strachey (London: Routledge and Kegan Paul, 1950), p. 143.
18 Jacques Lacan, *Écrits: A Selection*, trans. Alan Sheridan (London: Tavistock, 1977), p. 199.
19 Slavoj Žižek, *For They Know Not What They Do: Enjoyment as a Political Factor* (London: Verso, 1991), p. 134.

20 Slavoj Žižek, *Looking Awry: An Introduction to Jacques Lacan through Popular Culture* (Cambridge, MA: MIT Press, 1991), p. 24.
21 Ibid., p. 24.
22 Ibid., pp. 24–5.
23 Jacques Lacan, *Seminar I: Freud's Papers on Techniques, 1953–1954*, ed. Jacques-Alain Miller, trans. John Forrester (London: Norton, 1988), p. 221. All subsequent references are to this edition, and are given in parentheses in the text.
24 Judith Feher-Gurewich, 'A Lacanian Approach to the Logic of Perversion' in Jean-Michel Rabaté (ed.), *The Cambridge Companion to Lacan* (Cambridge: Cambridge University Press, 2003), pp. 191–207 at p. 191.
25 Michel Foucault, *The History of Sexuality, Volume I: An Introduction*, trans. Robert Hurley (New York: Vintage Books, 1990), p. 43. All subsequent references are to this edition, and are given in parentheses in the text.
26 Jeffrey Weeks, *Sex Politics and Society: The Regulation of Sexuality since 1800* (London: Longman, 1981).
27 Ian McCormick, *Secret Sexualities: A Sourcebook of 17th and 18th Century Writing* (London: Routledge, 1997), p. 109.
28 Ibid., p. 115.
29 Ibid., p. 123.
30 Ibid., p. 152.
31 George E. Haggerty, 'The Horrors of Catholicism: Religion and Sexuality in the Late Eighteenth Century', *Romanticism on the Net: An Electronic Journal Devoted to Romantic Studies*, 36–7 (Nov. 2004–Feb. 2005), p. 15. www.erudit.org/revue/ron/2004/v/n36-37/011133ar.html (accessed 14 September 2006).
32 Anon., *An Antidote Against Popery: Or, The Principal Errors of the Church of Rome Detected and Confuted*, 2 vols (Edinburgh: n.p., 1779). All subsequent references are to this edition, and are given in parentheses in the text.
33 McCormick, *Secret Sexualities*, p. 173.
34 Ibid., p. 73.
35 Clara Tuite, 'Cloistered Closets: Enlightenment Pornography, The Confessional State, Homosexual Persecution and *The Monk*', *Romanticism on the Net: An Electronic Journal Devoted to Romantic Studies*, 8 (Nov. 1997), p. 7. http://users.ox.ac.uk/~scat0385/closet.html (accessed 12 May 2002).
36 Brian Fothergill, *Beckford of Fonthill* (London: Faber and Faber, 1979), pp. 129–34.
37 Jerrold E. Hogle, 'The Ghost of the Counterfeit – and the Closet – in *The Monk*', *Romanticism on the Net: An Electronic Journal Devoted to Romantic Studies*, 8 (Nov. 1997) http://users.ox.ac.uk/~scat0385/closet.html (accessed 20 May 2002).
38 Haggerty, 'Literature and Homosexuality in the Late Eighteenth Century', p. 349.
39 Žižek, *Looking Awry*, p. 24.

40 Tim Dean, 'Lacan and Queer Theory', in Jean-Michel Rabaté (ed.), *The Cambridge Companion to Lacan* (Cambridge: Cambridge University Press, 2003), pp. 238–52, at p. 241.
41 Moe Meyer (ed.), *The Politics and Poetics of Camp* (London: Routledge, 1994), p. 1.
42 Ibid., p. 3.
43 Dean, 'Lacan and Queer Theory', p. 240.
44 Feher-Gurewich, 'A Lacanian Approach to the Logic of Perversion', pp. 203–4.

3
'Do you share my madness?':
Frankenstein's queer Gothic

Mair Rigby

> What is peculiar to modern societies, in fact, is not that they consigned sex to a shadow existence, but that they dedicated themselves to speaking of it *ad infinitum*, while exploiting it as *the* secret.
>
> Michel Foucault, *The History of Sexuality* (1976)[1]

Since Gothic horror texts have long been perceived to enjoy a privileged role in the representation of sexual fantasies and fears, it is little wonder to find that queer scholarship has paid attention to the genre.[2] In recent years, there has certainly been a steady proliferation of academic publications addressing the extent to which Mary Shelley's *Frankenstein* (1831) can be read as a tale of dangerous queer desire. My object in this chapter is not to argue, yet again, that queer meanings are present in *Frankenstein*; it is, rather, to consider how the text creates an impression of deviant and dangerous sexual possibility. I want to build upon the question of *Frankenstein*'s engagement with nineteenth-century sexual rhetoric in order to explore some of the ways in which the signifying practices of queerness have been written into the signifying practices, or *language*, of Gothic fiction. Taking a broadly Foucauldian approach, I propose that many of the conventions, signs, codes, linguistic figures, lexical devices and rhetorical tropes that have come to be recognisable to readers as 'Gothic' can be recognised also as signifying 'queer'. In this respect, *Frankenstein* is a productive text for discussing modern western culture's tendency to produce the possibility of sexual nonconformity as a Gothic horror story.

Frankenstein was first published in 1818. Mary Shelley revised it for the 1831 third edition upon which this chapter is based.[3] Presented in epistolary form as a series of framed narratives, the text opens with Captain Walton finding Victor Frankenstein in the Arctic Circle. At Walton's urging, Victor recounts the scientific obsession that led him to animate a monstrous creature. Contained within his narrative is the Monster's own tale of abandonment, rejection and revenge. After killing Victor's younger brother, the Monster demands a companion from his creator; but, when Victor refuses to complete the task, he murders his friend Clerval and bride Elizabeth. The two then pursue each other into the Arctic where Victor dies and the repentant Monster, swearing that he will burn himself to death, disappears into 'darkness and distance'.[4]

The homosexual connotations and camp sensibilities discernible in film and theatre adaptations from the 1930s onwards indicate that *Frankenstein* was subject to queer reading long before the advent of academic queer theory.[5] But in terms of the novel, recent queer scholarship draws largely upon the work of Eve Kosofsky Sedgwick, developing her analysis of male homosocial culture, homoerotic desire, homosexual panic and homophobia within the nineteenth-century 'paranoid Gothic': the 'literary genre' in which she argues that 'homophobia found its most apt and ramified embodiment'.[6] As the male relationships in *Frankenstein* range from Victor's affectionate, arguably homoerotic, friendships with Henry Clerval and Captain Walton, to the repressed desire, homosexual panic and homophobia readable in his deadly bond with the Monster, the text does seem particularly concerned with desire between men.

Building upon this critical trend, I propose that *Frankenstein*'s 'queer' and 'Gothic' textuality has something further to reveal about the relationship between the language of Gothic fiction and the language of sexual 'deviance'. As Troy Boone observes, popular Gothic texts still 'have much to teach us about the regulation of sexuality' and, as I will argue, about the *deployment* of sexuality.[7] In his *History of Sexuality*, Michel Foucault contends that, from the seventeenth century onwards, sexual material has not been 'repressed' in the way traditionally thought. Instead, methods of speaking about sex have proliferated and 'around and apropos of sex, one sees a veritable discursive explosion' and, moreover, 'a whole rhetoric of allusion and metaphor' has been 'codified' (17). If Gothic texts often appear to be speaking to us, more of less indirectly, about 'sex' of the most dangerous, deviant and perverse varieties, a Foucauldian reading would suggest that the genre does not simply 'reflect' or 'represent' the construction of the desires, identities and behaviours which have since come to be dubbed 'queer'. Rather, this aspect of Gothic fiction takes part in the discursive *production* and even *dissemination* of cultural 'knowledge' about sexual nonconformity, and it is perhaps in the deployment of a coded, figurative language of sexual allusion and metaphor that Gothic fiction speaks to us about modern sexual discourse.

'OF WHAT A STRANGE NATURE IS KNOWLEDGE!'

Most twenty-first-century western readers probably would not find it difficult to agree that Gothic narratives can usually be read as sexual nightmares on some level, not least because such texts appear so adept in the creation of sexually charged atmospheres. In relation to Gothic fiction, Sedgwick notes that there are 'habits of reading, habits of recognising and responding to fictional character and plot, habits of knowing'.[8] Certain 'habits' of recognition, response and knowing have developed around sexual meaning in the Gothic, to such an extent that the genre often appears to invite, and even encourage, us to read queerly. David Greven argues that some nineteenth-century texts make use of a kind of 'winking rhetoric', through 'coded and specific lexical devices' whereby 'queer content' is potentially communicated to the reader.[9] This is a useful theory and evidently there have always been readers consciously 'in the know' and on the look out for codes which speak their 'language'. But it is also interesting to think how the Gothic has developed a form of textuality which most readers, from the past to the present, have been able to experience as sexually disquieting and exciting. What I want to cultivate here is a sense of how the language of Gothic fiction works to create an atmosphere of sexual danger and transgression. In putting into play signs and codes such as forbidden knowledge, recognition, paranoia, the unspeakable, madness, monstrosity, death, disease, social ostracism and strange, symbolic space, *Frankenstein*, for instance, can be read as mobilising conventions which have come to double as both Gothic tropes *and* tropes within the language of sexual 'deviance'. But queer reading possibilities are not simply inscribed 'in' *Frankenstein* or, for that matter, 'in' the reader. They are produced, rather, through a reciprocal relationship, a kind of transaction, if you will, between the text and the reader's conscious or subconscious awareness of the conventions through which 'queerness' has been made available as a coded language.[10]

The homoerotic energy underscoring Walton's response to Victor Frankenstein has been much discussed but, in terms of sexual rhetoric, the eroticised quality of his desire for Victor's *knowledge* is also striking.

He waits, with baited breath and pen poised, for Victor's story to begin: 'as I commence my task, his full-toned voice swells in my ears; his lustrous eyes dwell on me with all their melancholy sweetness' (29). Victor warns Walton that he is a dangerous outcast, but, like much Gothic fiction, before and since, *Frankenstein* depends upon a cultural awareness that the prohibitive law actually produces the desire *to know* which it is supposed to repress. Scholars following Foucault have discussed the various ways in which 'sex' has become a privileged site of 'truth' in western culture, noting that non-normative sex is particularly subject to epistemological pressure. In this respect, Gothic fiction tends to confirm the Foucauldian view that not only has sex been exploited as the secret, but supposedly forbidden, desire but also that identities and behaviours have actually been produced as *more* interesting and *more* subject to the demand for truth than those posited as sexually 'normal'.[11] I would hazard a guess that nobody reads Gothic fiction in order to pursue the 'truth' of acceptable, regular desire. Such texts have always allowed readers to enjoy a sense of having got away with reading something subversive in relative safety and, as such, have been viewed with suspicious disdain in some quarters since the eighteenth century. Fred Botting notes that such texts were 'attacked throughout the second half of the eighteenth century for encouraging excessive emotions and invigorating unlicensed passions'. They:

> were also seen to be subverting the mores and manners on which good social behaviour rested … Gothic fictions seemed to promote vice and violence, giving free reign [*sic*] to selfish ambitions and sexual desires beyond the prescriptions of law or familial duty.[12]

For early twenty-first century readers, the Gothic preoccupation with 'forbidden knowledge' is likely to suggest more than a hint of dangerous sexual possibility. The close tropological proximity of the term 'forbidden' with the term 'knowledge' engages the cultural production of sexual deviancy as a kind of prohibited knowledge, something so tempting that it must be kept secret lest it spread.

Victor tells Walton that he is 'exposing' himself 'to the same dangers which have rendered me what I am' (29), expressing a weighty anxiety that 'the gratification of your wishes may not be a serpent to sting you as mine have been' (28). What Walton apparently cannot perceive is the potential stigma attached to his act of recognition, if that act identifies him with Victor and, by implication, the Monster and all it represents. Within the phobic logic of the maxim 'it takes one to know one', the 'one' who sees always risks being implicated in the forbidden knowledge.[13] Although his own recognition of Walton is likewise erotically inflected, Victor also communicates the panic of one who has come to appreciate the dangers of knowing 'too much': 'a groan burst from his heaving breast and he spoke in broken accents – "Unhappy man! Do you share my madness?"' (27). Walton's desiring recognition of one such as Victor, who has already 'fallen' through the pursuit of forbidden knowledge and his persistence in desiring to know him is, as Victor himself warns, 'madness'. *Frankenstein* presents a familiar triple-bind in relation to 'forbidden knowledge': one desires to know because knowledge is desirable; moreover, one does need to know in order to protect oneself from certain dangers, but it is dangerous to know, or admit to knowing, too much.

The sexually tense knowledge/power relationships between characters in *Frankenstein* encourage a simultaneous sexually 'tense' knowledge/power relationship between the reader and the text. Much of the queer Gothic reading pleasure lies in experiencing the play of recognition, knowledge and ignorance in these narratives and in being put in the alarming, but also thrilling, position of the other 'one' in the text who might recognise the meaning and who might, therefore, be reading in dangerous proximity to the sexual code. The reading experience is both enjoyable and alarming, for the one who dares to admit to recognising the danger that is implicated in the forbidden knowledge. Victor Frankenstein's question addressed to Walton, 'Do you share my madness?' (27), also appeals to the reader who has been allowed to come dangerously close to recognising her or his own desire for the abnormal. But of course the reader does not *have* to admit to knowing or recognising anything because the dispersal of queer meaning into coded language and connotation always allows her or him to remain officially and safely 'ignorant'. The deployment of sexually connotative language is a means to achieve a thrilling subversive effect or, rather, to *affect* subversion while decreasing the risk of censorship. Student readers, coming quickly to the conclusion that Gothic texts are really all about 'sex' and setting themselves the task of liberating (speaking about) the apparently repressed meaning in Gothic fiction may be missing a crucial point. Gothic fiction has always appealed precisely because its deployment of coded language allows its readers to experience the thrills of sexual connotation without having to openly admit to recognising the possible meaning in the text. In so doing, the genre has always produced a pleasurable dynamic of excitement, fear and expectation.

The language of sexual deviance has long been linked to the language of recognition, for, in a world in which certain desires have been coded 'unspeakable', the reading of queerness has become largely a question of recognising signs and codes. There is often something queer about recognition in Gothic fiction. Uncanny, potentially erotic, overwhelming and paranoia-inducing, one consistent quality of the condition I would like to call 'queer Gothic recognition' is a sense of enthralment to a more powerful, more knowing figure, one who wields an inexplicable and dangerous power to arrest and dominate. In this respect, *Frankenstein* can be situated in relation to other nineteenth-century Gothic texts featuring moments where characters are powerfully affected by an indefinable, frightening sense of recognition.[14] The erotic energy of queer Gothic recognition is well expressed in Victor's linguistically climactic recognition of the Monster during their final pursuit over the Arctic ice: 'I … uttered a wild cry of ecstasy when I distinguished a sledge, and the distorted proportions of a well-known form within. Oh! with what a burning gush did hope revisit my heart!' (200). The Monster also disrupts Walton's journey. The 'strange sight' of this unnamable unknown moving across the Arctic ice arrests his attention, excites his 'unqualified wonder' (23), and throws into doubt all his preconceptions about what is natural, normal and possible. The Monster's appearance is 'queer', undoubtedly, in the *strange* sense of the word, but the queerness of his effect deepens through his capacity to cause a disruption to 'narrative equilibrium' and set in motion 'a questioning of the status quo, and … the nature of reality itself'.[15] While Walton cannot identify the creature, he recognises that something important is happening. The narrative depends upon an illusion of disrupted progress as readers are encouraged to feel that they, too, are about to take an 'alternative' journey into thrilling and frightening realms of experience. I am struck by the fact that this recognition, that the story proper has begun, occurs at the same moment as the text makes it possible for readers to recognise that 'something queer' is happening. As it is the sense of perspective-shifting queer arrest which warns us that we are about to embark upon a Gothic journey, perhaps this sense of 'queerness', in the broadest sense of the word, actually makes the text recognisable as 'Gothic'.

'THINGS FEARFUL TO NAME'

Yet another reading of *Frankenstein* that argues that the novel illustrates anxieties about relationships between men might seem superfluous, but I do want to look again at the way an impression of homosexual and homophobic meaning is conveyed in the language of this text. The early nineteenth century was an intensely homophobic period in England, and *Frankenstein* appears to put into play the language of sexual allusion and metaphor which has coded desire between men as a cause of paranoia, an unspeakable possibility, a threat to masculine autonomy, a source of madness, an unnatural, diseased and an abject deathly condition, well into the twenty-first century. The trope of 'paranoia', for instance, represents an exemplary convergence of Gothic and homophobic conventions. With twenty-eight trials for sodomy between 1805 and 1818, the year *Frankenstein* was first published, men in Mary Shelley's England had reason to be paranoid.[16] When Gothic narratives present men who are paranoid in relation to other men, it is not difficult to read their condition as 'homosexual panic': 'the fear and loathing that set in whenever a man suspects either himself or another man of feeling homosexual desire'.[17] Victor's incipient paranoid subjectivity is brought to 'life' at the same moment as his monster. Admitting he had 'desired it with an ardour that far exceeded moderation', as soon as he sees 'the dull yellow eye of the creature open', he finds 'the beauty of the dream vanished, and breathless horror and disgust filled my heart' (56). When his friend Clerval arrives in Ingolstadt, Victor fears that the Monster will be waiting for them in his bedchamber, but they find the room 'freed from its hideous guest' (60). His relief is premature, however, for in *Frankenstein* the monster of desire with its terrifying power of disclosure is always a haunting presence in the 'bedchamber' of paranoid male subjectivity. The Monster's body may have vanished but the fear remains: 'I thought I saw the dreaded spectre glide into the room; "*he* can tell. – Oh, save me! Save me!" I imagined that the monster seized me' (60). It often seems that more than one 'monster' haunts nineteenth-century Gothic narratives, and *Frankenstein*'s unnameable creature can stand for this other speaking unspeakable: the patched together, heterogeneous and massively overdetermined textual monster *of* homosexuality, a spectral presence that stalks culture as persistently as the Monster pursues Victor.

The fact that 'unspeakable' is one of the most famous code words for sex between men and, as Sedgwick notes, one of the most distinctive Gothic tropes again suggests a relationship between the conventions of Gothic textuality and historically determined discourses about homosexuality.[18] Of course the code 'unspeakable' does not actually reflect a *repression* of homosexual meaning; it illustrates, rather, the *production* and dissemination of oppressively homophobic rhetoric figuring desire between men as unspeakable, unnameable and unthinkable. The Latin formulation is probably the most famous example: '*peccattum illud horrible, inter Christanos non nominandum*' – 'the horrible sin not to be named among Christians'. When we see this code put into such insistent play, it is difficult to escape the impression that Gothic textuality has developed as a form of cultural production which exploits the discursive construction of male same-sex desire as a proscribed possibility. Although the 'unspeakable' is probably more commonly associated with later nineteenth-century fictions such as *The Picture of Dorian Gray* (1891) and *The Strange Case of Dr Jekyll and Mr Hyde* (1886), the theme is already established in *Frankenstein*. From the moment of his monster's animation, Victor is locked in a psychic closet: 'How they would, each and all, abhor me, and hunt me from the world, did they know my unhallowed acts' (179). He repeatedly claims that his feelings are both unspeakable and unthinkable and the Monster, who embodies his 'unhallowed acts', is actually hunted from the world for the duration of the narrative.

Yet, the flip-side to unspeakability is a powerful inducement to confess. Confession is another common Gothic convention and, according to Foucault, an important knowledge/power relation through which sexual 'truth' has been constituted in Judeo-Christian culture. Confession, he observes, 'was, and still remains, the general standard governing the production of the true discourse on sex' (63). In this context, non-normative desire is supposedly rendered unspeakable but it is also mandated that 'you will seek to transform your desire, your every desire, into discourse' (21). *Frankenstein* can be read as a text which reveals something about the apparently, but not actually, opposing cultural imperatives constituting deviant desire as *both* a verbal prohibition and an inducement to confession. Take, for instance, the madness-inducing tension between the 'unspeakable' and the desire to confess experienced by Victor Frankenstein. He claims, 'I would have given the world to have confided that fatal secret', but at the same time feels, 'I could not bring myself to disclose a secret which would fill my hearer with consternation, and make fear and unnatural horror the inmates of his breast' (180). But the double-bind is not contradictory within the logic of the deployment of sexuality outlined by Foucault. The tension between the need to keep dreadful secrets and the compulsion to speak about them might contribute to a sense that the text is really speaking to us about sex, in so far as deviant sexual meaning has been produced as a secret one feels compelled to confess.

When Victor panics as he 'catches' the Monster's 'opening eye', the text calls to mind a fearful threat to masculine autonomy. In *Frankenstein* the language of the male gaze is a penetrative language; or, to put the point another way, it could be said that the language of penetration makes itself felt most forcefully through the language of the gaze. D. A. Miller observes that 'where homosexuality is concerned', the male gaze often assumes penetrative qualities: 'the object beheld may penetrate, capture and overwhelm the beholder's body consciousness like a smell'.[19] If *Frankenstein* can be read as engaging nascent discourses about homosexuality, the clustering of desires and anxieties surrounding the sign of the male gaze in the text is striking. Take, for example, Victor's response to the Monster's first approach: 'He held up the curtain of the bed; and his eyes, if eyes they may be called, were fixed on me ... one hand was stretched, seemingly to detain me, but I escaped' (57). From Victor's paranoid perspective, he cannot help but read the Monster's desire as a sexual threat and its gaze, together with the physical reach through the curtains towards his body, figures his bedchamber as a potentially 'sodomitical' space. Theorists of homosexuality, such as Leo Bersani, Ellis Hanson and Lee Edelman, have addressed the longstanding perception of anal sex as a shattering of male subjectivity leading to the 'dissolution of the self'.[20] If the boundaries of male subjectivity have been homophobically constituted as a refusal to be penetrated by another man and if same-sex desire is frequently conveyed through the 'look', the Monster's gaze fixed intently upon Victor's vulnerable body represents a madness-inducing threat.

In the convoluted logic of homophobic reading, homosexual desire is read through reading the sign of the male gaze, but of course it is the nature of queer coding to render the meaning conveyed ambiguous and, ultimately, unreadable. The deployment of sexually coded language creates anxiety and excitement precisely because it is always impossible for the reader to know for sure if they are reading what they suspect they might be reading. In this discursive context, it is quite apt that in his nightmares Victor can hardly distinguish between the eyes of his dead friend Clerval and those of the Monster. He sees 'nothing but a dense and frightful darkness, penetrated by no light but the glimmer of two eyes that glared upon me', which appear sometimes 'the expressive eyes of Henry, languishing in death ... sometimes it was the watery clouded eyes of the monster, as I first saw them in my chamber at Ingolstadt' (176). Such nightmares 'speak' of a world in which all male relations are subject to a hermeneutics of suspicion which threatens to read them as literally monstrous.

The language of abjection, profanity, death, disease and the unnatural, so pervasive in *Frankenstein*, further compounds a sense of doubling between the conventions of Gothic fiction and conventionally phobic responses to the possibility of sexual deviance, especially male homosexual deviance. The idea of 'crimes against nature', for instance, has long been linked with non-reproductive sexual relations. Victor's desire to create the Monster is presented as unnatural from the beginning: 'profane', 'unhallowed', 'filthy' and 'unwholesome' (53). As the project begins to affect his health, his 'slow fever' (53) and 'incipient disease' (55) hint at the sickness and contagion also associated with 'unnatural' desire. Notably, Victor's ill-health stems from his courting of abjection, and from his penetrative 'dabbling' 'among the unhallowed damps of the grave' (53) emerges a Monster. This equation, non-reproductive desire equals death, is doubly apt during a period in which the death penalty for sodomy was used more widely in England than at any other time. Until 1835, when the last execution for sodomy took place, if a man's body or behaviour did 'speak' of homosexuality, it could indeed lead to his death under the law, and same-sex desire has continued to be associated with death in homophobic rhetoric to this day.

Frankenstein's film and theatre progeny have continued to put the language of homosexual deviance into play, presenting audiences with numerous paranoid, secretive, effeminate, unhealthy, nervous, death-obsessed, insane Frankensteins who repeatedly abandon their families and neglect their women in favour of 'monsters'. Benshoff finds the 'core idea – that of a mad male homosexual science giving birth to a monster ... to a greater or lesser degree in almost every filmic adaptation' (18). James Whale's *Frankenstein* (1931), for instance, features a coded homosexual subtext. The film opens in a graveyard, and the camera's focus upon a Memento Mori statue sets the scene for a double-voiced Queer Gothic narrative: remember death/remember homosexuality. For 'knowing' audience members, it also contains a warning: remember that homosexuality has been constructed as a deathly condition; remember, in other words, homophobia. Given the quantity of homosexual connotation and homophobic signification available in the text, McGavran reads Shelley's novel as 'a secret yet scarcely disguised gay adventure' (60). If the text does contain a 'gay adventure' it has a telling conclusion when the Monster finally decides to burn himself to death. Burning is, after all, the classically recommended punishment for sex between men.[21] Burning remains the 'recommended' punishment for the Monster in *Frankenstein* films, as in the famous scene in Whale's version where the villagers finally trap him in a burning windmill.

'A VOYAGE OF DISCOVERY'

An attention to the sexual textuality at work within Gothic space further illustrates the extent to which a coded language of sexual deviance has become a kind of Gothic convention. Gothic fiction has always used space to communicate fears and desires which cannot be spoken directly. As Botting notes, it is often presumed that the 'gloom and darkness of sublime landscapes' function as 'markers of inner mental and emotional states' (91–2). Indeed, the overt psycho-sexual symbolism of crumbling castles, sinister monasteries, deep dark forests, dungeons and subterranean passages sometimes seems a little too obvious to be especially interesting. That said, a queer approach could offer a fresh perspective on what sometimes seems a rather hackneyed generic convention. Of particular interest in *Frankenstein* are moments where the representation of unorthodox desire, strange knowledge and marginal space intersect. Located on the social, cultural and sexual peripheries of the narrative, such liminal spaces are never entirely exterior to the normal world, but can be recognised as constituting places of *difference*. Gothic texts are replete with marginal spaces, the kind of spaces which might be considered ambivalent sites of queer possibility, critical power and danger, because, away from the hegemony of dominant institutions, sexual subjects are least stable.[22] Moreover, the strange wanderers and outcasts journeying through the narrative may function also as markers of a larger sexual and epistemological journey undertaken by culture during this period. In this respect, it is again important not to read *Frankenstein* as simply repressing or pushing queer meaning into the language of Gothic landscapes and journeys, leaving it there for the reader to discover. Instead, we should consider how the text engages and takes part in the production of certain spaces as queer and queer desires as marginal, strange, deathly and even 'Gothic' conditions.

In spatial terms, *Frankenstein* opens in a strangely appropriate place, a dangerously unstable shifting sea of ice. I would propose that it is only from a space such as this that a tale such as *Frankenstein* can be told. This place, if it can be called a place, where nothing is certain, predictable or known, sets the scene for the entire novel, forewarning of the uncertain boundaries and dangerous desires to be found within. Walton's narrative begins with an optimistic spatial fantasy: 'What may not be expected in a country of eternal light?' (13). Instead, he finds himself presented with limitless ice, liable to crack at any moment, over which passes the warning figure of the Monster. Victor draws attention to the relationship between space and previously unimaginable possibilities when he says to Walton, 'Were we among the tamer scenes of nature, I might fear to encounter your unbelief, perhaps your ridicule; but many things will appear possible in these wild and mysterious regions' (29). His presumption links the space to the production of the narrative itself, by which I mean, the liminal (neither land nor sea) space of the Arctic is a wild zone, which opens the possibility for telling 'mysterious' narratives of 'wild' desire.

Although it is not specified precisely what becomes possible in this location, both Victor and Walton imply that things may be said and may occur that are different to 'normal' expectations. Moreover, as the alternative possibilities that Walton had hoped to discover are found not in the North Pole but in his relationship with Victor, this space encompasses potential for a different relationship between men, as well as the bestowal of knowledge other than that which Walton originally envisioned. But the opening of *Frankenstein* can also stand as an indirect comment on the perceived cultural function of Gothic fiction as a kind of generic wild zone, an alternative space which is supposed to offer reading experiences that differ from more mainstream literature. If we were not in this Gothic space, says Victor to the reader, I might expect to encounter your unbelief, but here, it might be possible to envision dangerous narrative possibilities. Such spaces also create possibilities for producing readings that differ from normal expectations, opening not only the narrative, but also the interpretative wild zone of queer reading.

Frankenstein presents a spatial allegory in which the dangerous desire and forbidden knowledge embodied by the Monster are diffused and expressed through the text's 'landscape of desire'.[23] Acting as a harbinger, ushering Victor in to tell his strange story, the Monster is symbolically central from the beginning. It is therefore his rightful place to precipitate the narrative and appropriate that Walton should see him first. The juxtaposition of the Monster's body with the Arctic setting implies a metaphorical relation between his body and the space he inhabits. The 'vast and irregular plains of ice', described by Walton, are traversed by the embodiment of 'vast', 'irregular', desire (23). Like the cultural construction of queer desire, the Monster is perceived to be 'out there', displaced away from the normal world, ultimately unknowable, and 'lost among the distant inequalities of the ice' (23). The strange space therefore heightens the sense of a queer allegory in the text. For the setting of the Monster's first appearance reminds us that non-normative desires and identities have a long history of relegation to the cultural and spatial edges, as monstrous sites where the known demarcations of sex, gender and desire begin to break down. In so far as he embodies a force of proscribed desire, the Monster's marginalised position also unmasks a violence that may be done to any desire, identity or body that deviates from the normativity of the period. The convergence, at this narrative moment, of a symbolically marginal dangerous space with a monster, and the forbidden knowledge he embodies, brings together space, desire and knowledge to produce a recognisably queer *figure* in both senses of the word. The Monster's 'figure' (his body) is strange, disruptive and frightening; it is also 'figurative' – packed with potential queer meaning.

Gothic texts abound with mysterious wanderers who seek knowledge, or have been forced to travel because they have been endowed with too much forbidden knowledge. The tropes of the journey and the wanderer present further points where it is possible to perceive a doubling of Gothic conventions and the conventions through which queerness has been made legible in the cultural imagination. Simply speaking, the Gothic wanderer's propensity to shift enacts his or her threatening sexual shiftiness. After all, endless travelling is not considered to be sexually normal, and Gothic texts often set up an opposition between the (hetero) normative stability of home, as against the queer traveller who literally refuses to be pinned down, and who has either rejected or been ejected from the cultural centre. In 1897, having been released from his prison sentence for homosexuality and forced into exile in France, Oscar Wilde pertinently signed his name as 'Sebastian Melmoth' in the register of the hotel where he was staying. In so doing he identified himself with the title character of Maturin's Gothic novel *Melmoth The Wanderer* (1820), a damned figure forced to wander the earth until the devil claims him for hell. As Baldick notes, 'Melmoth' is the 'badge of the eternal outcast'.[24] But Wilde tapped into another aspect of Gothic mythology; his self-nomination is also, appropriately enough, the 'badge' of the *queer*. Exiled and forced to wander, Wilde found that he had become a cultural monster, and his pseudonym calls upon a longer tradition linking Gothic authors with transgressive sexuality. This mythology stretches at least back to Lord Byron, who was famously forced to travel abroad in 1816 to escape rumours about his relationship with his half-sister and his liking for young men. Wilde, Byron, Walton, Victor's Monster and Victor himself are all variously Gothic 'wanderers, outcasts and rebels' 'condemned to roam the borders of social worlds', as 'bearers of dark truth or horrible knowledge' (98). Little wonder, then, that back at home in London, Walton's sister Margaret regards his journey with 'evil forebodings' (13). In terms of both queer and Gothic conventions, she has good reason to be worried.

The relationship between Victor and his Monster is realised through their journey into ever more strange, sublime and hostile environments, as they move through glacial mountains, appalling islands and graveyards. Ultimately, they are forced out to the Arctic where, as Rosemary Jackson observes, 'in a sterile polar region – the condition of their intimacy is a progressive alienation from society'.[25] It is difficult to escape the impression that, at the symbolic level, this allegorical journey progresses towards the production of queer desires as paranoid, dangerous, sterile and socially alienating forms of intimacy and identity. If the deployment of sexuality from the seventeenth century onwards paved the way towards a language charged with sexual connotation, the Gothic journeys undertaken in texts such as *Frankenstein* might stand in allegorical relation to the sexual/epistemological journey taken by society in the late eighteenth and nineteenth century. The space in which Victor and Walton are situated becomes increasingly dangerous as the narrative progresses. By the end, the ship is 'encompassed by peril ... I am surrounded by mountains of ice, which admit of no escape, and threaten every moment to crush my vessel' (205). Walton survives, albeit drifting and disillusioned, but for others the Gothic journey leads inexorably toward a figurative 'dead end'. Where else is there to go in a culture in which social and sometimes actual death were penalties for non-normative sexual activities? As Foucault notes, by the nineteenth century there was a feeling that 'strange pleasures ... would eventually result in nothing short of death' (54). It is a feeling that is well expressed in the deathly destination of many early nineteenth-century Gothic journeys.

QUEER AND GOTHIC

In terms of queer reading, Gothic fiction presents a productive point of departure for discussing the way we have come to speak about the possibility of sexual nonconformity and points towards commonplace but often unspoken links between entertainment and the construction of 'deviancy'.[26] It is worth noting that *Frankenstein* quickly attracted an aura of queer Gothic transgression. On viewing the first theatrical adaptation entitled *Presumption: Or the Fate of Frankenstein* in 1823, Mary Shelley took note of the decision to leave the name of the actor playing the Creature signified by a blank in the programme. In a letter to a friend, she observed, 'this nameless mode of naming the un[n]ameable is rather good'.[27] As the Monster's very namelessness is produced by the world that refuses him a name, the signifying of his presence with a meaningful silence is, as Shelley puts it, 'rather good'. Such a small hint of unspeakability may not seem very remarkable, but it gains more weight when considered in relation to the wider furore surrounding the production of *Presumption*. When tickets went on sale, 'some zealous friends of morality' took it upon themselves to protest. They distributed pamphlets advising the public not to view the 'monstrous drama', founded upon an 'improper work', warning readers, 'Do not take your wives and families – The novel itself is of a decidedly immoral tendency; it treats of a subject which in nature cannot occur.'[28] This pamphlet takes part in a larger tradition of contemporary anti-theatre protest, and perhaps the pamphleteers intended to refer only to the novel's arguably blasphemous subtext. But, even so, the language of the text steers close to another popular subject for pamphlets during this period, namely, those sexual behaviours considered immoral, unnatural, monstrous and dangerous to family life.[29]

The theatre responded with a successful repudiation, but the protests had already encouraged ticket sales. As one contemporary commented, 'You only have to tell a Cockney that an Exhibition is shocking – abominable – impious, and off he starts to bear witness to the fact'.[30] If Gothic fiction engages the discursive production of sexual nonconformity, it has come to depend upon the fact that desires considered 'queer' in the cultural imagination are also those considered to be especially exciting. 'Queerness' is thrilling precisely because it is supposed to be prohibited. In 1824, another theatre manager planning to stage *Presumption* took note and designed a hoax 'Caution to Playhouse Frequenters', apparently hoping to boost box office sales. This text described the play as 'impious', 'horrid and unnatural', a 'piece publicly exposed by the Society for the Suppression of Vice and Immorality', concluding with 'The Wages of Sin are Death' and referring to the theatre as a 'Grave of the Soul'.[31] The ploy backfired, perhaps partly because the text steered a little too close to the language of sodomy for even the most curious of Cockneys to stomach. What is interesting is that people were attempting to sell Gothic entertainment with a language recognisable as 'queer'. Through its association with *Frankenstein*, the theatre space itself has become, like Victor's laboratory in the novel, located as the site of deviance and productivity: from this space the monstrous queer meaning of the play *Presumption* is to be produced.

Gothic texts such as *Frankenstein* do not really hide dangerous sexual meaning; they take part in the constitution of sexual deviance as that which is supposed to be repressed, that which can only be made legible through coded language. In this respect, the genre is indicative of a society which has found many ways to speak about sex while pretending to maintain silence on the subject.

Although I have used homophobic discourse as the primary example in this chapter, Gothic texts still have much to reveal about the language of sexual nonconformity more generally. *Frankenstein* reminds us that modern sexual discourse has constructed queerness as forbidden knowledge, as something that must be recognised, but which is dangerous because, once recognised, it is imagined to infect and overwhelm the subject. The 'truth' of sexual nonconformity is depicted as a secret that should remain hidden, but despite the supposed prohibitions remains so fascinating that we feel compelled to try and speak about it. The text engages a world in which to be 'queer' is thought to lead to madness, death and social ostracism and is to risk becoming a strange wanderer, forced to travel, outcast on the edges of society in marginal, dangerous spaces. The fact that all of the above assumptions about what it means to be 'Queer' continue to inform ideas about sexual nonconformity into the twenty-first century suggests again that we encounter not the repression of sexual meaning in Gothic textuality but its ongoing production and proliferation.

NOTES

1 Michel Foucault, *The History of Sexuality, Volume 1: An Introduction*, trans. Robert Hurley (Harmondsworth: Penguin, [1976] 1998), p. 35. All subsequent references are to this edition, and are given in parentheses in the text.
2 Queer scholarship's affinity with Gothic horror fiction is evident in early groundbreaking publications such as Sue-Ellen Case's 'Tracking the Vampire', *Differences*, 3 (1991), 1–20. For more recent work developing the field of 'queer Gothic' studies see George Haggerty's book *Queer Gothic* (Urbana and Chicago: University of Illinois Press, 2006) and the special issue of *Romanticism on the Net* edited by Michael O'Rourke and David Collings, 'Queer Romanticism', 36–7 (2004–5), www.erudit.org/revue/ron/2004/v/n36-37/index.html (accessed 7 Nov. 2005).
3 I have chosen to use the 1831 revised edition because I think it remains the version with which most readers will be familiar. For the debate concerning the relative merits of both versions see Nora Crook, 'In Defence of the 1831 *Frankenstein*', in Esther Schor (ed.), *The Cambridge Companion to Mary Shelley* (Cambridge: Cambridge University Press, 2003), pp. 3–21; and James O'Rourke, 'The 1831 Introduction and Revisions to *Frankenstein*: Mary Shelley Dictates her Legacy', *Studies in Romanticism*, 38 (1999), 365–85.
4 Mary Shelley, *Frankenstein: or The Modern Prometheus* (1831), ed. Maurice Hindle (London: Penguin, 1992), p. 215. All subsequent references are to this edition, and are given in parentheses in the text.
5 See Michael Eberle-Sinatra, 'Readings of Homosexuality in Mary Shelley's *Frankenstein* and Four Film Adaptations', *Gothic Studies*, 7/2 (2005), 185–202.
6 See Eve Kosofsky Sedgwick, *Epistemology of the Closet* (London: Harvester Wheatsheaf, 1991), p. 186. In *The Coherence of Gothic Conventions* (London and New York: Methuen, 1986), Sedgwick calls the nineteenth century the 'Age of Frankenstein', a period 'distinctly and rhetorically marked by the absolute omnipresence of homophobic paranoid tableaus such as that of Victor and the Monster pursuing each other across the Arctic Ice' (x).
7 See Troy Boone, 'Mark of the Vampire: Arnod Paole, Sade, Polidori', *Nineteenth-Century Contexts*, 18 (1995), 349–66 at p. 365.
8 Sedgwick, *Coherence*, pp. x–xi.
9 See David Greven, 'Flesh in the Word: Billy Budd, Sailor, Compulsory Homosociality and the Uses of Queer Desire', *Genders*, 37 (2003), www.genders.org/g37/g37_greven.html, paragraph 14.
10 My thinking here has been influenced by Inge Crosman-Wimmers in her book *Poetics of Reading: Approaches to the Novel* (Princeton: Princeton University Press, 1988). See especially pp. xiii–xxii.
11 In the *History of Sexuality*, Foucault argues that, as the eighteenth and nineteenth centuries progressed, efforts to find out the secrets of 'heterosexual monogamy' were abandoned, while all manner of 'perversions' were identified and came under increasing scrutiny (38).

12 See Fred Botting, *Gothic* (London and New York: Routledge, 1996), p. 4. All further references are to this edition, and are given in parentheses in the text.
13 'One', as Sedgwick notes in *Coherence*, 'can always "also" have the specific meaning of "homosexual"' (viii). According to Lee Edelman, the act of recognition is charged with the homophobic logic 'it takes one to know one', a presumption which carries 'with it the stigma of too intimate a relation to the code and the machinery of its production'. See *Homographesis* (New York and London: Routledge, 1994), p. 7.
14 In Charles Maturin's 1820 novel *Melmoth the Wanderer* (Oxford and New York: Oxford University Press, 1989), for instance, Stanton becomes obsessed with Melmoth and, when he finally recognises him again, finds, 'There was nothing particular or remarkable in his appearance, but the expression of his eyes could never be mistaken or forgotten'. Stanton's heart 'palpitated with violence, – a mist overspread his eyes, – a nameless and deadly sickness, accompanied with a creeping sensation in every pore' (43). James Hogg's 1824 novel *The Private Memoirs and Confessions of a Justified Sinner* (Oxford and New York: Oxford University Press, 1999) contains another striking example when Wringhim first meets Gil-Martin: 'I felt a sort of invisible power that drew me towards him, something like the force of enchantment, which I could not resist. As we approached each other, our eyes met, and I can never describe the strange sensations that thrilled through my whole frame at that impressive moment' (116).
15 Harry M. Benshoff, *Monsters in the Closet: Homosexuality and the Horror Film* (Manchester: Manchester University Press, 1997), p. 5. All subsequent references are to this edition, and are given in parentheses in the text.
16 Eric Daffron, 'Male Bonding: Sympathy and Shelley's *Frankenstein*', *Nineteenth-Century Contexts*, 21 (1999), 415–35 at p. 515.
17 James Holt McGravan, '"Insurmountable Barriers to our Union": Homosocial Male Bonding, Homosexual Panic, and Death on the Ice in *Frankenstein*', *European Romantic Review*, 10 (1999), 46–67 at p. 48.
18 See Sedgwick, *Between Men*, p. 94.
19 D. A. Miller, 'Anal Rope', in Diana Fuss (ed.), *Inside/Out: Lesbian Theories, Gay Theories* (London and New York: Routledge, 1991), p. 131.
20 As Hanson notes, in psychoanalytic terms, to engage the gaze of another man 'would be a form of madness, an embrace of narcissism and death' leading to a 'dissolution of the self'. He continues, 'it becomes extremely important to avoid the gaze of the gay man. For a man, to fear the gay male gaze is to fear the Evil Eye or, rather, the Evil Not – I, the dissolution of the self in narcissistic looking'. See 'Undead', in Diana Fuss (ed.), *Inside/Out: Lesbian Theories, Gay Theories* (London; New York: Routledge, 1991), pp. 328, 329. Leo Bersani's groundbreaking work also remains pertinent. See 'Is the Rectum a Grave?' in Douglas Crimp (ed.), *AIDS: Cultural Analysis, Cultural Activism* (Cambridge, MA and London: MIT Press, 1988).

21 Louis Crompton, *Byron and Greek Love: Homophobia in 19th-Century England* (Berkeley: University of California Press, 1991), p. 13.
22 I am here drawing upon Richard Phillips and Diane Watt in their 'Introduction' to *De-Centring Sexualities: Politics and Representations Beyond the Metropolis* (London and New York: Routledge, 2000), pp. 1–17.
23 The phrase 'landscape of desire' is taken from David Bell and Gill Valentine's 'Introduction' to *Mapping Desire: Geographies of Sexualities* (London; New York: Routledge, 1995), p. 1.
24 As Baldick comments, 'Upon his release from prison in 1897, Oscar Wilde travelled to France under an assumed name carefully contrived to announce him as both martyred saint and blasted sinner: it was "Sebastian Melmoth"'. See his 'Introduction' to *Melmoth the Wanderer*, p. vii.
25 Rosemary Jackson, *Fantasy: The Literature of Subversion* (London: Methuen, 1981), p. 100.
26 See Edward Ingebretsen, 'When the Cave Is a Closet: Pedagogies of the (Re)Pressed', in William J. Spurlin (ed.), *Lesbian and Gay Studies and the Teaching of English: Positions, Pedagogies, and Cultural Politics* (Urbana: National Council of Teachers of English, 2000), pp. 14–35 at p. 18.
27 See Betty T. Bennett (ed.), *The Letters of Mary Wollstonecraft Shelley: Volume 1* (Baltimore and London: Johns Hopkins University Press, 1980), p. 378.
28 The full text is reprinted with commentary on the incident in Stephen Earl Forry, *Hideous Progenies: Dramatisations of Frankenstein from Mary Shelley to the Present* (Philadelphia: University of Pennsylvania Press, 1990), pp. 3–11.
29 Rictor Norton's website, 'Gay History & Literature', is a good resource for examples of eighteenth- and nineteenth-century pamphlets on the subject: www.infopt.demon.co.uk/gayhist.htm (accessed 30 Sept. 2006).
30 Quoted in Forry, *Hideous Progenies*, pp. 6–7.
31 The text is available in ibid., p. 8.

4
Daniel Deronda's Jewish panic

∼

Royce Mahawatte

> Theodora ... As for the Jewish element in *Deronda*, I think it a very fine idea; it's a noble subject. Wilkie Collins and Mrs Braddon would not have thought of it, but that does not condemn it. It shows a large conception of what one may do in a novel.
>
> Henry James, '*Daniel Deronda*: A Conversation' (1876)[1]

George Eliot's 'large conception' was perhaps greater than Theodora, or even Henry James, could have imagined. With half of its narrative concerned with the Jewish people in England, *Daniel Deronda* (1876) was clearly more socially orientated than it was sensational or popular. But, the question must be asked, were Jewish subjects out of place in the fiction of the railway stands or the periodical? If Eliot did not engage with the subjects of her sensational contemporaries, then it is possible to detect in her work the aesthetics of their Gothic predecessors. Daniel Deronda's slow realisation that he is Jewish is accompanied by tropes usually found in the Gothic novel. This consists of Mordecai's passionate entreaties to him; his unswerving belief in Daniel's Jewish heritage (in spite of Daniel's denials) is also accompanied by images of possession and sickly hands. Mordecai offers Daniel a Melmoth-style pact for everlasting life via Cabbalistic mysticism: 'You must be not only a hand to me, but a soul – believing my belief.'[2] Daniel is as fearful of Mordecai's attempts to grasp at him as he is of his own unknown origins. It is possible to read a 'Jewish panic' alongside an erotic one: the so-called 'homosexual panic' that has powered so much of Eve Kosofsky Sedgwick's work. In her final novel, George Eliot created an eroticism of fear around Daniel and his Jewish identity, one that eventually becomes quite explicit. When viewed against the other plot in the novel, Gwendolen Harleth's resistance to her husband's 'empire of fear' (395), Eliot's handling of Daniel's Jewish realisation certainly does demonstrate high ambitions, not only for the novel but also for the erotic capabilities of different novelistic languages.

It might seem impossible to separate the Gothic from the queer. After all, the title to this book itself provokes the question, 'when is the Gothic anything *but* queer?' Since the publication of Sedgwick's *The Coherence of Gothic Conventions* (1980) and more crucially *Between Men: English Literature and Male Homosocial Desire* (1985) and *Epistemology of the Closet* (1991), the Gothic novel has been revised, by Sedgwick's reading of Claude Lévi Strauss and René Girard, from being a metaphor for the repressed to a more sociologically complex articulation of 'homosocial' power exchange via marriage, and the homosexual desire and acts that might lurk around the corner. The Gothic is an experience of managed difference, often authored by sexual dissidents and, in terms of literary style, manifested by the grotesque surfaces and, more curiously and in erotic terms, by the understatements and the absences in the narrative.[3] As Sedgwick points out, in Charles Maturin's *Melmoth the Wanderer* (1820), the unspeakable demands of the immortal induce panic into those who hear him. The omissions in his manuscript are at times more suggestive than the violent narratives found later on.[4] The Gothic is its own closet and the closet is fundamentally fashioned from metaphor. That homosexual desire might leak into male political relations is a part of the Gothic that finds a particular expression in affect, namely fear. And these fears are represented by bodily events: the starts, the swoons, the ashen aspects and dead faces.[5] Sedgwick offers an interpretation of the Gothic's tendency towards silence as a way of accessing the literary depths between the surfaces whilst also connecting with a society where homophobia is becoming systematised as social fraternity develops.

GEORGE ELIOT AND THE CONTRADICTIONS OF GOTHIC CONVENTIONS

To position George Eliot within both a Gothic tradition and under queer investigation might seem surprising, irreverent or, at the very least, anachronistic. Gordon Haight fiercely stresses that George Henry Lewes's love for Eliot 'left no room for' the passions of her female admirers, but, as the range of biographical evidence would suggest, 'George Eliot's extraordinary attraction for women is seen throughout her life'. Miss Lewis, Eliot's teacher, activists Barbara Bodichon and Bessie Parkes, and most famously Edith Simcox who, amidst other fanatical behaviour, kept a handkerchief that had been used to wipe Eliot's tears, are all examples of these. Some of these women would be identified as having a lesbian sexuality, while others would not.[6] All that can really be said here is that, to extend Terry Castle's reading of '[S]ororal or pseudo-sororal attachments' in Jane Austen's period, Eliot was a product of her time and her time was one where the sexes were segregated and same-sex intimacy was practised very differently and clearly had a range of meanings.[7]

George Eliot's correspondence with Edith Simcox and some of her other female friends has not survived, so there is no primary evidence that might be used to categorise Eliot's sexuality as being anything but heterosexual. But, of course, 'queerness' is a product of cultural definitions and consensus, and in her personal life Marian Evans was not conventional. As the common-law wife of George Henry Lewes, she was shunned by her brother and unvisited by most women of her status up until her marriage to Walter Cross in 1880. Marian Evans, in her private life, held a position that could be easily described as sexually dissident or 'sensational'. Her relationship with John Chapman at 142 The Strand, as editor of *The Westminster Review*, would attest to this. In her public life, however, as 'George Eliot', she was a secular and liberal realist and the sage writer of moral fiction. Although she was considered in some circles an adult novelist, she was deeply committed to widening the sympathies of her readers to include the experiences of the middle and lower orders of society.[8]

But elements of the Gothic and its descendant, the Sensation novel, appear in Eliot's writing: in her plots, character types, lexical elements and literary allusions. Besides her Gothic novella 'The Lifted Veil' (1859), Maggie Tulliver, Dorothea Casaubon and Gwendolen Harleth all have fearful experiences that would not be out of place in a Gothic or Sensation novel. And just as it is Gothic, Eliot's fiction is packed with closets. Characters have to negotiate provincial social environments where the public and the private threaten the other's territory, bringing havoc, the sins of the past, anxiety and very often exclusion. Alexander Welsh's important work on blackmail sees the Sensation novel as an expression of Victorian anxieties concerning secularisation and knowledge. For Welsh, Eliot uses the techniques of Sensation fiction, and themes of scandal and presumed immorality, in order to rationalise and ironise a secular society obsessed with information, reputation and approval.[9] In *The Mill on the Floss* (1860), after her quasi-elopement with Stephen Guest,

Maggie Tulliver finds that Doctor Ken can not come to her aid now that she is viewed as a fallen woman. After Nicholas Bulstrode's corruption is exposed, the gossiping town of Middlemarch turns on Casaubon's nephew and, in effect, casts him out: '"Young Ladislaw the grandson of a thieving Jew pawnbroker" was a phrase which had entered emphatically into the dialogues about the Bulstrode business.'[10] These examples make the connection between Welsh's and Sedgwick's work clear. Sedgwick points out that blackmail and the fear of scandal serve homosociality and feelings of homosexual panic; at the same time, the treatment of Ladislaw shows that Eliot wanted to show that racial or religious identity also operates within a system of secrecy and suspicion.[11] The public and the private, the present and the past, exert strong shaping influences on identity and on how it might be managed within society.

It is perhaps unsurprising, then, that Eliot's final novel exhibits elements of the Gothic and the queer in that it draws affective strategies both from the Sensation writers of the period and also from the Gothic tradition proper. In addition to the paranoid male plot and vampiric homoeroticism in Daniel's narrative, the attention-grabbing story of Gwendolen Harleth's wavering fortunes, blackmail and murder, albeit of a psychological kind, certainly had economic benefits for the publisher. When it was part published between February and September 1876, the novel captured an awaiting audience: Blackwood, Eliot's publisher, wrote: 'Deronda has evidently hooked his fish at the first start and is keeping him steadily on the line all through the run.'[12] The unlikely relationship between *Daniel Deronda* and Gothic aesthetics has been picked up by critics. Anne Cvetkovitch sees Gwendolen's narrative as a Sensation novel plot and relates it to Eliot's engagement with mass culture; Marlene Tromp sees 'incorporation of the images and methods of the sensation novel into her drama' as a way of coding domestic violence in a middle-class setting; and Sarah Gates writes: 'I do think the Gothic plot has to be the black romance played out between Grandcourt, the brute-turned-gentleman, and Gwendolen, the maiden-in-flight, and that … Lydia Glasher … is a figure of the hidden or elided violent woman – the Dracula's wife.'[13]

Surprisingly though, *Daniel Deronda* has not been discussed in terms of Gothic aesthetics. The novel quite clearly explores secrecy in relation to desire, sexual or economic – the two are morbidly linked for Gwendolen and Grandcourt. At the same time, Jewish identity is a secret that cannot help but be revealed, if not exposed. Daniel's story of self-discovery in many ways yields much to queer interpretation, especially when the

Gothic register that is used to describe him is considered. His awakening Jewishness can be read as a narrative of otherness – a Gothic 'coming-out' story full of fear, dread and startling coincidences.

A NARRATIVE OF CABBALISTIC VAMPIRISM?

It is possible to read Daniel Deronda's journey to self-awareness, and to Jewish realisation, as a unique reworking of the vampire narrative and the paranoid male trope. Recent critical readings of the figure especially in the fiction of Sheridan Le Fanu and Bram Stoker, show how the vampire is a significant site of contestation. Anxieties about modernity, homosexual anxiety and theories of degeneration all seem to coalesce around the figure.[14] Carol Margaret Davison's work on anti-Semitism and the Gothic tradition tracks the immortal wanderer at the beginning of the nineteenth century to the figure of Count Dracula towards the very end and interprets this lineage as a representation of 'the Crypto-Jew narrative'.[15] Gothic and Sensation fiction have always included Jewish stereotypes. The Wandering Jew is a stock stereotype of Gothic fiction – a symbol of loneliness, expulsion and ostracism. Henry James's Theodora was partially correct to say that Jewish subjects did not appear in the work of Collins or Braddon, but in fact, in Sensation fiction, Jewish stereotypes hover on the fringes of a corrupt society – exploiting the follies of the fallen respectable. In Mary Braddon's Sensation novel *Birds of Prey* (1867), as in *Daniel Deronda*, Jewish moneylenders aid the heiress-hunting gamblers.[16] Whether feeding on life-force in the earlier nineteenth century, or on bank balances and blood in the middle and later period, the figure of the Jew is associated with rather worldly attempts to feast on the untouched vitality of the living.

With respect to Eliot's final novel, Davison picks out Daniel's progression from 'benighted self-estrangement to self-enlightenment' as a feature of the 'traditional Gothic character' and sees the vampire motif displaced on to Grandcourt and Lapidoth, Mirah's father.[17] While her argument is entirely convincing, Davison seems reluctant to associate the vampiric with Mordecai, the European wanderer, settled in London, who wants to bring Daniel into his world of Cabbalistic and transcendent spirituality. At the same time, Daniel is a virgin figure, thirsty for an understanding that might release him from his 'neutral life' (567). He, too, is a wanderer, but in his case amongst the English upper classes. Interestingly, however, Eliot seems to invoke the figure of the vampire in Mordecai and all the fears that accompany it in order to effect a transition on Daniel, one that he himself cannot initiate. In keeping with the tradition of the vampire, Mordecai is a morally ambiguous and uncannily enlightening figure and Daniel cannot help but be sympathetic towards him.

On this last point, characterisation of Daniel has come under severe criticism. Oliver Lovesey points out that Daniel Deronda is 'a curiously absent character' and Leslie Stephen famously described him as a woman's hero.[18] Lovesey gives a convincing defence for Daniel's position as a humanist symbol that 'must continually demonstrate the capacity to accommodate another'.[19] It appears that Daniel is more 'feminine' than most critics would like. The famous argument levelled at him by critics such as Mary Wilson Carpenter, K. M. Newton and Cynthia Chase is that his self-realisation might have come about a little faster had he just peeked into his own underpants. Even Carol M. Davison writes that 'Eliot's Crypto-Jew long remains Crypto, especially to himself'. All of these critics are responding to the link between Daniel and what might be termed Gothic aesthetics – mysteries and apparent dread that lie in their solution. The medical historical work of Ronald Hyam and Ben Knights has done much to answer the question of Daniel Deronda's circumcised penis. Routine infant circumcision was widespread amongst the English upper and middle classes of the late nineteenth century as an anti-masturbatory measure, rather than as the mark of the Covenant of Abraham. Daniel Deronda or George Eliot would not have necessarily related a circumcised penis exclusively to a Semitic heritage. The fact still remains, though, that Daniel seems to be bafflingly unable to grasp his masculinity.[20]

When viewed within the terms of the Gothic, however, Daniel's masculinity reveals much about Eliot's creative intentions for him. His sensitivity, his deferral of self, his compassion, these all function, at least in literary terms, as affective indicators of both his morality and his racial difference. Like many Gothicists before her, Eliot explores Deronda's heritage by invoking family portraiture. Paintings in Gothic fiction often act as a interface between the present and the past, recording lineage and physiognomic continuity. 'But in the nephew Daniel Deronda the family faces of various types, seen on the walls of the gallery, found no reflex' (205). Deronda is outside history, his face absent from the family tradition. He is a mystery. More tellingly, Daniel is separated from his own reflection: 'His own face in the glass had during many years been associated for him with thoughts of some one whom he must be like – one about whose character and lot he continually wondered, and never dared to ask' (226). In Lacanian terms Daniel is the perfect subject for panic as he quite literally identifies himself, not only with *the* other, but with *an* other 'some one'. The Other, which is both enticing and threatening, elicits fear. In Lacanian psychoanalysis, the Other, which often coincides with the maternal, intimates the prelinguistic state that is both comforting and unsettling. Daniel's 'desire to know his own mother, or to know about her, was constantly haunted with dread' (246), we are told, so, rather than confronting his future, Daniel hides from it, and so the Gothic registers that Eliot uses here are singularly suited to him. As an adult, Daniel experiences the isolation and introspection of a Melmoth figure:

> He was ceasing to care for knowledge – he had no ambition for practice – unless they could both be gathered up into one current of his emotions; and he dreaded, as if it were a dwelling place of lost souls, that dead anatomy of culture which turns the universe into a mere ceaseless answer to queries ... But how and whence was the needed event to come? – the evidence that would justify partiality, and make him what he longed to be yet was unable to make himself – an organic part of social life, instead of roaming in it like a disembodied spirit, stirred with a vague social passion, but without fixed local habitation to make it real? (336)

Daniel's world is subtly conveyed through images of death and desolation: 'a dwelling place of lost souls'. The feeling of being an outsider, a Gothic feeling, is transferred to a dissatisfaction with his social life. In his English environment, 'that dead anatomy of culture', Daniel is a rootless ghost. The lack of social connection in his past and in his present have uncanny ramifications: events and significant occurrences find their way to him, rather than the other way round. As with Maturin's Monçada, happenings and coincidences advance Daniel's life: Mirah on the banks of the Thames; unknown men who identify Daniel as Jewish; Mordecai turning out to be the 'Ezra' that Mirah speaks of, the sudden letter from Daniel's mother. Daniel inhabits a world which tends towards meaning rather than towards dissolution. A part of this tendency, this narrative Gothic gravity, is bound up with the relationship between Daniel and Mordecai and the erotics of affect that are found there.

Eve Kosofsky Sedgwick's view of the doppelgänger plot as a literary manifestation of the worrying interplay between homosociality and homosexuality has a particular bearing on Daniel's dawning identity.[21] The image of the protagonist fearing the presence or pursuit of another male who seeks an unwanted intimacy with him punctuates Daniel's narrative and the intimacy sought out is racial. Before Daniel even meets

Mordecai he is approached when walking in the Jewish quarter in Frankfurt, by a man who asks him about his parentage. Daniel's response is telling: 'He had a strongly resistant feeling: he was inclined to shake off hastily the touch on his arm; but he managed to slip it away and said coldly, "I am an Englishman"' (417). Daniel is able to remove the touch, but he can not remove the feeling he has of anxiety and revulsion. Eliot uses the hand as a type of conceit as it conveys a sense of the uncanny, while also indicating the idea of the 'grasp', a body held by a deathly hand and yet also a feeling or position that needs to be understood.

The deathly hand reappears in Daniel's first meeting with Mordecai in the bookshop:

> Deronda felt a thin hand pressing his arm tightly, while a hoarse, excited voice, not much above a loud whisper, said –
> 'You are perhaps of our race?'
> Deronda coloured deeply, not liking the grasp, and then answered with a slight shake of the head, 'No.' The grasp was relaxed, the hand withdrawn, the eagerness of the face collapsed into uninterested melancholy, as if some possessing spirit which had leaped into the eyes and gestures had sunk back again to the inmost recesses of the frame; and moving further off as he held out the little book, the stranger said in a tone of distant civility, 'I believe Mr Ram will be satisfied with half-a-crown, sir.' (437–8)

Again Daniel rejects this second proposition, and this time he blushes. Instead of being described as a 'touch', there is something all the more challenging in 'the grasp' and the understanding it suggests. Eliot sets up a contrast of physicalities that can only add to the erotic suggestiveness of this meeting. Mordecai is clearly physically compromised with his 'hoarse, excited voice'. On the other hand, blood rushes into Daniel's face and after the rebuttal, the grasp, the need to understand that it implies, retreats. The imagery of possession and 'recesses' invoke the Gothic that then lingers over the mundane monetary transaction. The underlying sense here is that Daniel's physicality, his sexuality is just as 'out of bounds' as his own racial awareness. Mordecai is cast as predatory. The dynamic between the men is metaphorical of racial shame as it is of internalised homophobia. When they meet, by coincidence hours later, the discomfort increases. Daniel and Mordecai register each other as two men who have shared something, but who do not wish to make reference to it: 'neither in his surprise making any sign of recognition' (448). Here is a connection of anonymity, a knowledge, a 'grasp' of some kind of connection that has morbid overtones.

To a degree, Mordecai's sublimity is manifested by his sickness, which, in turn makes his interest in Daniel, his intense and rather overly emotional behaviour, metaphorically vampiric and predatory. When the narrator turns to Mordecai, he is described as someone 'whose figure had bitten itself into Deronda's mind' (528). Mordecai himself finds that his 'passionate desire had concentrated itself in the yearning for some young ear into which he could pour his mind as a testament'. His ailing condition, we are told is diverted by 'the current of this yearning for transmission':

> He wanted to find a man who differed from himself ... he imagined a man who would have all the elements necessary for sympathy with him, but in an embodiment unlike his own: he must be a Jew, intellectually cultured, morally fervid ... but his face and frame must be beautiful and strong, he must have been used to all the refinements of social life, his voice must flow with a full and easy current, his circumstances be free from sordid need; he must glorify the possibilities of the Jew, not sit and wander as Mordecai did, bearing the stamp of his people amid the signs of poverty and waning breath. (528–9)

Mordecai's spiritual desires seem like desire nevertheless, the search for a lover. This feeling is suggestively racialised and inflected with concerns about the nature of identity. The vision is of an idealised face, which is fulfilled by Daniel, 'a face and frame which seemed to him to realise the long-conceived type' (536). Mordecai wants someone Jewish but assimilated, someone spiritual but physical. He has a desire that tries to correct social exclusion and the text blurs the distinction between both the dream and the wider vision which tries to seek and locate Daniel. 'It was Deronda now who was seen in the often painful night-watches, when we are all liable to be held with the clutch of a single thought' (537). This ability to locate Daniel approaches the clairvoyant when Mordecai watches him from Blackfriars Bridge and says that 'I expected you to come down the river. I have been waiting for you these five years' (590). He has 'Cabbalistic' 'Jewdar'.

Up until this point, Daniel's response to Mordecai has been an anxious one. Once Mordecai starts revealing his hopes for what he and Daniel might achieve together, Daniel's response is not to panic but to explore with a degree of scepticism: 'he could not but believe that this strangely-disclosed relation was founded on an illusion' (590). The ensuing conversation where Daniel and Mordecai discuss the prospect of preparing Mordecai's spiritual revelations for publication seem in part to be like the healthy humouring the ramblings of a sick man, and yet also as the genuine expression of a need to pass on an inheritance. Within the terms of repressed and projected homoerotic desire, it is the Melmoth-like pact between the living and the non-living. Daniel ensures that he can help Mordecai publish his work – 'If you will rely on me, I can assure you of all that is necessary to that end' (557). Clearly this is insufficient:

> 'That is not enough,' said Mordecai, quickly, looking up again with the flash of recovered memory and confidence. 'That is not all my trust in you. You must be not only a hand to me, but a soul – believing my belief – being moved by my reasons – hoping my hope – seeing the vision I point to – beholding a glory where I behold it!' – Mordecai had taken a step nearer as he spoke, and now laid his hand on Deronda's arm with a tight grasp; his face little more than a foot off had something like a pale flame in it – an intensity of reliance that acted as a peremptory claim, while he went on – 'You will be my life: it will be planted afresh; it will grow. You shall take the inheritance; it has been gathering for ages ... But I have found you. You have come in time. You will take the inheritance which the base son refuses because of the tombs which the plough and harrow may not pass over or the gold-seeker disturb; you will take the sacred inheritance of the Jew.' (557)

Here, the language is highly stylised and blends the melodramatic with Old Testament imagery via the idioms of the twelfth-century Spanish poet Judah Halevi (c.1085–1140) that Eliot read during her preparation for writing the novel. Within this complex interplay of literary influences, Eliot takes the reader back to the Gothic motifs of the grasping hand and the transferral of one ebbing life to the vital existence of another.

Arguably, Eliot is reworking a theme that is common to her later fiction, that of the intellectual inheritance being passed down to a younger generation that is doubtful of its relevance or significance. Dorothea Casaubon has to search her motives carefully before accepting her husband's request to continue with his 'Key to Mythologies' after his death. In *Middlemarch* (1871–72), Eliot treats the theme similarly with the reference to Casaubon's 'Dead Hand' controlling the life that Dorothea might share with Will Ladislaw. Daniel's response is as intricate as Dorothea's, encompassing both a fear of being pressured to agree to something and the fear that he might give Mordecai unrealistic expectations. These fears melodramatically appear on the men's faces, and again the motif of the clutching hand appears:

> Deronda had become as pallid as Mordecai. Quick as an alarm of flood or fire, there spread within him not only a compassionate dread of discouraging this fellow-man who urged a prayer as of one in the last agony, but also the

opposing dread of fatally feeding an illusion, and being hurried on to a self-committal which might turn into a falsity. The peculiar appeal to his tenderness overcame the repulsion that most of us experience under a grasp and speech which assume to dominate. (558)

Daniel's response, his defence, is to repeat what he has always maintained. That is, his position as regards his identity: '"Do you remember that I said I was not of your race?"' '"It can't be true," Mordecai whispered immediately, with no sign of shock. The sympathetic hand still upon him had fortified the feeling which was stronger than those words of denial.' This time, the hand is one of fellow feeling rather than one of coercion. Mordecai may be sure of Daniel's origins – 'what is my life else?' – but, as his certainty increases, Daniel rationalises this within a psychiatric paradigm. To him, at least during the later sequences of the novel, Mordecai is a monomaniac, a description that, at least within the realms of literature explained erratic and single-minded behaviour (568). This relationship is constructed through fixed binaries – the dying pursues the living; the outsider propositions the insider; the insane tries to convince the sane; the lustful pursues the chaste. All of these dynamics have an erotic manifestation denoted by the clutch and the grasp and then the subsequent horror, the brushing off and the denial.

Although the fears subside, the complications of public and private identities never leave Daniel's side. If Daniel's dawning awareness of his Jewishness can be read as an awakening sexuality, then his realisation involves a psychological readjustment. According to the reading I am giving here, the maternal space that was so fearful when suggested by Mordecai's advances finds its own appropriateness when Daniel actually meets his mother and reconnects with the heritage he was missing so much. Both the Gothic and the Sensation novel have a tendency to focus on private acts and how they make their effects felt on women. In *The Woman in White* (1860) Mr Fairlie's sexual misdemeanours are responsible for Laura Fairlie's incarceration and loss of identity. For Eliot, the Gothic interface with the past is problematic as she wants to show the role of matrilineal descent. The novel's climax here places Daniel's Jewish panic not so much at the feet of his dead father as at the skirts of his dying mother's racial shame. In revealing his heritage to Daniel, the Princess uses the imagery of subjugation:

'I relieved you from the bondage of having been born a Jew.'
   'Then I am a Jew?' Deronda burst out with a deep-voiced energy that made his mother shrink a little backward against her cushions. (689)

Here fear, indicated by 'shrink', is transferred back to the mother. Daniel is thankful for what his mother is deeply ashamed of and, in rediscovering his inheritance and demystifying it, he can redirect his energies into nation forming.

The closure of Daniel's narrative functions to resolve the queer Gothic text. Where there is the Gothic, it seems that there is homosexual panic, and where there is panic there is homosociality. The future of nations in the novel is enacted out through the reorientation of homosocial bonds and the rechannelling of erotic networks in the novel. Prior to meeting with Mordecai, Daniel had a homosocial connection with Hans Meyrick. Between these two men are similar themes of sacrifice and transferred life. Daniel sacrifices his career at university for Hans and continues to support him emotionally in his love for Mirah in spite of his own feelings for her. Through Mirah, both men connect, both romantically and adversarially. Of course Mirah allows Daniel to connect homosocially with Mordecai and she becomes one side of two erotic triangles between which Daniel can choose. If Mordecai is vampiric, then the opium-smoking Hans is most likely worse. As a self-indulgent, nihilistic and notionally anti-Semitic character, he represents the kind of egotistical dysfunction Eliot liked to warn her readers against. In 'coming out' as Jewish, Daniel can renegotiate his bonds and can connect to Mordecai via familial bonds rather than by erotic adumbrations.

Consequently, these new bonds require a coming-out process. Daniel has to reveal his identity as being born Jewish to his family and friends, and the response is again very suggestive. Hans Meyrick has already been told by his mother who could not keep a secret; Hugo Mallinger advises Daniel not to 'go into eccentricities' (785), by which he implies any form of activism. Most interestingly, Gwendolen Harleth says '*You* are just the same as if you were not a Jew' (873) and presents a flattening liberal argument that, in spite of acknowledging difference, sees fit not to distinguish it.

UNQUEERING THE GOTHIC

The reading of the text that I have given here is, I trust, persuasive, but it is complicated by some small but significant details in Eliot's prose. The panic, the anxiety that is so important to queer readings, depends largely on the literary capacity of language to suggest. The grey area between the darkness and the brightness that cuts across both the homosocial and the homosexual must remain within the shadows. Like much of the fear experienced within the Gothic narratives of the period, the exact source of homosexual panic, if one can be identified at all, is not written down, not least because of social taboos, but, more existentially, because fear needs to be unknown. The Gothic of the nineteenth century is a genre of feeling and a writing of the implicit.

Eliot did not care for the effects of the Gothic. In her literary reviews, letters and journal entries, the work of Mary Braddon, Charles Reade and even Wilkie Collins, an acquaintance of the Leweses, was treated with scorn for its commercialism, 'exaggerated contrasts' and dreariness.[22] In a manner that is similar to her much-loved Jane Austen – Eliot read *Northanger Abbey* (1818) in 1857 – she introduced Gothic elements into her fiction only to deflate them. As suggestive as the vampiric is in *Daniel Deronda*, and I believe that it is highly suggestive, Eliot makes a number of attempts to illuminate her readers by revealing what is happening between the two men. Just before their conversation about Mordecai's visions the narrator describes the pair:

> In ten minutes the two men, with as intense a consciousness *as if they had been* two undeclared lovers, felt themselves alone in the small gas-lit book-shop and turned face to face, each baring his head from an instinctive feeling that they wished to see each other fully. (552, my emphasis)

What the Gothic offers, this sentence attempts to retract. 'Lovers' allows gender to be unspecified and allows a suggestion of homoeroticism, but by likening the men to lovers who are hidden, to themselves, each other or to wider society, Eliot switches on the light in the closet. She demonstrates that what the genre illuminates with a metaphor can be dimmed with a simile. In doing so, she invites the reader to consider that, no matter how *nearly* they might be, Daniel and Mordecai are *not* in an erotic relationship and that the complexities of their homosociality are of a different kind. Earlier, when explaining Mordecai's vision of his disciple, the narrator uses another simile:

> Reverently let it be said of this mature spiritual need that it was akin to the boy's and girl's picturing of the future beloved; but the stirrings of such young desire are feeble compared with the passionate current of an ideal life straining to embody itself, made intense by resistance to imminent dissolution. (531)

Though this information does not clearly identify what Mordecai is feeling, his desire has a childlike object orientation but it is 'ideal' and spiritually inflected, rather than lustful. As ambiguously as it may be conveyed, the subject of desire is something Eliot wanted the reader to consider.

Eliot's writing is ambivalent about the Gothic, but it seems to be less so about the erotic overtones of male friendship. It poses a problem for queer Gothic readings, which significantly want to work against the grain of the text. The obstruction lies in the fact that the body of Eliot's writing already engages with literary closets and sexual dissidence. Although George Eliot was a moral and social novelist, she was also a writer who was able to touch confidently on sexual topics. Within the cultural codes of the period any discussion of these subjects had to take place within strict controls and Eliot used literary techniques to indicate her subject matter. In *Adam Bede* (1859), the changing seasons indicate Hetty waiting for her missed menstrual period, and the birth of her child and the subsequent infanticide are disclosed via the statement of witnesses in court, a format that can be seen to pre-empt Wilkie Collins's narrative strategy in *The Woman in White*. In *Middlemarch*, Dorothea Casaubon's tears in Italy and her incarcerated existence in Lowick Manor, surrounded by snow and haunting rooms, re-create her existence as a virgin heroine in a Gothic environment of her own making. Eliot cannot tell us that Dorothea's marriage has not been consummated, but she can indicate as such with a deployment of Gothic images and sensations. In *Daniel Deronda*, Gwendolen's marriage is blighted further by Grandcourt's sadistic sexuality which is indicated not least by the Gothic images that surround him but by his delight 'in making the dogs and horses quail' (482). Whenever George Eliot tackles the subject of sex, not only does she rely on metaphor, she also wants to use Gothic aesthetics – hauntings, mysteries, fearful responses. The often painful experiences of adulthood invite the uncanny into her social realist world. At no point does Eliot make explicit reference to how the reader should see these sequences. The writing stays within the realm of metaphor and not as simile. When Eliot writes about sex, she keeps her subject firmly in the closet and makes the most of suggestion through closed doors.

When it comes to Daniel and Mordecai, the hints at what their relationship might be perceived as works against the Gothic, which, in this particular context, flourishes as metaphor and partially collapses as simile. It is, of course, impossible to say if Eliot is trying to double-bluff, but if she wanted to hint at an erotic concern, and considering her skill in suggestion, it is unlikely that she would be relatively explicit and largely 'unqueer' the relationship between Daniel and Mordecai.

Although a reader can retroactively read a homosexual identity over a Jewish one in *Daniel Deronda*, it would seem that Eliot is not actually coding a reference to homosexual desire and its problematic articulation within male social bonds. Discussing Racine's reworking of the Book of Esther, Eve Kosofsky Sedgwick notes that 'the Story of Esther' constitutes 'a certain simplified but lightly potent imagining of coming out and its transformative potential'.[23] The subsequent discussion Sedgwick lays out points out the differences between anti-Semitism and homophobia, and these differences are important, but not eternal. Sedgwick's discussion is admittedly artificial as the juxtaposition of Old Testament narrative and Racineian drama, but Sedgwick does not place the analogy within the context of the texts she uses (with a Biblical text it would be virtually impossible to do so). Erotic undercurrents and the Gothic have an important role within the affective structures of George Eliot's work, but they need to be viewed within the wider context, the 'large conception' of Eliot's creativity. After 'dehomosexualising' the panic in the novel, she can get on with the ostensibly real business of developing the visionary Jewish spirituality that allow her to pose questions about nationhood and individual identity. The criticism levelled at the Jewish plot of the novel is very much a response to the fact that this section of the novel is a quasi-fantastical exploration of ideas. There is a passing on of belief between Daniel and Mordecai which William Baker sees as David Friedrich Strauss's transmigration of souls, but the experience is also mixed with Eliot's reading of Cabbalism. Eliot was attracted to Strauss's work in so far as *Das Leben Jesu* (1864–65) enabled her to conceptualise a feeling for the greater humanity rather than for the nation or the group.[24]

By the time she came to *Daniel Deronda*, Eliot was able to project homosociality into something altogether more national. Eliot emphasises the friendship between Mordecai and Daniel as a turbulent channel for this transference and adapts the connotations of the vampiric plot to further this purpose. The racial shame of the past is present in the erotic anxieties of the present, and the tenderness and fraught emotions in the men's interchanges operate as an affective medium for Eliot's humanist ideas and also her philosophical worries about superstition and irrational belief. At the same time, Daniel's act of connection is as powerful, ambiguous and as energised as if it were an erotic and charged form of intimacy.

If the male paranoid plot communes with the past, then Gwendolen's plot is one where the future is speculated on the outcomes of the present. She finds that secrecy, illegitimacy and violent sexual acts inhabit her present. Her life leads to breakdown and her realisations hopefully will lead her to break through. Where there is inheritance, be it cultural or economic, the Gothic seems to exist on the fringes. And where there is the Gothic, there are almost invariably the power imbalances of the erotic.

Proposing this interpretation does not minimise the importance of reading against the heterosexism of Victorian literary fiction. The political history of queer theory, in the early years of the western AIDS epidemic, necessarily thrived on the seeking out of sexually dissident writers and unveiling the construction of sexual categories and concepts. Queer readings have a tendency to place erotic tension in the position of a signified. In linking queerness to the Gothic, especially within a text that uses the Gothic in a liminal way like much of Eliot's fiction, it is possible to see that both the Gothic and the queer act as a process, or a language that operate within a historical and aesthetic context. This process is one where racial identities and same-sex bonds, erotic or otherwise, can be negotiated and advanced within a greater conception and vision of social evolution.

NOTES

1 Henry James, '*Daniel Deronda*: A Conversation' (1876), in D. Carroll (ed.), *George Eliot: The Critical Heritage* (London: Routledge and Kegan Paul, 1971), pp. 417–33 at pp. 422–3.
2 George Eliot, *Daniel Deronda* (1876), ed. B. Hardy (Harmondsworth: Penguin, 1967), p. 557. All subsequent references are to this edition, and are given in parentheses in the text.
3 Eve Kosofsky Sedgwick, *Between Men, English Literature and Male Homosocial Desire* (New York: Columbia University Press, 1985), p. 92.
4 Ibid., p. 94.
5 Eve Kosofsky Sedgwick, *The Coherence of Gothic Conventions* (New York: Methuen, 1980), pp. 12–13.
6 Gordon S. Haight, *George Eliot, A Biography* (Harmondsworth: Penguin, 1968), pp. 493–7.
7 Terry Castle, 'Reading Jane Austen's Letters', in Jane Hindle (ed.), *London Review of Books, An Anthology* (London and New York: Verso, 1996), pp. 138–48 at p. 141.
8 Lyn Pykett, 'Introduction' to Mary Braddon, *Aurora Floyd* (1863) (Oxford: Oxford University Press, 1996), p. xviii. Pykett writes that whilst the Sensation novels of Mary Elizabeth Braddon were permitted in the school-room, George Eliot's were not.
9 Alexander Welsh, *George Eliot and Blackmail* (Cambridge, MA: Harvard University Press, 1985).

10 George Eliot, *Middlemarch* (1871-72), ed. David Carroll (Oxford: Clarendon Press, 1986), p. 761.
11 Sedgwick, *Between Men*, p. 89.
12 John Blackwood to George Eliot, 11 May 1876, in *The George Eliot Letters, The Yale Edition*, ed. G. S. Haight (Oxford: Oxford University Press; New Haven: Yale University Press, 1954-78), vol. VI, 250.
13 Ann Cvetcovich, *Mixed Feelings: Feminism, Mass Culture and Victorian Sensationalism* (New Brunswick: Rutgers University Press, 1992), p. 130; Marlene Tromp, 'Gwendolen's Madness', *Victorian Literature and Culture*, 28/2 (2000), 451-7; Sarah Gates, '"A Difference of Native Language": Gender, Genre and Realism in *Daniel Deronda*', *ELH*, 68 (2001), 699-724.
14 For a discussion of the figure in relation to *fin-de-siècle* sexology see Robert Mighall, *A Geography of Victorian Gothic Fiction, Mapping History's Nightmares* (Oxford: Oxford University Press, 1999), pp. 227-35.
15 Carol Margaret Davison, *Anti-Semitism and British Gothic Literature* (London: Palgrave, 2004), p. 12.
16 Charles Maturin, *Melmoth the Wanderer: A Tale* (1820), ed. Douglas Grant (Oxford: Oxford University Press, 1968), chapter 12, passim; see also Mary Braddon, *Birds of Prey: A Novel*, 3 vols (London: Ward, Lock and Tyler, 1867), vol. I, pp. 37-8.
17 Davison, *Anti-Semitism and British Gothic Literature*, p. 12.
18 Leslie Stephen, *George Eliot* (London: Macmillan, 1902), p. 190.
19 Oliver Lovesey, *The Clerical Character in George Eliot's Fiction* (Victoria, BC: University of Victoria, 1991), p. 103. See also Edgar Rosenberg, *From Shylock to Svengali: Jewish Stereotypes in English Fiction* (London: Peter Owen, 1960), pp. 181-2.
20 C. Chase, 'The Decomposition of the Elephants: Double-Reading in *Daniel Deronda*', *PMLA*, 93/2 (1978), 215-27; K. M. Newton, '*Daniel Deronda* and Circumcision', *Essays in Criticism*, 31 (1981), 313-26; Mary Wilson Carpenter, '"A bit of her flesh": Circumcision and the Significance of the Phallus in *Daniel Deronda*', *Genders*, 1 (1988), 1-23; Davison, *Anti-Semitism and British Gothic Literature*, p. 12. For historical and cultural discussions of circumcision see Ronald Hyam, *Empire and Sexuality: The British Experience* (Manchester and New York: Manchester University Press, 1992); O. Moscucci, 'Clitodectomy, Circumcision and the Politics of Sexual Pleasure' in A. Miller and James Eli Adams (eds), *Sexualities in Victorian Britain* (Bloomington and Indianapolis: Indiana University Press, 1996) and Ben Knights, 'Men from the Boys: Writing on the Male Body', *Literature and History*, 3/1 (2004), 25-42.
21 Sedgwick, *Between Men*, pp. 91-3.
22 See George Eliot to John Blackwood, 11 Sept. 1866, in *Letters*, IV, 309-10, and George Eliot, 'Harriet Beecher Stowe's *Dread*, Charles Reade's *It is Never Too Late to Mend* and Frederika Bremer's *Hertha*', first published in *Westminster*

Review, Oct. 1856, in *Essays of George Eliot*, ed. Thomas Pinney (London: Routledge and Kegan Paul, 1963), pp. 239-330.

23 Eve Kosofsky Sedgwick, 'The Epistemology of the Closet', in H. Abelove, Michele Aina Barale, and D. M. Halperin (eds), *The Lesbian and Gay Studies Reader* (New York and London: Routledge, 1993), p. 21.

24 William Baker, *George Eliot and Judaism* (Saltzburg: Institut für Anglistik und Americanistik, Universität Saltzburg, 1975), pp. 26-9.

5

'That mighty love which maddens one to crime': medicine masculinity, same-sex desire and the Gothic in Teleny

Diane Mason

Best known today for its alleged association with Oscar Wilde, *Teleny, or The Reverse of the Medal* (1893), is a classic erotic and, in many respects, Gothic novel that charts the brutal and tragic progress of an obsessive homosexual passion.[1] The novel, though, is not necessarily, as Alan Sinfield suggests, nothing more than the celebration of 'an emerging – though far from available – queer subculture'.[2] Rather, it is a medical as well as an erotic work, and one which, when read through the discourses of its age, problematises the pathology – as well as the position – of the homosexual or invert. Indeed, in the first edition of *Teleny*, the novel is subtitled 'A Physiological Romance of Today', which appears to give the work a somewhat clinical or scientific emphasis.[3] Far from being gay icons, as modern criticism has suggested, the eponymous hero, René Teleny and his lover Camille Des Grieux are mobilised by a curative rather than a celebratory discourse – a discourse whose implications limit rather than liberate the individuals and practices described. The language here is as much that of the case study, mobilised in more recognisably Gothic texts such as J. S. Le Fanu's *In a Glass Darkly* (1872), as that of the titillating pornographic novella. In *Teleny*, Des Grieux relates his torrid tale in retrospect to an enigmatic and anonymous interviewer who may be another gay man or, indeed, a doctor.

This chapter will consider the constructions of Teleny and Des Grieux through the filter of late nineteenth-century medical writing. It will not merely address the perceptible link between the discourses of medicine and the writing of pornography but will suggest that it is the medical content of the novel which inhibits and shapes its depiction of homosexual acts and relationships. Notably too, this, apparently medicalised portrait of a same-sex liaison contains some strikingly Gothic elements whose presence seems to censure rather than commend the characters and their sexuality. The Gothic aspects of *Teleny* will be considered with reference to Eric, Count Stenbock's short story 'The True Story of a Vampire' and George Du Maurier's *Trilby*, both published the year after *Teleny* in 1894.

Central to the medical question is the blurring of boundaries between seemingly 'unspeakable' medical conditions – in this case homosexuality, styled as invertism or uranism, and masturbation. Both, as it were, are crimes against nature and society, crimes which seemingly carry a burden of both guilt and inevitable punishment. In an 1892 commentary on the 'disgusting details' of 'Sexual Perversion', Norman Connolly suggests that, 'For the purpose of the physician it seems sufficient to look upon them as *varieties of masturbation*'.[4] What Connolly implies, perhaps, is that onanism was perceived as by far the lesser 'sin', and thus it provided a euphemism more suited to general consumption. Similarly, for Edgar J. Spratling, masturbation is the 'arch enemy' which 'hand in hand with its *boon companion*, sodomy … stalks through every ward, entangling its victims more hopelessly with each passing night'.[5] The 'sin' of Onan, here, is clearly equated with contamination – one is infected through practice of the vice – and, thus infected, the tainted individual is likely to be easily initiated into other, even more perverse sexual practices, in this case, sodomy. This is analogous, in many ways, to the twentieth-century myth that 'soft drugs lead to hard drugs'.

In falling victim to the '*syren* vice'[6] of onanism, the degraded male crucially risked the loss of his virility, a quality the physician R. V. Pierce describes as 'the *very essence of manhood*'.[7] Virility is expressly the opposite of effeminacy or impotence, denoting not only masculine strength but also the power to procreate. In the physician's rhetoric, this 'virility' is not merely a desirable quality to possess but the '*very essence*' – meaning 'that which makes [a thing] to be what it is' – of manhood.[8] The notion of virility here, however, not only stands for a man's ability to father children but also serves as an indicator of his fitness for the task. Arguably, the key issue is one of self-control. As Lesley Hall asserts, 'Mastery over the baser lusts was seen as appropriate and desirable behaviour (a form of internalised moral policing) for the middle classes or would-be respectable', and the lionising of self-control as an advantageous, if not essential, masculine virtue is patently reflected in *fin-de-siècle* advice manuals for young men.[9] Writing in *The School of Health* (1908), Alfred B. and M. Ellsworth Olsen contend that 'secret vice, besides consuming the vitality and strength of all the bodily organs, deadens the moral sensibilities ... and *completely unmans* its victims', the 'unmanning' occurring as a consequence of the fracture in masculine self-restraint.[10]

In order to combat effeminacy, then, the male had to retain an awareness of his own virility and employ a manly self-control against the perverse practices which could lead to its breakdown. Admittedly, as Krafft-Ebing notes, those in same-sex communities – schoolchildren, prisoners and forces personnel – may take up mutual onanism, sodomy or tribadism owing to a lack of other sexual outlets. Nevertheless he maintains that in 'the *normally* constituted, *untainted*, mentally healthy individual ... No case has been demonstrated in which perversity has been transformed into perversion, – into a reversal of the sexual instinct.'[11] In other words, if one is physically and intellectually sound – and hales from robust stock – the occasional sensual aberration will cause no lasting harm. Self-control, though, is still an important factor as Krafft-Ebing seems to imply that only the normal or healthy individual will have the willpower necessary to resist improper temptations and revert, instead, to more normative means of fulfilling desire when they become available.

Sensuality, it appears, may be either transmitted to succeeding generations or controlled by the power of the self in the present. There was a high degree of medical unanimity on the influence of heredity in cases of sexual inversion, and it is notable that, in *Teleny*, the pianist, René, and his male lover, Camille Des Grieux, are constructed as men with distinctly unfit pedigrees. Des Grieux, twice recalls that his father 'died mad', potentially as a consequence of alcoholism.[12] Writing on 'Perversions of the Sexual Instinct', the physicians L. Thoinot and Arthur W. Weysse assert that '*Intoxications*' and 'especially ... *alcoholism* ... plays a great rôle in the procreation of degenerates'.[13] To compound the felony, Des Grieux's mother is loath to place her son as a boarder in school – 'hotbeds of vice' according to many Victorian doctors – because, as he states, she is 'frightened lest I might have *inherited* my father's *sensual disposition*' (33, my emphases).[14] By inference, the word 'sensual' emphasises that which is 'carnal', 'voluptuous; [and] lewd' – surely an allusion then to something more than merely an excessive appetite for alcohol.[15] In his 1889 clinical lecture on 'Sexual Perversion, Satyriasis and Nymphomania', G. Frank Lydston asserts:

> It is probable that few bodily attributes are more readily transmitted to posterity than peculiarities of sexual physiology. The offspring of the abnormally carnal individual is likely to be possessed of the same inordinate sexual appetite that characterizes the parent. The child of vice has within it, in many instances, the germ of vicious impulse, and no purifying influence can save it from following its own inherent inclinations. *Men and women* who seek, from mere satiety, variations of the normal method of sexual gratification, stamp their nervous systems with a malign influence which in the next generation may present itself as true sexual perversion.[16]

Lydston's words seem particularly appropriate in the case of Des Grieux, who is, arguably, constructed as the progeny of *two* 'abnormally carnal' parents. His mother is said to be 'somewhat light and fond of pleasure' (22), and, as John McRae asserts, 'there are grounds for suggesting that the nebulous father-figure was driven mad, and then to death, by his young wife's sexual excesses'.[17] Although this is a matter of conjecture, a similar pattern of family relationships may well be discernible in the case of René Teleny. His father, however, is not so much 'nebulous' as non-existent in that he is never mentioned in the text. What is apparent though is that Teleny's mother is a woman prone to illicit lascivious indulgence. Recalling his childhood, Teleny tells Des Grieux: 'My mother actually rode a gentleman under my very eyes' (98). Taking into account this textual evidence, both Des Grieux and Teleny can be viewed as the offspring of sexually rapacious progenitors – and are therefore, the inheritors of their defective heredity.

In the construction of Teleny, the pianist's faulty ancestry is further intensified by dint of his racial origins. He is a concert pianist of Hungarian descent. His nationality appears to be particularly relevant when examined in the light of late nineteenth-century writing on sexual inversion. In their consideration of the frequency of '*uranism in men and women*' (333, emphasis in the original), Thoinot and Weysse cite the 1880 work of K. Ulrichs, who 'claimed that there was on average one adult invert for 200 adult heterosexual men, and that the proportion was *even greater among the Magyars*' (334, my emphasis).[18] A *fin-de-siècle* dictionary definition of 'Magyar' is 'A Hungarian, allied in race to the Turks'.[19] In *Teleny*, the foreign 'otherness' and exoticism of the eponymous protagonist's background is further underlined when he tells Des Grieux, 'the gypsy element is strong in me' (17) and emphasises that there is '*Asiatic blood* in my veins' (18, my emphasis).[20] This 'Asiatic blood' is visibly manifested in the shape of his oriental and voluptuous mouth (135). This connection with the Arab world is compelling inasmuch as in the nineteenth century, as Rudi C. Bleys asserts, 'the image of widespread sodomy was disseminated in handbooks about the world of Islam and its countries'.[21] Writing in 1864, the German forensic physician J. L. Casper claims that the practice of 'paederastia' is 'of Asiatic origin'.[22] Arguably, these racial signifiers can be seen not only to indicate his nationality but also to disclose his propensity for licentious or deviant sexual behaviour. The Orient and Asia were favoured locations for pornographic texts in the period, with titles such as *The Lustful Turk* (1828), *Venus in India* (1889) and *A Night in a Moorish Harem* (1900) having a particularly enduring currency.

In Gothic literature too, the vampiric or predatory 'other' was frequently figured as a being of eastern origin. In George Du Maurier's *Trilby* (1894) and Eric, Count Stenbock's 'The True Story of a Vampire' (1894), the malevolent mesmerist, Svengali, and the vampire, Count Vardalek, distinguished by his 'effeminacy' of countenance, have eastern, and particularly Hungarian, connections.[23] To compound Svengali's ancestry in the 'poisonous East', Trilby receives an image of him 'in the military uniform of his own Hungarian band'.[24] Vardalek, as his 'Hungarian' name implies, might well have his roots in that same country. In Stenbock's tale, Vardalek preys exclusively on a young member of his own sex. In *Trilby*, although Svengali has a 'sinister' (11) aspect, he is capable of enthralling men and women in equal measure, ostensibly with his music. Indeed, an exceptional talent for playing the piano is a further common characteristic in the fabrications of Vardalek, Svengali and Teleny.

By profession, Teleny is a concert pianist, Svengali plays piano with the aplomb of a 'master' (13) and Vardalek, despite his protestations that he plays but 'a little' (167), nevertheless performs 'very beautifully' (169). Not only does musical accomplishment have its place in the medical discourse on sexual inversion but also musicianship was perceived to be synonymous with homosexuality in a cultural discourse that was current well into the twentieth century.[25] As Alkarim Jivani asserts in *It's Not Unusual* (1997), a contemporary history of gay and lesbian Britain, 'Between the wars' one of the most 'popular' phrases 'to inquire whether someone was gay or not' was 'Is he musical?'[26] These notions appear to be encoded in Stenbock's 'The True Story of a Vampire'. Gabriel, Vardalek's adolescent male victim, is a gifted violinist who is captivated by the vampire Count. Notably, when Vardalek pronounces 'in a very sad voice' that Gabriel has 'the soul of music within' him, the *female* narrator of the tale cannot comprehend why the Count is 'commiserat[ing]' with rather than 'congratulat[ing]' the boy on his 'extraordinary talent'.[27] It could be argued that she exists outside the homosexual community of feeling and experience and does not understand the implications and possible consequences of, to use the 'Swinburnian euphemism' for same-sex passion, *'strange'* love.[28] Although, on the surface, the tale is merely about a creature compelled to feed on blood to survive and has nothing whatsoever to do with homosexuality, on a deeper level this does not explain why the Count should feel 'sad' about his victim's musicality. It does not ring true that a ruthless monster, driven only by his hideous appetite, would feel remorse about depriving the world of an accomplished individual. Significantly, Vardalek enjoys a tender and intimate relationship with his 'beautiful' (164) victim, he is seen 'walking about hand in hand' (167) with Gabriel and the youth 'kiss[es] him on the mouth' (168). Though reticent when compared with the uncompromising language of *Teleny*, Vardalek's relationship with Gabriel is ambiguous and can be read in several ways. It can be viewed as a stereotypical story about the corruption and contamination of (the, perhaps, not quite so) innocent by the (vampiric) sexually predatory older man or, alternately, as a cautionary tale about the possible repercussions of indulging rather than repressing (or exercising masculine self-restraint over) unconventional or perverse sexual desires. Either way, the outcome is the same and the consummation of their union leads to the, seemingly inevitable, demise of one of the parties involved.

In choosing the name Vardalek for his central character, Stenbock, 'a slightly demented Russian aristocrat'[29] in the words of Matthew Bunson, may have drawn inspiration from the word *'vourdalaks'*.[30] According to the Russian author, Alexis Tolstoy, writing in 1884, this is the 'name given to vampires by Slavic peoples'.[31] Although, 'like all types of vampire', they 'suck the blood of the living', they are particularly 'terrifying' as they prefer to prey on 'their closest relatives' and 'most intimate friends' and 'once dead, *the victims become vampires themselves*' (257, my emphasis). Stenbock's story deviates from the familiar script, however, as there is no evidence to suggest that his victim, Gabriel, comes back to haunt – or feast on – the living. This seems to add a further layer of ambiguity to Stenbock's tale, hinting that it may be rather more than, as Bunson asserts, a 'poorly written work' about vampires.[32] As a representative of his type, Vardalek appears to be a complete failure. He is, symbolically at least, impotent, in the matter of perpetuating his kind.

Returning here to the medical symptoms in *Teleny*, a particularly telling visible indicator of the eponymous pianist's physical health (as well as the health of Vardalek and Svengali) is his complexion, described as being 'of that warm, *healthy paleness* which ... artists often have in their youth' (8, my emphasis).[33] The concept of 'healthy' pallor is something of a misnomer when examined in the light of Victorian medical discourse. Pallor can be a signifier of many afflictions, including consumption and syphilis. Most appropriately here though, according to the physician R. V. Pierce, a 'pale' face is one of the primary symptoms of spermatorrhoea, a male physiological disorder characterised by involuntary emissions and a resultant seminal weakness 'generally induced by the early habit of masturbation'.[34] This is important inasmuch as it impacts on the pathology of sexual inversion. Many practitioners including Havelock Ellis and Krafft-Ebing identified what the latter terms 'neurasthenia sexualis'[35] or 'marked hyperaesthesia or irritable weakness' of the ejaculation centre in 'a considerable proportion' of male sexual inverts, and this is clearly a pertinent factor in both Teleny and Des Grieux.[36]

When Des Grieux encounters Teleny for the first time at a 'grand charity concert' (7), he is 'spellbound' by Teleny's interpretation of 'a wild Hungarian rhapsody', experiencing 'the strangest visions' (9), all of which are Orientalist, exotic and sensual in character, and redolent with references to same-sex pleasures. Significantly, Vardalek and Svengali too are capable of charming members of their own sex with similar music. In *Trilby*, Svengali plays music to 'madden just for a moment', 'czardas, gypsy dances, [and] Hungarian love-plaints' (14). Of his three male listeners, the Laird and Taffy are 'wild in their enthusiasm' while Little Billee experiences 'a silent enthusiasm too deep for speech' (14). In 'The True Story of a Vampire', Gabriel is left with 'his eyes dilated and fixed' and his body 'quivering' when Vardalek plays 'wild, rhapsodic' 'Hungarian csardas', described by the tale's female narrator as 'the music which makes men mad' (167). In *Teleny*, Des Grieux longs to feel 'that mighty love which maddens one to crime' (10) – a magnification upon the more celebrated 'love that dare not speak its name' – and recalls, 'the pianist's notes just then seemed murmuring in my ear with the panting of an eager lust, the sound of thrilling kisses'. Although he claims to have been 'sat still, like all the crowd around me' (10), he remembers that his 'whole body was convulsed and writhed with mad desire' (10). This culminates in a further and more explicit masturbatory experience as

> *a* heavy hand seemed to be laid upon my lap, *something* was bent and clasped and grasped, which made me faint with lust. The hand was moved up and down, slowly at first, then faster and faster it went in rhythm with the song ... and then, *some drops* even gushed out. (11, my emphases)

Note here Des Grieux's tone of detachment from, and denial of, any participation in this activity. It is '*a* heavy hand' – the indefinite article, a hand which might belong to the self or to another – which clasps '*something*'. The whole is ambiguous. Admitting that one indulged in 'solitary vice' could be seen as pejorative enough in the Victorian period but masturbation in a public place would have been perceived as even more perverse, obscene and anti-social. Given that *Teleny* is set in Paris, it should be remembered that, in French territories, '*public* acts of ... *solitary or reciprocal immodest manipulations*' were included in the legal definition of '*public offences against decency*'.[37] The implication is that what he is experiencing is within him, a figment of his imagination, and he is explaining a *spontaneous* ejaculation – symptomatic of his 'neurasthenia sexualis' – by way of the language of auto-eroticism. After Teleny's performance he is undoubtedly 'spent', to use a context from the spermatic economy. As he recalls, 'I was powerless to applaud, I sat there dumb, motionless, nerveless, exhausted' (11). This is characteristic of both the post-orgasmic state and the man rendered, in the physician, James Cantlie's words, 'sleepless, listless, nervous, [and] anaemic' as a result of excessive involuntary emissions.[38] Des Grieux's mother observes how 'pale' her son looks and asks if he feels 'ill' (11).

Des Grieux's lascivious reaction to Teleny appears to be unerringly accurate when measured against the prototypical behaviour of male inverts recorded by Krafft-Ebing. The physician claims that:

> simply *embracing* and kissing, or even only the *sight* of the loved person, [will] induce the act of ejaculation. Frequently this is accompanied by an abnormally powerful feeling of lustful pleasure, which may be so intense as to suggest a feeling of *magnetic currents* passing through the body. (225, my emphasis)

Krafft-Ebing's words are further borne out when, after the concert, Des Grieux meets Teleny face-to-face. The effect here is even more profound. The mere touch of Teleny's hand sets Des Grieux's emotions 'on fire' and 'Priapus, re-awakened, uplifted his head' (13). Des Grieux recalls, 'I actually felt I was being taken possession of [by Teleny], and I was happy to belong to him' (13). The 'carnal hunger' in Teleny's eyes makes him 'feel faint' and, when the pianist hugs him 'tightly', he feels 'something hard press and move against [his] thigh' (19). This results in Des Grieux experiencing a second and more powerful orgasmic involuntary emission, his penis 'spout[s] one or two drops of that *creamy, life-giving* fluid' (19, my emphases). Teleny too appears to undergo a simultaneous reciprocal orgasmic ejaculation or spasm as a result of their physical contact. He '*shuddered* as if he had received a *strong electric shock* ... All the colour ... fled from his face, and he became *deathly pale*' (19, my emphases).

The morning after the concert, Des Grieux's identity appears to be closely bound up with that of Teleny and this is described in the 'occult' terminology of demonic possession. He claims that 'the image of Teleny' haunts him and, moreover, when he looks in the mirror he '[sees] Teleny in it instead of myself' (22). He feels 'a grudge against the male musician who had *bewitched*' him (25, my emphasis) and, although he tries not to think of Teleny, 'the more I tried not to think of him, the more I did think ... he actually *haunted* me' (26, my emphasis). He hears the pianist's voice and has 'hallucinations' of a sexual nature which give him 'a strong erection' (26). Moreover, his mother is 'struck with the change in [his] appearance' and asks if he feels 'unwell' (22). This scenario is reminiscent of an encounter with the vampire in Gothic fiction. In 'The True Story of a Vampire', consequent to his first meeting with Vardalek, Gabriel not only gradually loses his 'general health and vitality' but also, on a psychological or mental level is 'utterly under the domination of' (168) the, ostensibly vampire, Count.

Rather like vampire and victim, a particularly striking feature of the relationship between Teleny and Des Grieux is their seemingly psychic linkage, a phenomenon which can be categorised among what Thoinot and Weysse termed 'The *psychic* symptoms, or, better, *stigmata*' (270, original emphasis), seen as a crucial factor 'in the immense majority of cases' (269) of sexual perversion. When Teleny asks Des Grieux to recall the first time their eyes met, Des Grieux confirms that 'there was a *current* between us, like a spark of *electricity*' (20, my emphases). The notion of 'electricity' here emphasises their psychic as well as physical affinity. Medical writing on sexual inversion frequently makes mention of the fact that male inverts are able to, in Casper's words, '*recognise one another*' and often 'at a single glance' (Vol. 3, 331, original emphasis).[39] Krafft-Ebing further observes that 'The psychical love manifest in these men is, for the most part, exaggerated and exalted in the same way as their sexual instinct is manifested in consciousness, with a *strange and even compelling force*' (225, my emphasis). When, in retrospect, Des Grieux is questioned by

∼81

the nameless interviewer as to whether Teleny had any 'peculiar dynamic quality' in his eyes, he confirms that *'For myself of course there was*; yet he had not what you would call *hypnotising* eyes' (8, my emphasis). Note, 'For myself', the implication here being that a heterosexual male or female would not have recognised, or would have been impervious to, the 'peculiar dynamic quality' of the pianist's gaze. In the words of William Lee Howard, the sexual invert's 'abnormality is seldom recognized except by those of similar psychical desires'.[40]

As Des Grieux begins to understand the significance of his 'natural feelings' for Teleny he purports to be 'staggered, horrified; and filled with dismay' (44). He agonises over his condition and is determined to 'stifle' (44) his feelings. This is not uncommon in medical discourse. Havelock Ellis recalls three cases of sexual inversion where the subjects 'have fought in vain against their perversion' (260). Notably, Des Grieux proceeds to read all he could find 'about the love of one man for another, that loathsome crime against nature' (45). One work in particular makes a very strong impression. He recalls:

> I ... read in a *modern medical book*, how the penis of a sodomite becomes thin and pointed like a dog's, and how the human mouth gets distorted when used for *vile purposes* [presumably, fellatio], and I shuddered with horror and disgust. Even the sight of that book blanched my cheek! (45, my emphases)

Des Grieux is paraphrasing freely from the Parisian physician Ambroise Tardieu's *Etude médico-légal sur les attentats aux moeurs*, first published in 1858, a work written 'with more ardour and fancy than with the necessary critical caution' (Vol. 3, 329) according to Johann Ludwig Casper. The fact that, in *Teleny*, Des Grieux gains access to Tardieu's clinical work raises interesting questions about the availability and dissemination of medical discourse on sexual inversion beyond the limits of specialist practitioners and suggests, perhaps, that such literature might have had a rather wider distribution. Given the undeniable medical accuracy of the anonymous author's depictions of Teleny and Des Grieux, it is difficult to believe that the novella was written in isolation and that such details are purely coincidental.

The 'consummation' of their union is, notably, described in terms reminiscent of a conventional heterosexual marriage. As Teleny welcomes Des Grieux into his home, the pianist's language is noticeably Biblical as he tells his lover-bride, 'My body hungereth for thee, soul of my soul, life of my life!' (89). This paraphrase of the Old Testament 'flesh of my flesh', said by Adam to Eve when he wakes to find her beside him in Eden, seems to function here as a kind of symbolic celebration of matrimony.[41] Notably, the same passage of Genesis 2: 23–4 appears to be adapted in 'The True Story of a Vampire'. In a particularly anguished encounter with Gabriel, who is 'walking in his sleep', Vardalek refers to the boy as 'my beloved! My life' and tells him 'thy life is my life' (169). Krafft-Ebing emphasises the element of parody characteristic of uranistic love in his assertion that 'since it is the exact opposite of natural feeling, it becomes a caricature' of conventional heterosexual passion (255). The marriage bond implicit in their relationship is later reinforced by Des Grieux, who asserts that 'had our union been blessed by the church, it could not have been a closer one' (130).

Despite Des Grieux's protestations, however, their relationship ends in tears. The issue here is rather one of fidelity – or the lack of it; Teleny's inability to be 'faithful' to Des Grieux is a characteristic of homosexual passion, according to Thoinot and Weysse. In their words, '*Constancy* is not a trait of uranistic love; inverts are, with rare exceptions, rather flighty and have temporary love affairs' (304, original emphasis). Although Teleny confesses to Des Grieux 'I do not care for a single girl in this world, I never did, I could never love a woman' (18), the pianist's fickleness is borne out inasmuch as he is portrayed having erotic interludes with partners of *both* sexes, most significantly with his lover's mother who is underwriting his debts, an 'affair' which was to have tragic repercussions. The fact that he can make love to a woman is not to contradict his self-confessed homosexuality. Havelock Ellis, among others, asserts that, in some cases, inverts can 'find sexual satisfaction both with their own and the opposite sex' (259). In certain respects, Teleny is depicted as something of a sexual predator and he is described in animal terms. His movement is 'characteristic of the Felidae' (93), or cat, and, as Des Grieux recalls, 'when he clasped himself to you he seemed to entwine himself around you like a snake' (93). These not overtly comforting images seem to have more in common with the 'serpentine' (165) figure of the vampire, Count Vardalek, than of a conventional romantic lover. When Des Grieux discovers the pianist and his 'own mother' (152) locked in a passionate clinch (at a time when his lover is supposed to be out of town), the sight not only wracks him with feelings of 'shame', 'terror' and 'despair' (152) but also drives him to attempt suicide by drowning. After recovering from an unsuccessful suicide bid, Des Grieux visits his lover to offer forgiveness, only to find Teleny on the brink of death by his own hand, lying in 'a pool of coagulated blood' with a 'small dagger' (155) protruding from his chest. Moreover, a suicide note, left by Teleny for Des Grieux, 'had got to be public property' (158), thus condemning the surviving partner to societal censure and opprobrium.

In conclusion, if one accepts that *Teleny* is a book ostensibly about same-sex desire but channelled through and informed by medicine, the calamitous ending hardly constitutes a big surprise. Because it participates in medical discourse, there is no way for sex to succeed. The language of medicine here is double-edged. Although it provides a framework which enables hypotheses or premises about sexuality to be articulated, it can operate only within the bounds of the permissible. Therefore, in a medical context, sex cannot be celebratory, it can only be pathological and problematic. Teleny has to die – he cannot face the shame of exposure – while Des Grieux is allowed to live but thereafter, like the 'cosmopolitan' vampire, Count Vardalek, 'a wanderer on the face of the earth' (167), he has to move on and conceal his identity. There is a distinct reversal of roles in *Teleny* though inasmuch as it is the one who is 'bewitched' (25) rather than the one who, as it were, cast the spell that survives. Quoting directly from Charles Lamb's 'confessional verse', 'The Old Familiar Faces' (1798), in which the poet 'reviews' the loss of family and friends 'sustained through his life', Des Grieux states, 'Earth seemed a desert I was bound to traverse' (158).[42]

Aside from the medical framing of the text, given this notion of exile and loss, the denouement of this pornographic novella seems to mobilise the Gothic motif of the Wandering Jew, in legend, a character 'condemned to wander over the face of the Earth till judgment day' for the sin of insulting or spurning Christ while he was bearing the cross to Calvary.[43] In a Gothic sense, this 'narrative motif ... deals with a person who has committed a serious transgression against the basic and sacred values ... of human society' whose 'punishment' is 'restless exile for an almost infinite time ... until his crime is atoned for or someone has taken the burden on him/herself'.[44] Des Grieux recalls the reaction of former friends and acquaintances when his homosexuality is revealed for public scrutiny in 'every newspaper' (158); 'Then, Heaven, having revealed my iniquity, the earth rose against me' (158). Sermons of an 'edifying' (158) nature are preached, presumably denouncing Des Grieux's perceived sins, using an uncompromising text from the Biblical Book of Job: 'He shall be driven from light into darkness, and chased out of the world' (158).[45] In allowing his transgressive sexuality to become public knowledge, in societal terms, Des Grieux is effectively rendered *persona non grata* and doomed to wander, having to move on periodically when his notorious past threatens to catch up with him. This is a narrative which undeniably discloses at least a lay appreciation of cause and effect. Whatever the truth of its origins, I hope the reading given here has shown that *Teleny* is a significant work in its own right rather than merely a colourful adjunct to the study of Oscar Wilde.

NOTES

1 As Patrick J. Kearney asserts, '*Teleny* has been habitually ascribed to Oscar Wilde'. See Patrick J. Kearney, *A History of Erotic Literature* (n.p.: Parragon, 1982), p. 120.
2 Alan Sinfield, *The Wilde Century: Effeminacy, Oscar Wilde and the Queer Moment* (London: Cassell, 1994), p. 18.
3 A facsimile title page of the first edition of *Teleny*, published by Cosmopoli in 1893, can be found in Anonymous, *Teleny: A Story of a Forbidden Relationship* (London: Icon Books, 1966), p. 5.
4 Norman Connolly, 'Sexual Perversion' in D. Hack Tuke (ed.), *A Dictionary of Psychological Medicine* (London: J. & A. Churchill, 1892), 2 vols, vol. 2, p. 1157, my emphasis. In his writing on 'Auto-Eroticism', Havelock Ellis asserts that '"Onanism" is largely used [as a term for masturbation], especially in France, and some writers even include all forms of homosexual connection under this name'. See Havelock Ellis, 'Auto-Erotism: A Psychological Study', *Alienist and Neurologist*, 19 (1898), 260–99 at p. 261.
5 Edgar J. Spratling, 'Masturbation in the Adult', *Medical Record*, 28 Sept. 1895, 442–3 at p. 442, my emphasis.
6 R. V. Pierce, *The People's Commonsense Medical Adviser* (Buffalo, NY: World's Dispensary Printing-Office and Bindery, 1883), p. 795, my emphasis. 'Siren' is, significantly, a term more usually used to describe 'an enticing woman': see P. Austin Nuttall, *Nuttall's Pronouncing English Dictionary* (London: George Routledge and Sons, 1894), p. 591.
7 Pierce, *People's Commonsense Medical Adviser*, p. 796, my emphasis.
8 Nuttall, *Pronouncing English Dictionary*, p. 226.
9 Lesley A. Hall, *Hidden Anxieties: Male Sexuality, 1900–1950* (Cambridge: Polity Press, 1991), p. 3.
10 Alfred B. Olsen and M. Ellsworth Olsen, *The School of Health: A Guide to Health in the Home* (Watford: International Tract Society, 1908), p. 127, my emphasis.
11 Richard von Krafft-Ebing, *Psychopathia Sexualis*, seventh German edition (1892), trans. C. G. Chaddock (Philadelphia: F. A. Davis Company, 1916),

p. 190, original emphases. All subsequent references are to this edition, and are given in parentheses in the text.

12 Anonymous, *Teleny, or The Reverse of the Medal* (1893) (Ware: Wordsworth Editions, 1995), pp. 100, 109. All subsequent references are to this edition, and are given in parentheses in the text.

13 L. Thoinot, *Medicolegal Aspects of Moral Offenses* (c.1895), translated from the original French and enlarged by Arthur W. Weysse (Philadelphia: F. A. Davis Company, 1911), p. 270, original emphases. All subsequent references are to this edition, and are given in parentheses in the text.

14 To cite but two examples (there are many more), in her medical advice book for women, Anna Longshore-Potts asserts that 'Boarding schools may become the very hot-beds of this terribly destructive vice', the 'vice' in question being masturbation. Likewise, in a chapter entitled 'Private Words for Men', Edward Bliss Foote considers the 'dangers of school-life', claiming that 'writers on this subject agree that boarding-schools and colleges are the main hot-beds for the planting of the seeds of early vice and perversions'. See: A. M. Longshore-Potts, *Discourses to Women on Medical Subjects* (San Diego and London: Published by the Author, 1895), p. 47. Edward Bliss Foote, *Home Cyclopedia of Popular Medical, Social and Sexual Science* (London: L. N. Fowler, 1901), p. 651.

15 Nuttall, *Pronouncing English Dictionary*, p. 575.

16 G. Frank Lydston, 'Sexual Perversion, Satyriasis and Nymphomania', *Medical and Surgical Reporter*, 61 (1889), 253–8 and 281–5 at p. 255, my emphasis.

17 John McRae, 'Introduction' to the Gay Men's Press edition of *Teleny*, attributed to 'Oscar Wilde and Others' (London, 1986), p. 18.

18 Although Thoinot and Weysse later concur that 'Only half credence can be given to the statements of Ulrichs, who is rather inclined to exaggerate the number of his kind' (334), Ulrichs's claims as to the particularly high proportion of inverts among the ethnic Hungarian population could nevertheless be seen as influential in the construction of Teleny.

19 John Ogilvie and Charles Annandale (eds), *The Student's English Dictionary* (London: Blackie & Son, 1903), p. 435.

20 To the twenty-first-century reader, Teleny's allusion to his 'gypsy element' could be seen to function as a further signifier of his sexual orientation. As Alkarim Jivani points out, in the early twentieth century, 'gay men used a secret language called Polari which would have baffled all. Although the origins of the language are obscure, it appears to have originated with show people and gypsies in the nineteenth century'. See: Alkarim Jivani, *It's Not Unusual: A History of Lesbian and Gay Britain in the Twentieth Century* (London: Michael O'Mara Books, 1997), p. 14.

21 Rudi C. Bleys, *The Geography of Perversion: Male-to-Male Sexual Behaviour outside the West and the Ethnographic Imagination 1750–1918* (London: Cassell, 1996), p. 163.

22 Johann Ludwig Casper, *A Handbook of the Practice of Forensic Medicine, Based Upon Personal Experience*, (London: The New Sydenham Society, 1864), 3 vols, vol. 3, p. 330. All subsequent references are to this edition, and are given in parentheses in the text.

23 Eric, Count Stenbock, 'The True Story of a Vampire' (1894), in James Dickie (ed.), *The Undead: Vampire Masterpieces* (London: Pan Books, 1973), pp. 162–70 at p. 165. All subsequent references are to this edition, and are given in parentheses in the text.

24 George Du Maurier, *Trilby* (1894) (London: Everyman, 1994), p. 330. All subsequent references are to this edition, and are given in parentheses in the text.

25 According to Krafft-Ebing, 'In the majority of cases', homosexuals are marked out by their 'brilliant endowment in art, especially music'. See: Krafft-Ebing, *Psychopathia Sexualis*, p. 225.

26 Jivani, *It's Not Unusual*, p. 14.

27 Stenbock, 'True Story of a Vampire', p. 167. Moreover, like Teleny and Des Grieux, the story hints that Gabriel may not spring from entirely sound progenitors, he has an 'innate wildness in [his] nature', said to be inherited from his late mother who was 'of gypsy race' (164). In common with Des Grieux too, the boy is not sent away to school but is educated at home by his Belgian governess, Mlle Vonnaert.

28 Nina Auerbach, *Our Vampires, Ourselves* (Chicago and London: University of Chicago Press, 1995), p. 40. There is a notable repetition of the word 'strange' in the music Vardalek plays to the, ostensibly sleepwalking, Gabriel. When the boy enters Vardalek's room the Count strikes 'one agonised and *strange* chord'; as Gabriel leaves, the tune becomes '*strange* and … heart-rending!' See Stenbock, 'True Story of a Vampire', p. 169, my emphases.

29 Matthew Bunson, *Vampire: The Encyclopaedia* (London: Thames & Hudson, 1993), p. 258.

30 Alexis Tolstoy, 'The Family of the Vourdalak' (1884), in Christopher Frayling (ed.), *Vampyres: Lord Byron to Count Dracula* (London: Faber and Faber, 1992), pp. 254–79 at p. 257, original emphasis. All subsequent references are to this edition, and are given in the text

31 Tolstoy, 'Family of the Vourdalak', p. 257.

32 Bunson, *Vampire*, p. 258.

33 Again, pallor is a feature not only of Teleny's physiognomy but also of Vardalek's and Svengali's. On her first meeting with Vardalek, the female narrator recalls that he is 'very pale'. See Stenbock, 'True Story of a Vampire', p. 166. In the case of Svengali, he is described as having a 'sallow' aspect. See Du Maurier, *Trilby*, p. 13. Given that one dictionary definition of 'Sallow' is 'a pale, sickly, yellow colour', Svengali's appearance might give rise to anxieties regarding his physical and mental fitness. See James Wood, *Nuttall's Standard Dictionary of the English Language* (London: Frederick Warne and Co., 1898), p. 577.

34 Pierce, *The People's Commonsense Medical Adviser*, pp. 800, 795.
35 Krafft-Ebing, *Psychopathia Sexualis*, p. 225.
36 Havelock Ellis, 'Sexual Inversion with an Analysis of Thirty-Three New Cases', *Medico-Legal Journal*, 13 (1895–96), 255–67 at p. 258. All subsequent references are to this edition, and are given in parentheses in the text.
37 Thoinot and Weysse, *Medicolegal Aspects of Moral Offenses*, p. 256, original emphases.
38 James Cantlie, 'Spermatorrhoea' in Richard Quain (ed.), *Dictionary of Medicine* (London: Longmans, Green, and Co., 1883), pp. 1449–50 at p. 1449.
39 This is further reinforced in the case of Herr N. recorded by the Vienna physician Julius Krueg. Krueg asserts that '[Herr N.] confirms the statement, repeatedly made by others, that individuals affected by this abnormality are able to recognise one another'. See Julius Krueg, 'Perverted Sexual Instincts', *Brain*, 4/15 (1881), 368–76 at p. 372. The notion that gay men are able to recognise one another indeed retains a currency among homosexuals to this day. This ability to spot a fellow homosexual is known as 'Gaydar' in twenty-first-century gay slang.
40 William Lee Howard, 'Psychical Hermaphroditism: A Few Notes on Sexual Perversion with Two Clinical Cases of Sexual Inversion', *Alienist and Neurologist*, 18 (n.d.), 111–18 at p. 114.
41 Genesis 2: 23–4. Notably, Bram Stoker uses a paraphrase of this Biblical verse to underline the Count's union with or possession of Mina in *Dracula*. See Bram Stoker, *Dracula* (1897) (Oxford: Oxford University Press, 1996), p. 288. For an earlier usage of the 'flesh of my flesh' analogy, this time used to illustrate a conventional husband and wife conjugal union, see Charlotte Brontë, *Jane Eyre* (1847) (London: Granada, 1983), p. 479.
42 Significantly, Lamb uses the poem as a vehicle to 'universalize his experience of the "day of horrors" when he arrived home [from work] to find his mother dead and his sister with a carving-knife in her hand'. See Duncan Wu (ed.), *Romanticism: An Anthology* (Oxford: Blackwell, 2006), p. 737. Stabbing is a pertinent motif in this context as, in *Teleny*, Des Grieux returns to the home he shared with the pianist to find him dying, in a 'pool of coagulated blood' with a 'small dagger ... plunged in his breast' (155).
43 Ivor H. Evans, *The Wordsworth Dictionary of Phrase and Fable* (Ware: Wordsworth Editions, 1993), p. 1138.
44 Hans-Ulrich Mohr, 'Wandering Jew (Ahasuerus)', in Marie Mulvey-Roberts (ed.), *The Handbook to Gothic Literature* (Basingstoke: Macmillan, 1998), pp. 249–51 at p. 249.
45 Job 18: 18.

6

Gothic landscapes, imperial collapse and the queering of Adela Quested in E. M. Forster's A Passage to India

∽

Ardel Thomas

INTRODUCTION: GEOGRAPHICAL MISCEGENATIONS
AND FORSTER'S HOMOSEXUALITY[1]

There were round white clouds in the sky, and white pools on the earth; the hills in the distance were purple. The scene was as park-like as England, but did not cease being queer.[2]

In his 1924 novel *A Passage to India*, E. M. Forster creates confused national boundaries, collapsed geographic settings and queer sexual and gender identities. In the opening scene of the novel, Forster describes Chandrapore as a city where 'The very wood seems made of mud, the inhabitants of mud moving' (7). In a 1915 letter to Syed Ross Masood, a close friend with whom Forster was in love, he describes his experience of Egypt (where he had been travelling) as a place where, 'the soil is mud, the inhabitants are of mud moving'.[3] One of Forster's biographers, P. N. Furbank, explains that 'Mud, the mud of the Nile, and moral "muddiness" were always to figure in his vision of Egypt. And in this and other ways his experience there [in Alexandria] was taken up into his Indian novel.'[4] In the December of 1922, Forster's book *Alexandria: A History and a Guide* was finally published by Whitehead, Morris & Co., only to be destroyed by a fire in the warehouse.[5] With the knowledge that his work on Alexandria might not ever reach his reading public, Forster may have consciously let the borders between India and Egypt slip. Or perhaps Chandrapore 'dresses in drag' as Alexandria because he had been working on the two texts simultaneously. Not only does Forster's setting conflate Egypt and

∽ 89

India but, as the epigraph for this chapter suggests, India also becomes 'as park-like as England'. The author's descriptive mixing of countries and cultures creates a 'queer' and miscegenated landscape.

While Forster's geography is made 'queer' through boundary slippages, we get another queer construction on a very literal level – the character of Dr Aziz. Forster creates an Indian doctor much the same way he creates India – out of a mix of India, Egypt and England. The book is dedicated to his long-time Indian friend and love, Syed Ross Masood, with whom Forster never had a sexual relationship. A British modernist historian, Peter Stansky, posits that Forster's 'continuing affectionate friendship with Masood set him on the course that led ultimately to his writing *A Passage to India*'.[6] Dr Aziz, though, is also drawn from Forster's Egyptian lover, Mohammed el Adl. Upon his return to England in March of 1922 after his stint as the Maharajah of Dewas's secretary, Forster was depressed and preoccupied because el Adl had become fatally ill – he died in May 1922.[7] (Forster had been able to make a quick trip to see his lover one last time before he began his journey back to England.) Forster wrote the following:

> Dear Mohammed   August 5th 1922
> This book is for you and me – I wish I could distinguish more clearly between us, but it was always difficult, and now you are not here to correct me when I think of you not as you are but as I should like to think you. I write with my mind on you and with the illusion that your mind still exists and attends. I pretend that you are still alive, because it only is thus that I can think of you as real, although I know that a putrid scrap in the Mansourah burial ground is all that was you. I write for my own comfort and to recall the past, but also because I am professionally a writer and want to pay you this last honour. ...[8]

Rustom Bharucha's essay 'Forster's Friends' argues that, in the relationship between Forster and el Adl, there was 'no otherness' because Forster 'can be made Egyptian by his friend'.[9] More precisely, through el Adl's death, he and Forster become each other; this concept becomes crucial at the end of *A Passage to India* when Aziz tells Mrs Moore's youngest surviving son that 'your mother was my best friend' (312). Forster writes of his inability to 'distinguish more clearly' between himself and el Adl because, through death, his lover exists only within his mind. Mohammed and Morgan are one, and the novel has become an extension of their friendship. If Forster sees himself as el Adl, and if el Adl did serve as a model for Dr Aziz, then Forster must also be part of the model for the Indian doctor. Thus, it is truly an interracial, queer (and here I do also mean homosexual as it refers to the relationship between el Adl and Forster) mix that gives life to Aziz.

The term 'queer' appears in numerous places throughout *A Passage to India*. The Indian landscape described as being 'as park-like as England' is 'queer' precisely *because* of this confusion over what comprises Oriental or Occidental terrain. The scene becomes 'queer' because India is England *and* England is India. Cyril Fielding reiterates this sentiment when he says, 'You can make India in England ... just as you can make England in India' (73). 'Queer' signifies oddness and a sense of disorder; Forster, however, utilizes the word to describe not only the scene but also his characters, and then, when he does, he most often refers to Adela Quested or Mrs Moore. I point to Forster's use of the term 'queer' because I think, in this novel, it signifies a critical turning point in definition. Forster's 'queer' is Victorian in its sense of the odd or strange, but his 'queer' also moves towards modern implications of homosexuality. As Stansky suggests, Forster may not necessarily have understood the term 'queer' to signify 'homosexual', but it becomes apparent that the idea was there as early as 1911. It was in this year that Roger Fry painted a 'Post-Impressionist' portrait of Forster. When a clergyman friend of his mother's saw the picture hanging in the home that Forster shared with her, 'he remarked to her after looking at the portrait that he hoped her son wasn't "queer"'. After this awkward incident, Forster removed the portrait, presumably out of his 'lack of ease about his sexuality' and gave it to his friend Florence Barger.[10]

Although the term 'queer' did not, according to the *Oxford English Dictionary*, become synonymous with 'homosexual' until the 1930s in Great Britain (and the 1920s in the United States), there does appear to be a sexual taint attached to the word as Forster uses it. Forster might have been aware of the American usage of 'queer'. 'Queer' carries contemporary, highly politicised sexual and gender meanings along with historical associations (not necessarily sexual, but possibly so) with the 'peculiar' and the 'odd'. In the years 1913–14 (two years following the clergyman's distressing comment to Forster's mother) Forster wrote *Maurice*, his homosexual novel, published posthumously in 1970. Forster's work on *Maurice* coincides with the time he *began* work on his Indian novel. While he created the homosocial and homoerotic Cambridge world of Maurice and Clive, he simultaneously constructed its opposite: Chandrapore, a town ruled by Anglo-Indian heterosexual norms. Beyond outward appearances, though, this Indian town, much like Cambridge, becomes the site of numerous 'queer' awakenings. The most obvious relationship of this type is the interracial, homoerotic one between Aziz and Fielding.[11] 'Queer' can certainly be used to describe the relationship between these two men, but it also defines Adela Quested and Mrs Moore's positionality. In this chapter, I focus mainly on Adela Quested (although Mrs Moore accompanies her in the process of a Gothic awakening), an often oversimplified character who, within hours of her arrival to Chandrapore, sets herself apart as 'queer' compared to the Anglo-Indians because she does not understand the rules of the colonised land; both she and Mrs Moore actually want to talk to and become friends with the natives. Through Quested and Moore's experiences, Forster deposits us on to the terrain of liminal existences where categories of nation, time, place, gender identity and sexual desire become a 'muddle'. For Adela Quested and Mrs Moore, this muddle begins with a confrontation they have with themselves in the bowels of a Gothic monstrosity – the Marabar Caves.

MARABAR CAVES

> The caves are readily described. A tunnel eight feet long, five feet high, three feet wide, leads to a circular chamber about twenty feet in diameter. This arrangement occurs again and again throughout the group of hills, and this is all, this is a Marabar Cave. (124)

What is the function of the caves twenty miles away from Chandrapore? In her essay, 'Forster's Imperial Erotic' (1995), Sara Suleri Goodyear writes that 'the category "Marabar Cave" roughly translates into the anus of imperialism'.[12] Wilfred Stone claims that the caves are 'the primal womb from which we all came and the primal tomb to which we all return'.[13] In both cases, the Marabar Caves do not sit as sublime entities outside of the body, encroaching like gentle fingers upon Chandrapore in the moonlight but, instead, become intimate as a gigantic, grotesque cavity.

The sections 'Mosque' and 'Temple' form dichotomous ends to the centrepiece of *A Passage to India* entitled 'Caves'. 'Mosque' and 'Temple' exemplify the tension between Muslim and Hindu, respectively, because the first section concentrates on Dr Aziz and his friends in a predominantly Muslim world, whereas 'Temple' focuses on Professor Godbole and the Hindu celebrations of the birth of God. In 'Temple', everything that has 'gone wrong' is 'righted' again. It stands to reason that 'Caves' represents a strange mix of not only Muslim and Hindu but also Christian, Buddhist and Jain theologies. These contestatory religions or philosophies bumping against each other in 'Caves' helps to create the 'queer muddle' at the core of Forster's text.

In *Delusions and Discoveries* (1972) Benita Parry explores a 'deeply pessimistic vision at the heart of Jainism' and Forster's use of it in his rendition of the caves. She claims that 'The archetypal quality of the Marabars is matched by the archaic mind they reawaken and the ancestral voices which the caves echo. The mood is that of the human soul plunged in a dark night of despair.'[14] Likewise, Gertrude M. White's mid-twentieth-century essay '*A Passage to India*: Analysis and Revaluation' (1953) also utilizes the terms of Jainism to interpret the Marabar Caves as 'the very voice of that union which is the opposite of divine; the voice of evil and negation.'[15] For Forster, the optimism of Hinduism (and Hindu caves) cannot completely work for his disturbing portrait of empire and queer awakenings in India, although the caves do embody a strong Hindu presence. This is exemplified in the chant 'Radhakrishna Radhakrishna' which soothes Aziz at the end of the novel and causes him to reach out his hand to Fielding, forgetting past hostilities and 'focusing his heart on something more distant than the caves' (311). Imagine if the British guests (Miss Quested and Mrs Moore) walked into a cave that resounded with the warmth, beauty and spirituality of a Hindu sacred space. They would leave having had an 'Indian experience' that would make it easy for both of them to romanticise India through imperial eyes. Instead, they frantically run out of the caves with a new awareness that forces them to turn their gaze inward to the horrors that await them there.

It is quite possible that the ambiguity of the Marabar Caves forces each person to interpret them in his or her own terms, regardless of preconceived notions of religion or spirituality. This could also explain Godbole's discomfort with the caves, for, to explain them, he would need to delve into Hinduism as well as a whole host of other theologies. Godbole may realise that, ultimately, it would be best to keep silent about the caves, for, as Forster writes, 'their reputation ... does not depend upon human speech' (124). The two English women must discover the caves for themselves.

To experience the Marabar Caves, though is not merely to experience 'evil' and the 'dark night of despair'. Although Parry does describe a Marabar cave as 'both the unfertilized womb of the race and the Nothing to which the Jain aspires'[16] and Richard Cronin writes that 'the caves reveal a world emptied of meaning and emptied of value',[17] Jainism alone cannot account for Forster's complicated description of the landscape of the Marabar hills with their enigmatic caves:

> There is something unspeakable in these outposts. They are like nothing else in the world, and a glimpse of them makes the breath catch. They rise abruptly, insanely, without the proportion that is kept by the wildest hills elsewhere, they bear no relation to anything dreamt or seen. To call them 'uncanny' suggests ghosts, and they are *older than all spirit*. Hinduism has scratched and plastered a few rocks, but the shrines are unfrequented, as if pilgrims, who generally seek the extraordinary, had here found too much of it. Some saddhus did once settle in a cave, but they were smoked out, and even Buddha, who must have passed this way down to the Bo Tree of Gya, shunned a renunciation more complete than his own, and has left no legend of struggle or victory in the Marabar ... Having seen one such cave, having seen two, having seen three, four, fourteen, twenty-four, the visitor ... finds it difficult to discuss the caves, or to keep them apart in his mind ... Nothing, nothing attaches to them. (124)

Cronin's analysis makes the point that the caves, though linked to multiple religions, adhere completely to none because the hills and the caves are older than *all* religion. In their Nothingness (which stretches beyond the nothingness of Jainism), the Marabar Caves exert their power. These caves have frightened off the Hindu pilgrims who sought 'the extraordinary' but found 'too much of it' there. These caves have even terrified Buddha who 'shunned a renunciation more complete than his own'. It is no wonder, then, that Forster ascribes to the caves an immense, destructive, Gothic power over individual actors and the greater Anglo-Indian community after the 'failed' trial of Dr Aziz, who is accused of raping Adela Quested: 'The Marabar caves had been a terrible strain on the local administration; they altered a good many lives and wrecked several careers, but they did not break up a continent or even dislocate a district' (237).

In their complex Nothingness 'older than all spirit', the caves wreak havoc upon individuals in a similar fashion to other, more well-known Gothic locations and monsters such as Transylvania, the House of Usher, Ayesha or Mr Hyde. Because of the 'incident' at the caves, the Anglo-Indians are prepared to face the monstrosity of uncontrollable Indian (hetero)sexuality (Dr Aziz's) and rally around the British victim. In fact, it is precisely Adela's victimisation that earns her approval from the Anglo-Indians who, initially, do not like her. With the shift in the trial, the British are forced, instead, to examine their own monstrous lies about allegiances, the heteronormative social structures of Chandrapore, empire and nation. Mrs Moore and Adela Quested are to blame for this shift in focus. If the caves frightened Hindu pilgrims and Buddha, what, then, could they do to two unsuspecting English women?

ADELA QUESTED

'This was Adela Quested, the queer, cautious girl whom Ronny had commissioned her to bring from England' (24). From Adela Quested's first night in Chandrapore, the elite circle of Anglo-Indian Ladies set her apart as 'peculiar' and 'other'. At a Club party following a bad production of *Cousin Kate*, Adela complains that she has '"scarcely spoken to an Indian since landing"' (26). One of the ladies replies, '"Oh, lucky you"' (26). Underneath Adela's longing to speak to an Indian lies an implication that Anglo-Indians bore her. At first, the ladies gather around Adela; amused at her naivety, they recount their own anecdotes about past encounters with Indians. Adela does not take the subtle social hint, and becomes more adamant only when she tells Turton the Collector (the highest official in town), '"I'm tired of seeing picturesque figures pass before me as a frieze"' (27). As her name suggests, Adela's 'quest' in India is also to become a collector (though of another sort than Turton) of different impressions of Indians and their landscape. The narrator explains that 'her impressions were of no interest to the Collector; he was only concerned to give her a good time' (27). When Turton suggests a Bridge Party to satisfy her curiosity, she makes the error of crossing an invisible social line when she says, '"I only want those Indians whom you come across socially – as your friends"' (28). Turton cuts her off with the reply, '"we don't come across them socially"' (28), but he fails to explain the situation, claiming that it is too late at night to go into all of the reasons. Unbeknownst to her, Adela has not only set herself apart from the crowd, but she has also deeply offended Mrs Turton, possibly the most powerful heterosexual matriarch in this corner of Anglo-India. Forster writes that 'At Chandrapore the Turtons were little gods' (28). Mrs Turton exclaims to her husband, '"Miss Quested, what a name!"' (28). In his unwillingness to speak against an Englishwoman, Turton turns the subject toward the wonders that India 'does for the judgment, especially during hot weather; it has even done wonders for Fielding' (28). This change of topic only bothers his wife further because Fielding, like Quested, refuses to play by Anglo-Indian rules: 'Mrs. Turton closed her eyes at this name and remarked that Mr Fielding wasn't pukka, and had better marry Miss Quested, for she wasn't pukka' (28).

After alienating Mrs Turton and consequently the other upstanding and good Anglo-Indian ladies of Chandrapore, Adela proceeds that very same evening to cause a rift between herself and her fiancée, Ronny Heaslop.

On the way to Ronny's home after the miserable play, cocktails and social talk at the club, Mrs Moore relates the story of her own encounter with a young doctor in a mosque. To his horror, Ronny learns that, between acts of the play, his mother 'stepped out'. Distressed, he tells her, '"But, mother, you can't do that sort of thing"' (30). To his further embarrassment and dismay, Ronny initially fails to realise that the young doctor about whom his mother spoke was Indian. Adela chimes in, exclaiming, '"A Mohammedan! How perfectly magnificent! While we talk about seeing the real India, she goes and sees it"' (31). With a totally different response, Ronny scolds his mother for answering the young doctor's request that she remove her shoes before entering the mosque. Instead of supporting him through silence, Adela comes to Mrs Moore's defence: '"Now look here ... wouldn't you expect a Mohammedan to answer if you asked him to take off his hat in church?"' (31). Ronny dismisses Adela by telling her that she does not understand. He does not say exactly *what* it is that she does not understand, but we are left with the impression that there exists an unwritten social code to which Anglo-Indians must adhere. In her defence of Mrs Moore and her lack of understanding of the imperial social structure (one could read here the hyper-heterosexualised imperial social structure), Adela once again treads on the fragile ground of proper British protocol, and, in so doing, causes Ronny to be more angry with her than with his mother, the actual 'culprit':

> He wished she wouldn't interfere. His mother did not signify – she was just a globe-trotter, a temporary escort, who could retire to England with what impressions she chose. But Adela, who meditated on spending her life in the country, was a more serious matter; it would be tiresome if she started crooked over the native question. (31–2)

Adela's desire to become acquainted with Indians and to treat them as fellow human beings (although she does, very problematically, exoticise them) means that she already has 'started crooked' in her new life at Chandrapore. In other words, Adela Quested has started off 'queer' or 'not straight' in a 'normal' environment. Here, it is possible to see Forster adding a bit of his own life experience and feelings to Miss Quested; in his own travels to Egypt and India, Forster had always felt 'crooked' because he could not be honest and open about his own homosexual desire. As Brenda R. Silver argues in her essay, 'Periphrasis and Rape in *A Passage to India*' (1995), Quested and Moore are dangerous because 'their resistance threatens to destroy the status quo through intimacy, not hatred'.[18] Adela and Mrs Moore both start out as 'rebellious' against patriarchal rule

(Ronny's) and feminine etiquette (as exemplified by Mrs Turton). Mrs Moore is given more leeway in making mistakes precisely because she is an older woman, a visitor and outside of the imperial, heterosexual economy of Chandrapore's Anglo-Indian community. Adela, on the other hand, must be 'brought up properly' if she is to take on the role of the City Magistrate's wife. As Mrs Moore says to her son while he's worrying over Adela not being Mrs Callendar's 'sort', "'I don't think Adela'll ever be quite their sort – she's much too individual'" (49). Later, when Ronny finds Adela smoking with Professor Godbole and Dr Aziz, he flies into a rage over her expressing this individualism. "'I won't have you messing about with Indians any more! If you want to go to the Marabar Caves, you'll go under British auspices'" (82). Adela's actions are perceived as a threat to Ronny as well as the British nation because she has begun to move toward a metaphoric queer miscegenation. Underlying the tension between Ronny and Adela as individuals and their separate representations of nation are the Marabar Caves because Adela want to explore their depths as a guest (an honorary Indian as it were) of India represented by Aziz and Godbole, but Ronny insists she go as a Briton 'under British auspices'.

Turton's Bridge Party (so named because it is an occasion to 'bridge the gap' between East and West) turns out to be a disaster, but it is there that Adela and Mrs Moore come into contact with Fielding, the Principal of Government College, and procure an invitation to his home to meet two 'real' Indians. When Adela comments that Ronny is 'hard-worked' and will not be able to drive them over to Fielding's, she notices the distant Marabar Hills that house the Gothic caves:

> How lovely they suddenly were! But she couldn't touch them. In front, like a shutter, fell a vision of her married life. She and Ronny would look into the club like this every evening, then drive home to dress; they would see the Lesleys and the Callendars and the Turtons and the Burtons, and invite them and be invited to them, while the true India slid by unnoticed. Colour would remain – the pageant of birds in the early morning, brown bodies, white turbans, idols whose flesh was scarlet or blue – and movement would remain as long as there were crowds in the bazaar and bathers in the tanks. Perched up on the seat of a dogcart, she would see them. But the force that lies behind colour and movement would escape her even more effectively than it did now. She would see India always as a frieze, never as a spirit. (47)

Adela longs to touch the Marabar Hills, but, in her realisation that she cannot, she sees a horrible 'vision of her married life'. This vision of despair at being for ever paired up with Ronny and the Anglo-Indian social expectations that come with this post leads her to break off her engagement. The above moment foreshadows Adela's coming experience of self-realisation in the Marabar Caves – the revelation that she cannot fit into the heterosexual economy of Anglo-India.

Just as the Anglo-Indians find Adela Quested peculiar, so, too, does Dr Aziz. After Aziz arrives early to Fielding's home and the two men have the intense homoerotic scene over the collar stud, the two English ladies enter a marginal situation, or what Aziz sees as an 'unconventional party' (68). At first anxious upon learning that the two ladies would be joining them, Aziz is put at ease when he sees Adela:

> Aziz found the English ladies easy to talk to, he treated them like men. Beauty would have troubled him, for it entails rules of its own, but Mrs Moore was so old and Miss Quested so plain that he was spared this anxiety. Adela's angular body and the freckles on her face were terrible defects in his eyes, and he wondered how God could have been so unkind to any female form. His attitude towards her remained entirely straightforward in consequence. (68)

However misogynous Aziz's assessment of Adela Quested may be, the fact that he does not find her attractive causes him to treat her like a man. Both Mrs Moore and Adela become marginalised in this scene because they do not fit into a heterosexual paradigm (one that would find Mrs Moore young enough and Adela pretty enough). Aziz views them equally because of these 'defects'.

It could even be argued that, during this visit, Adela actually pursues Aziz, not sexually but as a cultural and spiritual guide to India. When Aziz invites the two women to come to his bungalow, he does so at first to be polite, though he does not expect them to accept. As discussed earlier, Adela's insistence upon the visit to the house causes Aziz to panic and to offer, instead, a visit to the Marabar Caves (74). Suleri Goodyear writes the following about this odd moment of misunderstanding:

> Aziz chooses the cultural anonymity of geography in order to keep concealed the privacy of his home, and the moment is illustrative of Forster's meticulous revision of a colonialist-as-heterosexual paradigm. Rather than the male seeking to possess a feminised territory, the female seeks to enter the habitat of the colonized domesticity, hereby forcing the 'little Indian' to retreat into the exotic but empty space of an unvisited cave.[19]

Forster creates, as Suleri Goodyear suggests, a queer moment in the text. Aziz and Adela have crossed the boundaries of gender binarisms. Not only does Aziz treat Adela like a man, but her insistence on entering his private space feminises him. If we are to believe Edward Said's assessment, found in *Orientalism* (1978), that a crucial part of the male imperial project was to feminise colonised men, where do Adela's actions on this occasion place her?[20] Has she merely become a man and Aziz a woman? Or does the moment render them both as interstitial, queer characters, neither completely male nor female?

I have concentrated on Adela Quested's actions (and people's perceptions of them) at the Club and at Fielding's house in order to exemplify her 'oddity' – her 'queerness'. She shifts from a woman who wants to meet 'real' Indians and to 'experience' India to a disgruntled fiancée to a woman who grudgingly accepts her fate as a future wife of Anglo-India. On the train en route to the caves – for Adela is decidedly *not* going under British auspices – her 'thoughts ever veered to the manageable future, and to the Anglo-Indian life she had decided to endure' (136). Obviously, she does not look forward to her future, but she tries to put her confusion aside and take on the proper role expected of her. On the surface, her attitude towards the Indians and the Marabar Caves has also changed. Adela's 'wish had been granted, but too late. She could not get excited over Aziz and his arrangements' (133). Upon their arrival at the Marabar Hills, both Mrs Moore and Adela are nonplussed by their surroundings: 'They did not feel that it was an attractive place or quite worth visiting, and wished it could have turned into some Mohammedan object, such as a mosque' (141). Both women underestimate the power that the Gothic landscape will have to permanently change their lives. It might be this very nothingness, the lack of expectations, that leaves them ill prepared for the encounter they each have with themselves.

Following their visit to the first cave (the one in which Mrs Moore has a horrifying vision), Adela, Dr Aziz, and a guide set off, without the older woman, for the other caves farther up the hillside. We are told that the three encounter 'several isolated caves, which the guide persuaded them to visit, but really there was nothing to see' (151). In this 'nothingness' Aziz worries over the breakfast he will serve the British guests once they finish looking at the unexceptional caves. Miss Quested's thoughts begin to turn to her future marriage. A 'rock that resembled an inverted saucer' causes her to question, 'What about love?' (152). Something as simple and domestic as a saucer comes to her mind, but it is an inverted one, an odd one. Forster's use of the term 'inverted' (and from there, it is an easy leap to 'inversion') would most certainly call to mind the sexologist Havelock Ellis's recent and popular essays on sexual inversion, or homosexuality. Only four years after *A Passage to India*'s publication, E. M. Forster advocated, in the face of an obscenity trial, that the Bloomsbury Group should defend Radclyffe Hall's groundbreaking lesbian novel, *The Well of Loneliness* (1928).[21] Even for readers not necessarily looking for homosexual or queer coded language within the text, Adela's exploration of an image that reminds her of an inverted saucer could also hint at a possible inversion on her own part.[22] The idea of the inverted saucer causes her to question her own domestic life to come. Adela suddenly realises, 'no, they did not love each other' (152). Aziz sees Adela's confusion and asks if he is walking too fast for her. Before she replies in the negative, she has the following realisation:

> The discovery came so suddenly that she felt like a mountaineer whose rope had broken. Not to love the man one's going to marry! Not to find it out until this moment! Not even to have asked oneself the question until now! ... she stood still, her eyes on the sparkling rock. There was esteem and animal contact at dusk, but the emotion that links them was absent ... Aziz held her hand ...
> 'Are you married, Dr Aziz?' she asked, stopping again, and frowning. (152)

With this question, Adela invites an intimacy between them, only to destroy good feelings in Aziz when she ignorantly asks him, '"Have you one wife or more than one?"' (153). Aziz lets go of her hand and flees into the nearest cave. Adela, unaware that she has offended him, wanders into a cave – presumably a different one from Aziz's – thinking about her marriage and her boredom with the trip. The next time we see Adela Quested, she is a broken, traumatised woman literally torn up by the cacti she encounters on her terrified run out of the cave and down the slope to Mrs Callendar's car.

Benita Parry claims that 'The Marabars compel the decent and honest Adela Quested, flat-chested, plain and sensually underdeveloped, to acknowledge her atrophied sexuality, a confrontation which is in itself an assault on her being'.[23] In a similar vein, Laura Kipnis writes that 'The hermeneutical question posed around Adela's sexuality means that narrative resolution will necessitate exposing Adela's sexuality to full public view, to full visibility. But what is exposed is illness, repression, and malady.'[24] Adela's 'atrophied' sexuality is atrophied heterosexuality. She encounters herself in the cave, and in the echo Adela must also hear that she cannot fulfil the role of an Anglo-Indian wife. The echo in the cave fills Adela with a 'queer' anxiety, and, in order to cover up her realisation, she lands on the most tangible explanation – that Aziz has raped her. An impossible-to-conceptualise queer female British sexuality compels a need to create a monster out of the Oriental 'Other'. If we are to take Kipnis's reading of Adela's sexuality as a sickness, she becomes queer in nineteenth- and early twentieth-century notions of the term. In eventually owning up to her lie and speaking the truth about the encounter in the caves, Adela's sexual orientation haunts the courtroom.

For some in the courtroom, and for Ronny Heaslop in particular, Adela's admission that nothing actually took place in the Marabar Caves also points to a strange metaphoric miscegenation. Earlier in the trial, we have McBryde's claim that the 'darker races' are 'attracted by the fairer, but not *vice versa*' (219). In her admission that Aziz did not touch her, Adela dispels this British myth about the 'fairer races' being attractive to the Indian. But to push the point even further, we need to remember that she and Mrs Moore were the ones who desired Aziz's company – they desired an 'experience' with the 'real' India. In their preference for an Indian excursion over an afternoon of polo at the Club, the two women have proved McBryde wrong, and they are both marginalised for their trespass.

In one other very strange way, I think we can glean a queer reading of Adela Quested, but in order to do this we need to turn back to P. N. Furbank's biography of Forster and look at Morgan's first strange homosexual encounter with a villager:

> One afternoon, in midwinter, he was sent for a walk on the downs, and on reaching the summit he came on a middle-aged man, in a deerstalker hat and knickerbockers, urinating in full view. When the man had finished, he spoke to Morgan and made him come and sit on his mackintosh, near some gorse-bushes, and after a moment or two of conversation undid his own flies and told Morgan to play with his penis. Morgan obeyed, being more puzzled than alarmed.[25]

Forster wrote to his mother about the incident, and she then consulted his principal, Mr Hutchinson. It seems that Hutchinson held young Forster mostly responsible, and the entire incident became a great embarrassment for him. Furbank writes that 'Morgan made an entry in his diary, <<Nothing>>, to remind himself that there had been something'.[26] Furbank also claims that Forster draws upon this incident in his writing *A Passage to India* in that 'it became a model for Adela's vengeful and confused behavior after she imagines herself molested by Aziz'.[27] While Furbank's argument further complicates the question – what happened in the cave? – it also highlights the ways that victims of molestation are often silenced and made to feel insane for having thought something happened to them. If Forster did, in fact, use this scene from his boyhood for his Indian novel, then we must question whether Aziz actually did enter Adela's cave and molest her. But this also complicates Adela Quested's queer positionality in that Forster uses his first homosexual encounter to create a strange heterosexual encounter. One could argue that Adela Quested becomes E. M. Forster, and the <<Nothing>> which means 'something' resounds in the echo in Adela's head. When she speaks out the 'nothing' to the court, the echo leaves her mind; meanwhile, her articulation of 'Nothing' renders her a nothing to 'her people' – the Anglo-Indians. As she leaves the courtroom, Adela disappears into a 'mass of Indians of the shopkeeping class' who carry her through the bazaar that smells 'sweeter than a London slum' (231).

Historically, queer lives and experiences have been silenced and erased (certainly prior to the Stonewall Riots in 1969 and our contemporary move toward gay, lesbian, bisexual, and transgender – or queer – pride) by our heteronormative and homophobic culture and society. It is as though queer people were a gigantic <<Nothing>>. Adela Quested is a woman who could have embodied nation and empire through her heterosexual union with Ronny Heaslop. Through her Gothic experience in the Marabar Caves, however, she becomes nothing and no one. Adela Quested returns to England, only to carry on for the duration of her life as *Miss* Adela Quested – a spinster who represents nothing because she has removed herself from the heterosexual economy at home and abroad.

NOTES

1 While the term 'miscegenation' is more properly utilised to describe a 'mixing of blood' negatively when referring to interracial relationships, I find it to be a useful term when exploring the collapse of landscapes, time and place – almost always the East and the West – as is often found in Gothic horror.
2 E. M. Forster, *A Passage to India* (1924) (New York: Harcourt Brace Jovanovich, 1984), p. 317. All subsequent references are to this edition, and are given in parentheses in the text.
3 P. N. Furbank, *E. M. Forster: A Life* (New York: Harcourt Brace Jovanovich, 1978), 2 vols, vol. 2, p. 22.
4 Ibid.
5 Ibid., vol. 2, p. 113.
6 Peter Stansky, *On Or About December 1910: Early Bloomsbury and Its Intimate World* (Cambridge, MA: Harvard University Press, 1996), p. 128.
7 Furbank, *E. M. Forster: A Life*, vol. 2, pp. 105, 108.

8 Ibid., vol. 2, p. 113.
9 Rustom Bharucha, 'Forster's Friends', in Jeremy Tambling (ed.), *E. M. Forster* (New York: St Martin's Press, 1995), pp. 115–32 at p. 123.
10 Stansky, *On Or About December 1910*, p. 128.
11 For an excellent discussion of the homoerotic relationship between Fielding and Aziz see Sara Suleri Goodyear's 'Forster's Imperial Erotic', in Tambling (ed.), *E. M. Forster*, pp. 151–70, *passim*. Here, Goodyear examines the two most erotically charged scenes between Fielding and Aziz (though it can be argued that there are many moments like this between them). The first is the introductory meeting between the two men when Fielding has just stepped out of the shower and Aziz helps him get dressed by offering him his own collar stud. The second, and most blatant, homoerotic scene comes in the last paragraph of the novel. In it, Fielding and Aziz are arguing over Indian nationalism while they ride their horses close together and Aziz 'half kisses' Fielding.
12 Ibid., p. 151.
13 Wilfred Stone, *The Cave and the Mountain: A Study of E. M. Forster* (Oxford: Oxford University Press, 1966), p. 301.
14 Benita Parry, *Delusions and Discoveries: Studies on India in the British Imagination 1880–1930* (Berkeley: University of California Press, 1972), p. 287.
15 Gertrude M. White, '*A Passage to India*: Analysis and Revaluation', *Publications of the Modern Language Association*, 68 (1953), 641–67 at p. 667.
16 Parry, *Delusions and Discoveries*, p. 288.
17 Richard Cronin, *Imagining India* (London: Macmillan, 1989), p. 188.
18 Brenda R. Silver, 'Periphrasis, Power, and Rape in *A Passage to India*' in Tambling (ed.), *E. M. Forster*, pp. 171–94 at p. 179.
19 Goodyear, 'Forster's Imperial Erotic', p. 159.
20 Edward Said, *Orientalism* (New York: Vintage Books, 1979), p. 45.
21 Claude J. Summer, 'E. M. Forster', in Claude J. Summers (ed.), *The Gay and Lesbian Literary Heritage* (New York: Routledge, 2002), pp. 263–7.
22 E. M. Forster would certainly not be the first queer author who felt more comfortable writing about homosexuality involving someone of the opposite sex. Although to write about homosexuality was taboo, there is a safe distance when a gay man writes about a lesbian and vice versa. Patricia Highsmith is another rich example of a lesbian author who puts her homosexuality into the male homoeroticism found in the Ripley thrillers. Only recently, has her pseudonym, Claire Morgan, been revealed. Under the name Claire Morgan, she penned an early 1960s lesbian love story, *The Price of Salt*, which has the honour of being the first lesbian novel with a happy ending. Highsmith was a lesbian. For many queer authors, the 'love that dare not speak its name' did – but it was cloaked in the homosexuality of the opposite sex, which made it safer, and yet still allowed the queer author to be queer.

23 Parry, *Delusions and Discoveries*, p. 294.
24 Laura Kipnis, '"The Phantom Twitchings of an Amputated Limb": Sexual Spectacle in the Post-Colonial Epic', *Wide Angle: Film Quarterly of Theory, Criticism and Practice*, 11/4 (1989), 42–51 at p. 47.
25 Furbank, *E. M. Forster: A Life*, vol. 1, p. 37.
26 Ibid., vol. 1, p. 38.
27 Ibid.

7
Antonia White's Frost in May: Gothic mansions, ghosts and particular friendships

~

Paulina Palmer

Antonia White's *Frost in May* (1933) is not generally regarded as a work of Gothic fiction. As Elaine Marks observes in discussing the novel, it belongs to the form generally known as fiction of the gynaeceum, which treats friendships between girls in the context of school or college life.[1] Locating her narrative in the imaginary Convent of the Five Wounds at Lippington on the outskirts of London, her representation of the institution based on the educational establishment that she herself attended as a child, White investigates the attempts made by her youthful heroine Nanda and her fellow pupils to explore their burgeoning sexuality in the repressive context of Roman Catholic culture and ideology. Emphasis is placed on the feelings of same-sex attraction the pupils experience and the erotic attachments that they form with one another. However the novel also displays pronounced Gothic affiliations, as White utilises Gothic imagery and motifs to represent the sexually repressive climate of convent life, the surveillance the nuns exercise and the efforts the pupils make to elude and resist their control. The novel relates in this respect to the kind of fiction known as 'lesbian Gothic'. In fiction of this kind, as I and other critics illustrate, Gothic conventions and motifs become a vehicle for representing the transgressive nature of lesbian desire in hetero-patriarchal culture, the homophobic construction of it as monstrous and unspeakable, and the strategies of resistance that the female subject employs to articulate and explore it.[2] This, as we shall see, is the role they play in *Frost in May* .

White's treatment of female sexuality, as the oxymoronic title of the novel signals, bristles with contradictions. On the one hand, the

~ 105

prohibition the nuns place on what they euphemistically term 'particular friendships', the draconian measures they employ to prevent their occurrence such as spying on the girls and forbidding them to walk in pairs or exchange gifts, and the sensuous and at times sensual imagery that White employs to describe the attachments the girls none the less succeed in forming serve to alert attention to lesbian desire and intense passions that it involves.[3] On the other hand, however, no explicitly sexual acts are described and neither the word 'lesbian' nor 'Sapphic' appears in the text. The homophobic attitudes prevalent in the era of the novel's publication, the repressive atmosphere of Convent life and the naivety of the youthful heroine Nanda, whom White positions as the focaliser of events, make their utterance taboo.[4]

White's description of the Convent and the pupils' experience of life within its walls involves other contradictions and anomalies. The rigid system of surveillance to which the nuns subject their charges and the focus they place on disciplining their minds and bodies construct the Convent as an oppressive social and psychological environment resembling the panoptic regimes described by Michel Foucault.[5] In contrast to this, however, the attractive, though confusing, interplay of the secular and the sacred that the Convent simultaneously displays causes it to exude on occasion a seductive atmosphere of worldly pleasure. The heady mingling of the religious and the erotic that pervades the establishment prompts Nanda, in fact, to comment appreciatively on its 'rare, intense element' (176). She discovers that the room currently termed the parlour was once a ballroom and regards the picture portraying the Virgin Mary in a bright pink dress that ornaments it as surprisingly sensuous. And on certain exceptional occasions, such as the fête celebrating the canonisation of the foundress, the Convent becomes transformed into a place of orgiastic revelry, with the girls dancing round the festive bonfire 'in a wild eddy, singing and leaping' (124). As a result, despite Nanda's complaints about the discipline enforced by the nuns and her occasional rebellious perception that 'the whole of religious life seemed a monstrous and meaningless complication' (135), when her father unexpectedly suggests terminating her residence there, she finds herself 'overwhelmed with a passionate affection for the place' (176) and firmly rejects his offer.

White utilises Gothic motifs and imagery to depict both the oppressive aspects of convent life and the pleasures of the erotic attachments that the pupils form. To convey the sense of claustrophobia that pervades the Convent, she describes it, sometimes seriously and on other occasions with a note of humorous parody, in terms of the classic Gothic castle or haunted house, while assigning to Nanda the conventional role of entrapped heroine. A key theme in Gothic narrative, works of female Gothic in particular as is illustrated by critical readings of the novels of Ann Radcliffe and Charlotte Brontë, is the heroine's experience of her awakening sexuality and the difficulties she experiences in acknowledging and expressing it.[6] White inventively recasts this theme with reference to same-sex desire and relationships. The strategies of indirection that the she utilises, far from striking the reader as an inadequacy or flaw, agree with and, in textual terms, subtly enact the problems and contradictions that, as Judith Roof points out, confront the writer who seeks to depict lesbian sexuality in the antipathetic context of phallocentric culture. Roof describes the writer as 'faced with the difficulty of representing perceptions unaccounted for in a phallic economy in terms of that economy'.[7] One particular problem the writer is likely to encounter, she observes, is 'locating the place of lesbian sexuality in relation to the requisite visibility of a phallocentric system of representation' (100). In order to solve this, White avoids on the whole foregrounding the visual or the explicitly descriptive. She utilises, instead, strategies of representation that are covert and indirect. Instead of describing the feelings of sexual attraction that exist between the girls explicitly, she depicts them in displaced form, mediating them through allusions and imagery appropriated from heterosexual culture or repositioning them on to descriptions of the natural world. She also utilises tactics of metonymy and metaphor. And, in a manner that looks forward to Luce Irigaray's analysis of female eroticism, she foregrounds the multiple and diffuse nature of female sexual response.[8] As a result, female sexuality becomes associated in the novel with the typically Gothic motifs of secrets, mystery and 'the unspeakable'.[9]

HAUNTED HOUSES AND LIVING BURIAL

The positioning of Nanda in the role of Gothic heroine, and reference to the risk of incarceration in a castle or haunted house that it carries with it, are introduced in the novel's opening pages. Here she is portrayed being escorted by her father Mr Grey, a recent convert to Roman Catholicism, through the wintry London streets to take up residence at the Convent. Commenting on the significance that the castle assumes in the fiction of Radcliffe, Cynthia Griffin Wolff observes that it is 'for the most part a safe place, but has as its foundations some complicated maze of underground vaults or dark passages'.[10] The Convent vividly exemplifies these contradictions of security or danger. Whereas Mr Grey regards it as a place of spiritual safety for his daughter, priding himself on the fact that his decision to send her there reflects his commitment to the Catholic faith, Nanda, herself, though initially thrilled to be entering such a holy and socially privileged establishment, is experiencing second thoughts. On approaching the Convent, Mr Grey falls into conversation with an Irish woman who, congratulating him on his good sense in educating his daughter there, expresses the wish that Nanda may experience a vocation to join the religious community as an act of thanksgiving to God for his conversion. Nanda listens to the conversation with feelings of growing unease. She is by no means certain that she wishes to sacrifice her life for the good of her father's soul. As White comments with quiet irony, 'She had heard a good deal about vocations and she wasn't at all sure that she wanted one' (14).

The impression the reader gains of the Convent as a Gothic edifice in which Nanda is about to be imprisoned is accentuated by the reference to the fog enshrouding the walls, the 'rattling of chains and bolts' (16) that accompanies her entry and the ominous 'slam' of the 'nail-studded front door' (17) as it closes behind her. On bidding her father farewell, she feels 'suddenly lonely and frightened' (17). Her spirits are by no means raised by the sight of the gruesome-looking painting portraying the mutilated body of Christ displaying its famous five wounds which greets her in the passage. It introduces both her and the reader to the ideology of the subjugation of the flesh and the emphasis on physical and mental torture that pervade the place. Perverse punishments and acts of cruelty, though ostensibly performed in the name of the Roman Catholic faith, are frequently described as performed by both nuns and pupils with an element of sadomasochistic glee, parodying the acts of torture at the hands of the Inquisition referred to in Gothic novels such as Matthew Lewis's *The Monk* (1796). Nanda has a taste of this puritanical and sadistically oppressive culture on her first night at the Convent. On entering the dormitory, she finds that it lacks a looking-glass as such objects are condemned as promoting vanity. An older pupil who has been assigned the task of initiating her into the nightly routine officiously insists that, before she go to bed, her hair be fastened in a neat plait. Nanda is forced to submit while the pupil, as White expressively describes, 'pulled her hair back and twisted it into an agonisingly tight rope. The efficient bony fingers tied it tighter still, until Nanda's eyes felt as if they would start from her head' (34). And, with the aim of preventing her from touching parts of the body defined by Roman Catholic ideology as sexually taboo, the presiding nun orders her to refrain from sleeping curled up in her usual 'comfortable ball' (35), insisting that, instead, she lie on her back with her hands crossed. White emphasises the unnaturalness and physical discomfort of this position by describing how, after Nanda has managed to maintain it for a few minutes, 'her lids grew heavy and her crossed hands began to uncurl' (36).

The Convent also resembles the typical Gothic castle or haunted house in the connection it displays with the uncanny. The classrooms and dormitories, though appearing normal and even homely, none the less conceal secrets and mysteries. Nanda learns with excitement that 'the frightened look in Mother Pascoe's pleasant, faded eyes' stems from the fact that she has seen a ghost. The Reverend Mother is portrayed on feast days recounting the event to certain privileged older children who, in turn, relay it to 'the horrified and delighted ears of the Junior School' (37). The episode alerts us to the important role that references to the spectral and the psychoanalytic concept of 'the return of the repressed' play in the novel.[11] As we discover, the Convent is, in fact, haunted in metaphoric terms by memories of the pleasures and sexual desires that, on entering its precincts, both nuns and pupils are supposed to renounce. Whereas Nanda nostalgically recalls the mundane pleasures of warm fires and buttered toast, her class mates tell stories of the romantic and pleasure-loving lives led by the nuns before they joined the ecclesiastical community. The tyrannical Mother Frances, for example, who makes Nanda's life misery by confiscating her copy of *Dream Days* and subjecting her friendships with her fellow-pupils to strict surveillance, is unexpectedly described as having been surrounded by a bevy of suitors in her youth. Rumour reports that she spent the night before she entered the Convent not in prayer but dancing at a fashionable ball.

The dialectic of pleasure/repression and freedom/restriction that this anecdote exemplifies is developed in Nanda's encounter with Lady Moira Palliser, the beautiful young heiress who, in defiance of her relatives' wishes, has decided to join the ecclesiastical community. Nanda first catches sight of this elegant and aristocratic figure kneeling in the chapel. As White comments, introducing the theme of same-sex attraction that features prominently in the text, Moira 'was a source of great distraction to Nanda, for she was very pretty, with a mass of golden curls piled on the top of her small head' (51). The next time Nanda encounters Moira, however, she is shocked to see her 'shorn of her soft silk frocks and wearing the hideous flannel blouse and serge skirt of a postulant' (52). In a subsequent episode she listens 'with painful attention as Lady Moira made her vows of chastity, poverty and obedience, and shuddered when the Reverend Mother led her out of the chapel with the novice's thick white veil flung over her orange blossom and tulle' (55). The enshrouding of Moira's youthful beauty in a veil carries connotations of entombment, introducing the Gothic *topos* of living burial.[12] And before being permitted to join the community Moira is subjected to an act of physical mutilation, one that Nanda finds especially scary owing to the fact that it occurs unseen. After the nuns have led Moira from the chapel, a fellow pupil nudges her elbow and 'whispers ghoulishly, "They're cutting her hair now"' (55).

The association of the Convent with the Gothic motif of living burial is extended from the metaphorical to the literal in the episode focusing on the demise of Mother Frances. The news that she is on her deathbed in the community infirmary prompts the impressionable Nanda to envisage the scene in her imagination. She pictures the attendant nuns anointing the Reverend Mother's eyes, ears and nostrils with holy oil and wonders how many candles they have placed round her bed. The thought of death both frightens and thrills her, and White portrays her spending the day of the funeral in a mood of 'alternate fear and excitement'. On entering the chapel where the corpse is lying in state, Nanda is surprised to see that the Reverend Mother's countenance has changed very little; she appears 'hardly paler than she did in life, still wearing her sweet disdainful smile' (90). Nanda and her fellow pupils are portrayed, in typically Gothic manner, as frightened as much by the thought that the deceased may suddenly open her eyes and return to life as they are by the fact of her death. White describes how 'they trod guiltily, as if fearing Mother Frances would wake' and portrays Nanda 'as feeling half relieved when Monica cried out in a hysterical whisper, "She moved. I saw her move!"' (91).[13]

Nanda proceeds from imaginatively picturing the scene of Mother Frances's death in the community infirmary to pondering the architectural structure of the Convent building and the mysteries that it conceals – a train of thought, she discovers, that raises more questions than it answers:

> But where was the community infirmary? Somewhere in the building, there must be, she knew, a hundred cells and a whole counterpart of the school,

libraries, classrooms, study-rooms and sick-rooms, where no lay person except the nuns' doctor was allowed to set foot. Even parents might not visit a dying daughter there. But where did this house within a house lie? She knew the forbidden stairs that led to the community quarters, but that was all. (89)

Nanda's fantasy image of the Convent as mysteriously comprising a 'house within a house', the interior design mirroring that of the exterior, is illuminated by reference to Anthony Vidler's study of what he terms 'the architectural uncanny'. Discussing buildings that furnish the setting for uncanny events, Vidler describes houses in which the labyrinthine exterior gives the effect of 'protecting the inner center from profane intrusion'.[14] He also refers to houses that are constructed around or resemble a tomb, citing as an example the mansion that furnishes the setting for Edgar Allan Poe's The Fall of the House of Usher (1839). Both kinds of edifice are pertinent to the fantasy image of the Convent that Nanda constructs. The maze-like structure of the building, with its interrelating corridors and classrooms, serves to protect the quarters inhabited by the nuns from the intrusion of the laity. Meanwhile the nuns, in choosing to retreat from the world and renounce physical freedom and sexual pleasure, appear, as is illustrated by the episode describing Moira Palliser making her vows in the chapel, to enter a tomb and experience a form of living death.

Vidler also describes a type of architecture in which the edifice, though constructed above ground, represents a copy or offshoot of an underground structure. He connects this 'buried architecture' with the Freudian concept of the navel of a dream, reminding us that Freud refused fully to explicate the concept, cannily preferring to leave it mysterious and unexplored.[15] Nanda's fantasy image of the nuns' living quarters as representing a hidden 'house within a house', invisible to the external world, can in addition be read as a metaphor for her own psyche and the mysteries of the unconscious and repressed desire that it reflects. Her evocative reference to the flight of 'forbidden stairs' (89) which links the familiar world of the school to the unseen, impenetrable world of secrets inhabited by the nuns, supports such a reading, as also do the questions she ponders about the nuns' lives. These are notably physical in content. She wonders, for example, if they wear nightgowns and, alluding by implication to her own lack of such aids to dressing and identity-formation, if they are permitted the use of looking-glasses.

Further questions, ones of a specifically sexual nature reflecting both her childish naivety and her lack of access to sources of information, are described entering Nanda's mind on other occasions. Though recognising that the concept of 'Purity' (68), a key feature of the ideology of femininity that the nuns seek to promote, must represent 'some mysterious possession' (68) associated with femininity, she puzzles fruitlessly over its exact meaning. And what, she wonders, is the impure word the utterance of which, so she has heard, caused St Aloysius Gonzaga to faint? The innocent Nanda conjectures that it must be 'belly', a word she regards as 'so dreadful that she only whispered it in her very worst, most defiant moments' (69). The reader, however, in the privileged position of enjoying access to adult discourses of knowledge, surmises that, like many of the other mysteries and secrets which White implants in the text, it has to do with sex.

PARTICULAR FRIENDSHIPS AND 'THE UNSPEAKABLE'

Nanda's anxiety about the word the impropriety of which caused the sensitive St Aloysius to faint and the qualms she experiences about uttering the word 'belly', though striking the reader as amusing, none the less introduce a serious topic. This is the concept of 'the unspeakable' which, along with the related idea of 'the incommunicable', features prominently in Gothic fiction. Eve Kosofsky Sedgwick states, with justifiable emphasis, that in classic Gothic texts such as Charles Maturin's *Melmoth the Wanderer* (1820) and Emily Brontë's *Wuthering Heights* (1847), 'People hurl themselves against the barriers of the incommunicable'.[16] Describing the two concepts as constituting 'an interpersonal barrier where no barrier ought to be', she demonstrates their connection, on a linguistic plane, to the motif of living burial.[17] As she argues, the inability to articulate or communicate an idea or an emotion whether through fear, modesty or simply lack of knowledge may result in entombing the subject in silence.

This position of inarticulacy and impotence is one to which Nanda is frequently reduced in the repressive world of the Convent of the Five Wounds where the topic of sex, and feelings of same sex-attraction in particular, remain a closely guarded secret. The fly leaf of *St Winifred's World of School*, a book she comes across while residing in the infirmary suffering from a bout of flu, bears the forbidding message: 'Certain pages of this book have been cut out, as the matter they contain is both vulgar and distasteful to the mind of a modest reader' (102). The book is mutilated in other ways as well since a number of passages, presumably those regarded by the nuns as immoral, have been inked out. And, like the book, the writing that Nanda herself produces is also subjected to mutilation. She makes the mistake of allowing her feelings of infatuation for the attractive Clare Rockingham, an older pupil in her teens who enjoys the distinction of being one of the few Protestants to attend the school, to spill over in a letter she writes to her parents. After dutifully requesting them to pray that Clare see the light and convert to Catholicism, she rashly remarks that, on returning from the holidays, Clare 'looks prettier than ever' and, in a sudden burst of romantic passion, compares her eyes, which she describes as exceptionally bright, to 'chips of emerald' (142). When summoned by the appropriately Gothic-named Mother Radcliffe to explain the passage, she naively assumes that it is her grammar which is at fault. The nun, however, though sarcastically agreeing that her grammar is indeed 'slipshod' (144), explains that it is the content of the letter that offends, specifically the reference it makes to 'particular friendships' and 'the dangerous and unhealthy indulgence of feeling' (144) that, in her view, this signifies. She informs Nanda that, as a result, she intends to destroy the letter. As Sedgwick argues in *Epistemology of the Closet* (1991), by the end of the nineteenth century 'there had in fact developed one particular sexuality that was distinctively constituted *as* secrecy'.[18] This is, of course, homosexuality, and, in openly expressing her feelings of attraction for Clare, Nanda breaks the code of secrecy attached to it. Not only does she admit to emotions which, as the nun implies, the Church and society condemn as 'morbid', but (an even greater sin) she makes them public by articulating them in a missive addressed to members of the laity beyond the Convent walls. A letter, generally one with sexual implications, that fails to reach its destination on account of being buried, purloined or destroyed, is, of course, a common motif in Gothic fiction.[19] The nun's destruction of Nanda's letter home and the attempted suppression of female eroticism that it signifies develop this tradition with reference to feelings of same-sex attraction.

Commenting on Radcliffe's depiction of Montoni's castle in *The Mysteries of Udolpho* (1794), Nichols describes the edifice as characterised, as is often the case in Gothic fiction, by a 'diffuse sensuality' and exuding 'an atmosphere both sexually reticent and perverse'.[20] Lippington, though an educational institution on the outskirts of London peopled by nuns and schoolgirls rather than a castle in the Apennines where a romantic heroine is incarcerated, displays a similar atmosphere. Here, however, it is same-sex female attraction which is to the fore. Prevented from expressing their feelings openly by the ban that the nuns place on particular friendships, the pupils, the older ones in particular, resort to covert means. Flirtation, and the indirect communication of sexual attraction that it facilitates, are honed into a complex and sophisticated art. It is one at which the teenage Clare is especially adept. This is illustrated in the episode in which, by exploiting her reputation as 'poor enquiring heathen' (110) and the ignorance of the tenets of the Roman Catholic faith that it implies, she attempts to tease Nanda into talking about sex. She plays mischievously on the verb 'convert', allowing it to acquire resonances of lesbian seduction. The episode illustrates the piquant interplay of the sacred and the secular that characterises White's description of convent life. It also exemplifies the way that the pupils succeed in articulating erotic attraction indirectly, mediating it through concepts and phrases that they appropriate, ironically, from Roman Catholic doctrine. By utilising this tactic, they create a form of Foucauldian reverse discourse.[21]

The encounter between the two girls opens with Clare requesting Nanda to explicate certain thorny Biblical passages, in particular the sexually suggestive phrase 'fornication and all wilful pleasure in the irregular motions of the flesh' (112) cited in the Ninth Commandment. Nanda, embarrassed, hedges. Taking refuge in ignorance, she replies that she has not yet studied this Commandment since she has heard that it involves 'some very disgusting sins that only grown-up people commit' (112). Laughing at her naivety, Clare repeats her request for spiritual instruction, playfully introducing the topic of conversion:

> 'You may be converting me. Who knows?'
> 'I shouldn't dream of trying, Clare,' asserted Nanda, 'Catholics don't try and convert people like that. They just answer your questions and ... and ... pray for you.'
> Clare leaned over and touched Nanda's arm with a hot quivering hand that burned through her holland sleeve. 'Do you pray for me, baby?'
> 'Of course', said Nanda in a very matter-of-fact-voice, but she blushed all the same. Clare's touch embarrassed and delighted her; it gave her the queerest shivering sensation in the roof of her mouth. Why was it that when everyone else seemed just face and hands, Clare always reminded one that there was a warm body under her uniform? (113)

Several different factors account for the pronounced erotic power of this passage. As well as describing Nanda's response to Clare's caress exceptionally vividly, White provocatively juxtaposes sacred love with profane. Clare asks with mock piety, 'Do you pray for me, baby?', while simultaneously touching 'Nanda's arm with a hot quivering hand that burned through her holland sleeve'. The passage also creates a lively dialectic between the desiring female subject and the repression of desire, the liberated body and the constricted, two motifs that recur frequently in the text. They are represented here by Nanda's sudden intense perception that forms the climax of the episode, of 'the warm body' that lies concealed under Clare's drab school uniform.

The sexually provocative humour of the episode is further accentuated by the ironic incongruity of the name 'Clare'. Associated in Roman Catholicism with the ecclesiastical order of Poor Clares, the name conjures up an image of extreme unworldliness and spirituality – attributes which are obviously alien to Nanda's flirtatious friend.

The teasingly ambiguous interplay that White constructs between the sacred and the profane, along with the utilisation of religious references to express erotic emotions and sensations, that characterise her account of Nanda's conversation with Clare also inform other episodes in the novel. On the occasion of her first communion Nanda is distracted from thoughts of God by 'the smell of Joan Appleyard's newly-washed hair above the lilies and the incense' (84) and the ambiguous expression of ecstasy (Does it signify religious or sexual passion, the reader wonders?) on her friend Theresa's face. She perceives that 'Theresa Leighton's head was thrown back; she had closed her prayer-book and was gazing at the altar with a rapt, avid look, her mouth a little open' (84). White's choice of the name Theresa is wittily appropriate since it recalls the mystic St Teresa of Avila and Bernini's famous sculptural representation of her in ecstasy. Jacques Lacan relates St Teresa's mystical experience to the distinctive nature of female eroticism, arguing that it illustrates woman's ability to enjoy 'a *jouissance* beyond the phallus'.[22]

Events of a religious nature that take place in the Convent also become, on occasion, a vehicle for the communication of erotic attraction. In fact the pupils' performance of *The Vision of Dante*, an expurgated version of *La Divina Commedia* (1308–21) written and directed by the nuns, becomes so sexually charged in rehearsal, with Clare's Virgil gazing 'with such fond admiration at Rosario's Dante that she forgot her cues' (163) and Rosario's scenes with Leonie's Beatrice emitting a 'strange electricity' (170), that the presiding nun decides to intervene. To the intense anger and frustration of the actors, she dismisses them from the production and substitutes an alternative cast who perform the roles with less passion.

White also utilises other strategies to represent the topic of same-sex eroticism. Whereas cropped or bound hair functions throughout the text as an image of sexual repression, hair that flows free signifies liberation.

One of the most overtly erotic episodes in the novel is that in which Nanda and her friends spend the evening together in the school infirmary. Rosario and Clare loosen their tresses and compare their respective lengths while Nanda and her friend Leonie look on with evident pleasure.

In addition, White displaces the erotic on to descriptions of the natural world. The garden where Nanda is portrayed meeting Leonie is depicted as 'small and secluded, spicy with smell of azaleas' (80). White's description evokes, of course, the motif of the *hortus conclusus* and the associations it traditionally carries with female sexuality. On keeping her tryst with her friend there, Nanda experiences a sudden impulse of *jouissance*: 'The warmth [of the sun] playing on her skin made her feel quite dizzy with happiness: she wanted to tear off her thick serge and shake her hair loose from its plait' (80–1). Needless, to say, she does neither. She remains prisoner to the codes of self-control and the subjugation of the flesh which, despite the pupils' spirited attempts at rebellion, dominate convent life.

STORYTELLING, FANTASY AND PERFORMATIVITY

Commenting on the fractured appearance of many Gothic texts, an effect she describes as accentuated by the frequent breakdown of communication between the characters and the emphasis placed on events and facts that remain unspoken, Sedgwick remarks wryly on 'the difficulty the story has in getting itself told'.[23] Problems of communication sometimes occur, she illustrates, not only between the actual characters but also between writer and reader. Her observations are relevant to *Frost in May*, the narrative of which, in accord with Gothic convention, displays an exceptionally large number of gaps and absences. These stem chiefly from the repressive atmosphere of convent life and the refusal of the nuns to countenance explicit reference to sexual matters, feelings of same-sex attraction in particular. As we have seen, pages are cut out and passages erased from the books the pupils read, while the letters they write home are sometimes confiscated or destroyed. The narrative is haunted, in addition, by certain words and concepts that are either unexplained or remain unspoken. These include the meaning of the term 'my Purity' (68) and the mysterious word that caused St Aloysius to faint, both of which puzzle and perplex Nanda; and the words 'lesbian' and 'Sapphic' which are excluded from the text. Gaps and absences also exist in relation to theatrical events and literary texts which, as a result of the nuns' brutal intervention, fail to materialise or achieve completion. These include the pupils' passionate performance of *The Vision of Dante*, stymied by the director by the simple but deadly device of changing the cast, and the erotically charged novel that Nanda is surreptitiously engaged in writing. On discovering the manuscript, the nuns predictably confiscate it (207). The event has dire consequences for Nanda, giving rise to her sudden expulsion from the Convent and, as a result, the loss of her friends. It has an equally drastic effect on White's narrative, bringing it to an unexpectedly abrupt close. The sudden termination of the novel encourages us, in fact, to identify with Nanda since it leaves us with a similarly frustrating sense of female desires that are thwarted and personal histories left truncated and incomplete.

Another feature of *Frost in May* that tends to impede the smooth flow of the narrative and to prevent direct communication occurring between writer and reader, one that again accords with Gothic textual convention, is White's utilisation of multiple narrators and storylines. Nuns and pupils, though frequently portrayed in a state of conflict, none the less share a common interest. Both enjoy storytelling and are enthusiastic raconteurs. The nuns recount improving, if far-fetched, stories of the lives of the saints, along with Gothic tales focusing on uncanny or gruesome events, while the pupils entertain each other with anecdotes about their holidays and exaggerated accounts of their parents' wealth. The more intellectual ones, such as a Nanda and Leonie, try their hand at creative writing. The stories narrated by both nuns and pupils interweave, transforming the text into a tissue of interlocking narratives. This intricate exercise in intertextuality is further complicated by the introduction of different literary forms and genres. The primary narrative line is frequently fractured by excerpts from letters, poems, diary entries and notes of religious retreats, as well as by literary allusions. The latter are remarkably eclectic, creating a wittily provocative interplay of the sacred and the secular, the serious and the frivolous. Quotations from the Magnificat, the poems of Francis Thompson and the French Romantics interact with allusions to the works of Oscar Wilde, Hans Andersen's *Fairy Tales* (1835–37), *The Arabian Nights* (c.800–900) and Farrar's *St Winifred's; or the World of School* (1862).

The stories the nuns recount frequently rework in miniature the Gothic themes that inform the novel as a whole. Topics of living burial and the haunted house are recapitulated in the tale told by Mother Poitier, a French nun admired by the pupils as a 'great repository of stories' (47).

She recounts the legend of an aristocratic young bride who, while playing hide-and-seek with her wedding guests, loses her way in the cellars of the family chateau and dies alone. Mother Poitier emphasises the macabre aspect of the bride's corpse. She describes how the flowers in her veil 'were all withered' and mentions the way that her skeleton, on being touched, 'crumbled into dust' (71). The description of the bride buried alive in the underground vault, as well as recalling the image of Moira Palliser making her vows in the convent chapel with her orange blossom and tulle covered by 'a thick white veil', also evokes the stifling effect that convent life has on Nanda and her friends.

The sadomasochistic atmosphere of the Convent, with its emphasis on perverse punishments and the spiritual value of suffering, is foregrounded in another of Mother Poitier's anecdotes. She recounts, apparently for the moral benefit of the pupils, the story of little Molly, a former student, who, on having her ear accidentally pierced by a large safety pin while being dressed in her Communion veil, refused to alert attention to her plight but chose to suffer in silence. This bizarrely masochistic tale is, ironically, extremely well suited to the place where the event it describes allegedly occurred: the Convent of the Five Wounds. Sadomasochistic incidents of this kind parody the acts of torture performed by the Inquisition in the name of the Catholic faith referred to in eighteenth-century Gothic texts.

Sadomasochism is also to the fore in the events depicted in *The Lives of the English Martyrs*, a collection of historical anecdotes describing in graphic detail the physical torments suffered by her fellow Catholics in the sixteenth century which Nanda is given to read in her free study-hour. As White sardonically comments, emphasising the scary effect of such gory reading material on her youthful heroine, 'the account of the pressing to death of the Blessed Margaret Clitheroe had nearly turned her sturdy stomach' (42).

However storytelling and literary allusions, as well as being employed by the nuns to promote the interests of Roman Catholicism, also furnish the pupils with strategies of resistance. They manifest their defiance by reading prohibited novels and engaging in creative writing. Nanda gives up composing 'laboured little lyrics about spring and the sea, with a tardy reference to God in the last verse', and instead devotes her energies to writing a 'full-length novel' (158). Feeling guilty about ditching religion entirely, she hits on an ingenious compromise: 'She decided to describe a brilliant, wicked, worldly society, preferably composed of painters, musicians and peers, and to let all her characters be sensationally converted in the last chapter' (158).

Another tactic of defiance the pupils adopt is to write poems and love letters to one other. Leonie addresses elegant little eighteenth-century-style verses to her adored Rosario, celebrating her in the pastoral guise of Celia or Lucinda. And, unconsciously or deliberately, they irreverently subvert passages from the Roman Catholic liturgy by giving them erotic significance. Listening to Lelita singing in the convent chapel, Nanda notes with enjoyment the way that her 'lazy veiled contralto voice would make the *O Salutaris* sound like a love-song' (107).

The fantasy narratives and images that the pupils create serve on occasion to destabilise gender. Nanda's initial impression of Leonie, the daughter of an ancient, wealthy Roman Catholic family who subsequently becomes her closest friend, is the romantic image of 'a young prince, pale and weary from a day's ride, with his lovelocks carelessly tied back in a frayed ribbon' (79). She also pictures her as 'a stern, handsome young man' (122) and, alternatively, as 'a young soldier fresh from an audience with the king' (85). These images, and the courtly romantic narratives they evoke, elaborate the gallantly boyish role that Leonie herself cultivates. She speaks, incongruously for an eleven-year-old girl, of intending to 'sow her wild oats' (93) and, when a fellow pupil makes the mistake of ridiculing the Spanish nationality of her beloved Rosario, 'without a word … shot out her fist and sent her sprawling' (109). In keeping with this virile act, Leonie favours a stylishly eye-catching, if somewhat bizarre, form of cross-dressing. White tells us that she leaves the Convent to attend 'a well-chaperoned tea at the Ritz … incongruously arrayed in a military-looking coat chosen by herself and an absurd, daisy-trimmed hat that her mother had bought in Paris' (108). The performance of gallant masculinity that Leonie herself enacts and that Nanda elaborates in the romantic image she constructs of her friend, instead of striking the reader as an imitation of an authentic gender, do the reverse. They challenge the binary construct masculine/feminine, serving, as Judith Butler observes, to 'bring into relief the utterly constructed status of the so-called original'.[24]

Appropriately, considering Leonie's transgressive disregard of conventions of femininity, White assigns to her the role of the champion of fairytale and Gothic fantasy as opposed to the humdrum world of realism and common sense. Admitting that her allegiance to the Roman Catholic faith is aesthetic rather than spiritual in basis, reflecting her enjoyment of the fantastic, Leonie nonchalantly announces to the shocked Nanda:

'I like the Catholic way of looking at things ... Any way of looking at life is a fairy story, and I prefer mine with lots of improbable embellishments. I think angels and devils are much more amusing than microbes and Mr Wells's noble scientists.' (148-9)

Leonie's flamboyant defence of the pleasures of fantasy and fairytale, as well as reflecting her outspoken personality, exemplifies a key feature of White's representation of life at Lippington. This is the emphasis she places on the fertility of the female imagination and the girls' ability to resist the rigid routine of convent life and its sexually repressive atmosphere by drawing on resources of fantasy, literary invention and role-play.

Leonie's speech also makes an apt conclusion to my discussion of White's novel and the contribution it makes to the tradition of lesbian Gothic. As illustrated above, motifs associated with Gothic fantasy, such as the entrapped heroine, the haunted mansion with its mysterious passages and stairways constructed around a tomb, and the concepts of 'the unspeakable' and 'the incommunicable', are utilised to evoke the Convent's oppressive climate. Feelings of attraction between the pupils, instead of being articulated explicitly, achieve expression through strategies of indirection and displacement. The division between the secular and the sacred is problematised, with phrases from the Roman Catholic liturgy and passages from the Ten Commandments being appropriated by the pupils as vehicles for erotic perceptions and flirtatious exchanges. Together, these strategies create the heady atmosphere of female same-sex eroticism and the ambiguous interplay of the mundane and the uncanny which typifies the text of *Frost in May*.

NOTES

1 Elaine Marks, 'Lesbian Intertextuality', in Elaine Marks and George Stambolian (eds), *Homosexualities and French Literature: Cultural Contexts / Critical Texts* (Ithaca: Cornell University Press, 1979), pp. 353-77.
2 Terry Castle, *The Apparitional Lesbian: Female Homosexuality and Modern Culture* (New York: Columbia University Press, 1993), pp. 28-65; Paulina Palmer, *Lesbian Gothic: Transgressive Fictions* (London: Cassell, 1999) and 'Lesbian Gothic: Genre, Transformation, Transgression', *Gothic Studies*, 6/1 (2004), 118-30; Mary Wings, 'Rebecca Redux: Tears on a Lesbian Pillow', in Liz Gibbs (ed.), *Daring to Dissent: Lesbian Culture from Margin to Mainstream* (London: Cassell, 1994), pp. 10-32.
3 Antonia White, *Frost in May* [1933] (London: Virago, 1978), p. 43. All subsequent references are to this edition, and are given in parentheses in the text.

4 Lesbianism became a topic of extreme sensitivity following the 1928 trial in which Radclyffe Hall's *The Well of Loneliness* was declared obscene and banned. See Laura Doan, *Fashioning Sapphism: The Origins of a Modern Lesbian Culture* (New York: Columbia University Press, 2001), pp. 185–94. Nanda is nine when she enters Lippington and fourteen when she leaves.

5 Foucault describes panopticism as 'a type of power that is applied to individuals in the form of continuous individual supervision, in the form of control, punishment and compensation, and in the form of correction, that is the molding and transformation of individuals in terms of certain norms': see 'Truth and Judicial Forms', in *Essential Works of Michel Foucault 1954–1984*, ed. James D. Faubion (London: Allen Lane, 1994), vol. 3, pp. 52–89. Foucault includes convents among the institutions which exercise this form of power.

6 See Nina da Vinci Nichols, 'Place and Eros in Radcliffe, Lewis and Brontë', in Juliann Fleenor (ed.), *The Female Gothic* (Montreal: Eden Press, 1983), pp. 187–92.

7 Judith Roof, 'The Match in the Crocus', in Marleen Barr and Richard Feldstein (eds), *Discontented Discourses: Feminism / Textual Intervention / Psychoanalysis* (Urbana: University of Illinois Press, 1989), p. 109.

8 Luce Irigaray, 'When the Goods Get Together', in Elaine Marks and Isabelle de Courtivron (eds), *New French Feminisms* (Hemel Hempstead: Harvester Wheatsheaf, 1981), pp. 107–10.

9 See Eve Kosofsky Sedgwick, *The Coherence of Gothic Conventions* (London: Methuen, 1980), pp. 13–19.

10 Cynthia Griffin Wolff, 'The Radcliffean Gothic Model: A Form for Feminine Sexuality', in Fleenor (ed.), *The Female Gothic*, p. 210.

11 Sigmund Freud, 'The "Uncanny"' (1919), in *The Complete Psychological Works*, ed. and trans. James Strachey with Anna Freud (London: Hogarth, 1955), vol. 17, pp. 217–53.

12 Sedgwick, *The Coherence of Gothic Conventions*, pp. 128–34.

13 Female characters in Gothic fiction who, though assumed to be dead, unexpectedly return to life include Edgar Allan Poe's Madeline Usher and Ligeia.

14 Anthony Vidler, *The Architectural Uncanny: Essays in the Modern Unhomely* (Cambridge, MA: MIT Press, 1999), p. 43.

15 Ibid., p. 134.

16 Sedgwick, *The Coherence of Gothic Conventions*, p. 68.

17 Ibid., p. 16.

18 Sedgwick, *Epistemology of the Closet* (Hemel Hempstead: Harvester Wheatsheaf, 1991), p. 73.

19 In Charlotte Brontë's *Villette* (1853) a letter is buried, in Poe's 'The Purloined Letter' (1845) a letter is stolen, and in Henry James's *The Turn of the Screw* (1898) a letter is, so the governess assumes, destroyed.

20 Nichols, *Place and Eros*, pp. 190, 193.

21 See Foucault, *The History of Sexuality, Volume 1: The Will to Knowledge*, trans. Robert Hurley (Harmondsworth: Penguin, 1978), p. 101.
22 Juliet Mitchell and Jacqueline Rose (eds), *Feminine Sexuality: Jacques Lacan and the Ecole Freudienne* (London: Macmillan, 1982), pp. 145–7.
23 Sedgwick, *The Coherence of Gothic Conventions*, p. 13.
24 Judith Butler, 'Imitation and Gender Insubordination', in Diana Fuss (ed.), *Inside/Out: Lesbian Theories, Gay Theories* (London and New York: Routledge, 1991), pp. 13–31 at p. 23.

8
Devouring desires: lesbian Gothic horror

Gina Wisker

The vampire is the queer in its lesbian mode.

Sue-Ellen Case[1]

Your body is not my food ... Your pleasure is my food.

Katherine Forrest[2]

Gender influences everything but determines nothing! Vampires transcend gender. We as a modern people transcend gender, though we can never escape it. Ours is a time for which there are no precedents with regard to gender and freedom.

Anne Rice[3]

Desire and devouring feature as twin motifs in lesbian Gothic horror. They enable an enactment of the threat, danger, disgust, the celebration and potential for new relationships of equal exchange and pleasure. They are explored, in my discussion here, through the metaphors of werewolf and vampire, each figure offering the opportunity of breaking out, expressing a hitherto hidden version of self, and all the desires, dangers and potential for change which such a breaking out, such exposure, such exchange offers. Threats come from within as much as without, from internalised and imposed notions of the abject, against which develops a notion of queer and queer theory, which offers new perspectives on sexuality and on gender as performance.

A double abjection: what could be more abject and disgusting, fascinating, a twinned embodiment of desire and deviancy, than the performance of the queer, of lesbian and gay in Gothic horror? How else to explore and explicate the strategies of this performance and representation, the enactment of the taboos, the celebration of Otherness than via queer theory? Julia Kristeva locates abjection 'at the doors of the feminine, at the doors of abjection ... the drive foundations of fascism'.[4] Kristeva exposes how identification and abjection problematise the conventional constraints of constructed roles based on culture and gender, spring from and valorise a fascism of culture and of the body. Responding to such Fascist Othering, both Anne Rice and Sue-Ellen Case (above) celebrate rescripting the figure of the vampire as carrier of liberatory potential, a boundary breaker who can expose and challenge the unnecessary and stifling worldviews and practices embedded in the constraints of normative gender roles and role-play. Figures of horror, of the abject, are ideally placed to be reimagined and rescripted as positive celebrations of otherness, utilising the strategies of the queer Gothic to do so.

This chapter uses queer theory to explore, explicate and celebrate the boundary-breaking refusals and testing of conventions which gay- and lesbian-oriented Gothic horror offers through the rescripting of the figures of the werewolf and the vampire. In so doing, it argues that writers such as Poppy Z. Brite, Anne Rice, Pat Califia, Amelia G, Katherine Forrest and Melanie Tem demonstrate both the terrible price to pay for being different sexually, challenging conventions, and the necessity of those challenges, the celebratory excess, carnival and creative potential, the fundamental testing of established norms, possible through queer theory in action in gay- and lesbian-oriented vampire and werewolf tales. Identity, classification and control are key elements here. The chapter will focus in the main on Melanie Tem's lesbian werewolf tale 'Wilding' (1996), and Katherine Forrest's 'O Captain, My Captain' (1993).[5]

Exploring queer Gothic horror embraces Judith Butler's views of gender as performative, developing her problematising of gender categories. It offers a movement beyond the terms of lesbian and gay, seeing, as does Anne Marie Jagose, that queer is not a single category subsuming gay and lesbian but a consistent becoming. De Lauretis initially promoted the term 'queer' over lesbian and gay, arguing that they had to some extent become normative categories, and that identity classification has conservative effects, while queer can instead be conceived as a category in constant formation. Continuing this argument, Judith Butler notes that:

> [It] will have to remain that which is, in the present, never fully owned, but always and only redeployed, twisted, queered from a prior usage and in the direction of urgent and expanding political purposes, and perhaps also yielded in favor of terms that do that political work more effectively.[6]

This chapter considers lesbian Gothic horror, using queer theory where appropriate, to demonstrate both the dangerous limitations of fixing lesbian identity and the potential for exploration, realisation and enactment of versions of lesbian relationships which enable flexible becoming and changing of gendered relationships. Constant formation (see De Lauretis, above) becomes not only a critical effect but an affect of the newly configured identities and relationships in some lesbian Gothic horror, in alignment with a positive reading of Deleuze and Guattari's notion (1988) of 'becoming woman', where the ability to metamorphose, transform and break boundaries and taboos leads to new versions of self and relationships.[7] In the first instance, Melanie Tem's werewolf tale 'Wilding' dramatises a constraint, a failure to change, which pays a terrible price, while Pat Califia's lesbian Gothic vampire tale 'Vampire' (1993) and Katherine Forrest's sci-fi vampire horror tale 'O Captain, My Captain' offer expression of the positive potential of a creative becoming of relationships; the pleasures of exchange.[8]

Lesbian horror was not always seen as so liberating and potentially celebratory. Historically it has represented the abject, the censored and the sexually exciting. In a very titillating fashion, Hammer horror movies of the 1970s, which consistently represent excitingly unlicensed sexuality as vampirism or other forms of the monstrous, wallow in the disgusting potential of twin lesbian female vampires in *Twins of Evil* (1971) where scantily clad pin-ups – constructed by a very conventional heterosexual imagination – prefer girl-on-girl sexual acts rather than the heterosexual coupling clearly seen as normative within the economy of the movie and its audience's values system.[9] Lesbian coupling is more terrifying to the conventional 1970s director, and, more importantly, to viewers, than any concern that these women are victims and perpetrators of the vampire curse. Their sexual *deviancy* is figured as vampirism, their vampirism both an excuse for and a projection of what is considered deviant. Once viewers have finished wallowing, they can sit in judgement alongside the director and the storyline, and condemn and despatch the doubly evil transgressors.

This Hammer horror movie resembles the trajectory and normalising imperative of that first lesbian vampire tale, Sheridan Le Fanu's 'Carmilla' (1872) which predates Bram Stoker's *Dracula* (1897).[10] A homeless itinerant noblewoman is left at and supported in the homes of a series of young women. But the young traveller, Marcella/Carmilla, is a vampire and her nature demands that she drains young women for her own survival. Feminist and queer theorists and critics might be troubled by the conventional critique of Carmilla as deviant, disgusting, to be exorcised from the family home, marginalised. It is a tale constructed by and valorising conventional patriarchal values which condemn lesbianism *as* a form of vampirism. Carmilla must be warded off by the forces of patriarchy, the father and the General, but what of her companion, Laura? This is where a less conventional reading which refuses to uphold the normalised constraints of heterosexuality can enter our discussions. After the disturbing frisson of a dreamlike memory of the potentially predatory visitor, Laura does not find Carmilla so threatening. Theirs becomes a close relationship of fondness and exchange. While relating to Laura (some might say keeping her under her spell), Carmilla deliberately restrains her vampire nature, focusing instead on village girls. Although the politics of this are dubious (are these girls a lower form of being to be so easily drained without any qualms?), the sexual politics are far more complex. At the juncture and revelation of her predatory nature, Carmilla is despatched, but her influence lingers on. Laura misses her, Carmilla fills her dreams and our imaginations as a surprising trace of sexual excitement perhaps, one marginalised by conventional readings of disgust at the female vampire, and one with the potential to be revived precisely because the attraction, seen as deviant, abject, has been exorcised along with its originator, Carmilla. This conventional horror turn, based upon investment in culturally agreed values, need not be Carmilla or Laura's fate if, in rereading, the complacency, repression and limited vision which produce and valorise it are refused.

The advances of the lesbian vampire represent dangerous sexual deviance, a challenge to patriarchal controls. Contemporary feminist critics and those influenced by queer theory, however, might find in Carmilla a literary role model of the excitement and potential of transgression, questioning patriarchal power relations and conventional identity constructions.

In the late twentieth and early twenty-first centuries, contemporary women writers of lesbian and queer Gothic have engaged directly with ways in which horror figures and boundary breakers can be portrayed and read in ways which further debate about lesbianism and conventional representations of sexuality. In their work, these writers explore, question and trouble the destructive strategies of conventional society, imaginatively acting out new possibilities of sexual identity and relationships.

Explorations of the queer Gothic involve notions of Othering and the recuperation of the Other. Queer theory offers opportunities to recognise and reconfigure difference as something to celebrate rather than fear and destroy. While this challenge is focused upon sexuality, it can also be seen in a broader political context. Insistence upon exclusivity and boundaries, differences and hierarchies, leads to dominance, war between nations, between men and women, between the culturally and variously different.[11] By recognising the Other and the abject as part of ourselves, refusing that borderline and opposition, we can, Kristeva argues, overcome the need to find victims, scapegoats and enemies. Kristeva's *Strangers to Ourselves* (1988) provides a political exploration of the way the West treats foreigners, based on an examination of racism in France. Here she links the need to expose the boundaries, rejections and repression of western patriarchal-based horror with the need for racial and political equality:

> Our disturbing otherness, for that indeed is what bursts in to confront the 'demons', or the threat that apprehension generated by the protective apparition of the other at the heart of what we persist in maintaining as a proper, solid 'us'. By recognising *our* uncanny strangeness we shall neither suffer from it nor enjoy it from the outside. The foreigner is within me, hence we are all foreigners. If I am a foreigner, then there are no foreigners.[12]

Contemporary women writers of lesbian and queer Gothic horror use a variety of scenarios and strategies to trouble conventional representations of gender relations. In particular, they use the vampire and werewolf myths to explore transgression, Othering and the celebration of same-sex relations, where these are socially constructed as dangerous, disturbing and destructive. Versions of lesbian and queer sexuality and relations can be seen as open to change, as becoming and celebratory rather than condemned.

Melanie Tem undercuts conventional horror's neat reinforcing of the status quo in its closure, its packing away and staking of that which is terrifying because Other, abject, threatening to that status quo. Her work exposes and refuses the demonising of our animal nature, our other selves, and the easy maintenance of taboos as ritual spells against any bit of questioning of this neat set of behaviours and beliefs. Family relationships are a prime location for such horror, an exposé of hypocrisy, simple repressive binary oppositions, rituals which prioritise some behaviours, exclude, demonise, punish others. Tem often remains with the quandary exposed through figures and events of horror. Metamorphosis is often painful, difficult, and potentially fatal. Tem's 'Mama' (1990) has a returned vampire mother eating flies in the kitchen to the disgust of her teenage daughter who, nevertheless, soon succumbs to her own vampire nature.[13] But it is with her lesbian Gothic horror werewolf tale 'Wilding' that she deals most sensitively with the problem of Othering, inclusivity and exclusivity, which lie at the heart of queer theory's explorations.

The werewolf myth is chosen by some feminist and lesbian Gothic horror writers because it focuses on borderline natures, boundary crossing, adolescence, sexuality and identity. So why does the werewolf myth appeal as a way of tracking and tracing relations and behaviours which challenge and contrast the conventional? Werewolves are historically figures of disturbance, boundary crossers, refusers of rules and regulations, transformative, and as such perfect metaphors of the gay or lesbian challenge to conventional construction and representations of sexual categories and behaviours. Historically, there is a visible equation between political and social problematising and challenge, exposure as a werewolf, and subsequent punishment. Political, like sexual, challenge must be demonised and destroyed. In 1521 two French peasants suspected of being werewolves were sentenced to death by burning, and more than thirty thousand werewolves met their fate beside witches. Some were religious dissenters, but official reports locate an outbreak of lycanthropy among radical thinkers. By the late 1700s, government-funded werewolf hunters worked in France and Germany, catching, charging and executing anyone whose lifestyle suggested lycanthropy (i.e. outlaws, political dissenters, robbers). In 1602, the British royal court banned 'illicit assemblies', punishing as scandalous counter-cultural youth movements. 'Profane' culture included disguises, cross-dressing, and 'werewolfery', or 'vouarouverie', derivations of which in Norman French mean 'in disorder'.[14] The eighteenth-century Norman peasantry labelled outlaws as 'varoux', existing outside the boundaries of humanity, damned, the property of devils. Much of this passed into popular myth and fairytale, cautionary teachings for the young. In 'Little Red Riding Hood', werewolves reappear as representative of the dangers of sexual ravishment or taboo relationships, controlled by patriarchal force. They are embodiments of an Oedipally based threat of being devoured, which marginalises female monstrosity (the cannibalistic witch, the grandmother), and foregrounds masculine sexuality embodied by both wolf (illegitimate) and woodman (legitimate). Marina Warner suggests links between witch and wolf, which identify both as sexualised predatory deviants:

The wolf is kin to the forest dwelling witch, or crone; he offers us a male counterpart, a werewolf who swallows up grandmother and then granddaughter. In the witch hunting fantasies of early modern Europe they are the kind of beings associated with marginal knowledge, who possess pagan secrets and are in turn possessed by them.[15]

Two main explanations of the fascination with werewolves and the beast within emerge from Darwinism and Freudianism. Darwinism explicates the identification in nineteenth-century eugenics of those of other than white races as inferior, less developed, beasts, terrifyingly Other, while Freudianism links the werewolf or Wolf Man to ways in which sexual histories affect adult sexuality and identity formation.

Werewolves are more conventionally considered to be male, but female werewolves are figures used by more radical contemporary writers, including Melanie Tem and Angela Carter, Suzy McKee Charnas and authors in Pam Keesey's 1996 collection *Women Who Run with the Werewolves*, to explore transgressive sexual behaviours which question conventional norms at moments of potential change, such as for teenage girls at puberty (Carter, McKee Charnas).[16] In this respect, Angela Carter's Rosaleen, Little Red Riding Hood, in 'The Company of Wolves' (1979) uses her sexualised (heterosexual) werewolf nature to provide a challenge to and escape from the rules of her conventional family and of the traditional tales, which would relegate her to the role of victim to be saved only by one force of patriarchy (the woodman) from another force of patriarchy (carnivorous male wolf).[17] Carter's Rosaleen embraces her werewolf lover and transforms herself in the process.

Although conventionally a creature of abjection, the werewolf figure can be reclaimed as a celebration of sexuality, whether heterosexual or, in the case of Melanie Tem's 'Wilding', lesbian. However, unconventionality can be dangerous, as can moments of change or becoming, in inhospitable contexts. In 'Wilding', the werewolf figure is used in several ways, to challenge the representation of lesbian identity and sexuality as abject, and to expose the very real dangers of revealing one's nature as different from that of one's group or family.

'Wilding' deals with several kinds of difference and revelation, to terrible results, and in so doing urges consideration of the damage, the dangers of challenging approved group behaviours, in seeking to 'become', to metamorphose as oneself, something Lydia, in 'Wilding', cannot ultimately achieve. As a social worker, Melanie Tem must have had many experiences of the closed cultures of families, each a law unto themselves, a dangerous space for others to enter into. Werewolfishness in this tale represents both the exclusivity of the family circle into which new partners are introduced at their peril, and Lydia's potential for transformation and celebration of her own nature through the mutual affirmation of love. However, any assertion of Lydia's sexual identity, her right to an existence beyond that of the closed family group, is ruled out. Presenting a lesbian lover to the family is literally throwing the loved one to the wolves.

Families are often a well-kept secret. Their unpleasant social habits and their ostensible welcome for (but actual propensity for interrogation and dissection of) strangers, particularly new friends and lovers, is the subject of soaps, comedies such as *Meet the Parents* (2000) and black comedies including Pinter's *The Homecoming* (1965). Lydia in 'Wilding' is the sole carer of her matriarchal family, keeping her own werewolf nature at home, and crossing the boundaries between the working everyday world and the charnel house of her domestic setting with ostensible ease. But she cannot introduce the two to each other. The story comments on what we hide, how we relate, and on the ultimate, conventionally submerged, hidden viciousness of the domestic. Lydia seeks her own salvation though her relationship with Pam, a work colleague, but the short-sightedness and small-mindedness of the average suburban family fascinated with a lesbian couple is as nothing compared with what faces Lydia and Pam. 'Do you love pets Lydia?' (152) might seem a very ordinary way to introduce your dog and your lover, but it cannot be anything other than ironic in Lydia's situation, for Lydia lives a life far beyond Pam's imagination and comprehension, with no space for pets, though dogs are abundant. The story operates a defamiliarisation and displacement of references which keeps the reader disturbed and confused, like Pam, the outsider, misreading signs. From the outset we are troubled but cannot imagine what the undercurrent of threat and fear indicates, as Lydia invites Pam to her house. We define as possibly excessive Lydia's assessment of the situation, or put it down to fear of being outed in her own home by her disapproving family: 'the profound risk, the really incredible defiance, frightened her. The fear exalted her and made her angry with her mother and daughter and grandmother, with Pam' (153). The build-up to this new relationship is a heady mixture of the delicate and the overwhelmingly erotic; pleasure mixed with a little pain but mostly a terrifying delight of dangerous behaviour in an inhospitable context. We do not realise what is inhospitable until further on, only imagining it to be the family's closed circuit, four houses in a courtyard, the intensely domestic. This is a coming-out story where discovery of a same-sex relationship might lead to ostracism and emotional cruelty. Tem delicately manages a disturbing dual response through Lydia's warring instincts. Accompanying the celebratory freedom of their love is the occasional print or leakage of some other set of references to the nature of this currently absent matriarchal family of wolves, to whom Lydia is a trapped, devoted nurturer, provider, cleaner. Lydia hopes of herself that through this secret love affair, 'Maybe she would transform into her true nature by falling in love. With a woman. With this woman' (158). The women become passionately involved. Hints of otherness accompany Lydia's gradual letting go. Her instincts are 'tangled and unreliable' (156), in this context, leading her back to check the house. Deadly threats underlie descriptions of everyday furniture, the 'clawfoot tub' the dust 'thick as fur' (156); later 'the whorl in the carpet contains wolf fur' (156). Lydia is caught between the deadly Otherness of her family, and the otherness of her lesbian sexuality, the latter offering potential for self-actualisation. Love represents metamorphosis to Lydia, who could remain unsure of her own divided nature, or transform, become, affirm herself with Pam, the loved one.

Tem switches normative value judgements about what is abject, figuring the cruelty of the oppressive family as werewolfish. Lydia's family return, sniffing out her guest. In a perverse replay of 'Goldilocks', where the three bears suspect invasion represented as the emptying of porridge bowls, so this matriarchal family sniff out subversion, rejecting lesbian love as they reject Lydia's right for self-definition. Pam's cries indicate that she could accept Lydia in any form, but Lydia's attempts to maintain a dual life are doomed. She loses the courage of her convictions as love and family vie for versions of self. As she slips in and out of her wolf/human nature, she finds she cannot choose and act decisively to save Pam, ultimately sacrificing her in her indecision: 'Neither wolf nor woman, Lydia ran away. She did not choose. In the house she left behind, the heart of her lover was devoured by someone else.'[18] In such an inhospitable context, the closed system of a disapproving family, Lydia cannot transform. Her body lurches between woman and werewolf, the union with Pam offers resolution, recognition of her mixed self, but the terminal disapproval of the family cuts off all possibilities, strands her mid-change, an abject creature now even in her own perception. In this tragic werewolf tale, Tem focuses on the impossibilities of 'becoming'.

Judith Butler's 1993 account of identity as socially constructed and performed provides a theoretical underpinning to discussion of tales of transformation, which use figures of the werewolf or the vampire to explore opportunities for personal and sexual 'becoming'. Both werewolves and vampires have traditionally been figured as outsiders, deviants, boundary crossers in conventional mythology, but for contemporary writers engaging with queer theory this very marginal outlaw position is one which exposes and troubles complacent conventions of relationships, gender and power. Use of these figures enables an exposure of latent and blatant oppression. Werewolfishness is the terror of what might lie beneath our civilised controlled skins. The abject figures of werewolf and vampire, however, also can valorise and celebrate, offering alternative and multiple relationships, showing all representations and constructions of gender and power to be no more than that: choices and constructions underpinned by conventions and values.

A winner of awards for gay-themed fiction with her *Lost Souls* (1992), Poppy Z. Brite, in *Love in Vein* (1992), celebrates the energies and freedoms which the taboo-breaking vampire offers us as readers: 'The vampire is everything we love about sex and the night and the dark dream-side of ourselves: adventure on the edge of pain, the thrill to be had from breaking taboos.'[19] Of all the figures of horror reappropriated by contemporary women Gothic horror writers, the vampire rises renewed and reinvigorated. Traditionally associated with the terrors of unleashed libidinal energies, imaged in the deadly fanged kiss which conveys ecstasy then condemns the beloved to an eternity of death in life as victim and victimiser, she is fascinating, troublesome. For Richard Dyer: 'The female vampire is conventionally represented as abject because she disrupts identity and order.'[20] And as Barbara Creed notes:

> Driven by her lust for blood, she does not respect the dictates of the laws which set down the rules of proper sexual conduct. Like the male, the female vampire also represents abjection because she crosses the boundary between the living and the dead, the human and the animal.[21]

Contemporary lesbian Gothic horror writing, particularly in the vampire genre, engages with Kristeva's theories about abjection and Othering of anyone perceived as different from a patriarchal and heterosexually defined and controlled version of self and sexuality (1982). The vampire offers the potential for celebration, transformation, becoming, moving beyond rigid constraints of socially constructed sexual and other identities.

Conventionally, the female vampire terrifies because of her ability to transgress norms and behaviours associated with gender difference: her actions (fangs piercing the skin) resemble those of penetration. The transgressive lesbian vampire becomes a powerful rescripted figure for such transformations. Not only does her existence as a vampire challenge male power but her sexual choice is perceived as a threat to normative sexual behaviour, both disgusting and titillating. In making *Brides of Dracula* (1960), for example, the decision to include lesbian scenes, building on the triadic relationship of the three women in Stoker's *Dracula*, produced voyeuristic fascination with what is ultimately considered utterly abject.[22]

It is through rescripting the demonic vampire with its bestial fanged kiss that contemporary women's horror enables a feminist erotic expression.[23] Pat Califia's 'The Vampire' (1993) is a good example of this rescripting, as is Amelia G's 'Wanting' (1994) and Katherine Forrest's 'O Captain, My Captain'.[24]

Vampirism is, in Rosemary Jackson's words, 'perhaps the highest symbolic representation of eroticism'.[25] Dyer locates the attraction of the vampire as a romantic, erotic metaphor in private settings, our beds and our innermost thoughts. Blood draining is equated with sexual ecstasy, domination, swooning, sensuality, both 'the hideous and terrifying form that sexual energies take when they return from being socially and culturally repressed' and the promise of eternal love and life: 'the vampire seems especially to represent sexuality … s/he bites them, with a bite that is just as often described as a kiss'.[26]

Vampires are popular figures in contemporary women's horror not merely because of their promise of eternal youth but also because of their naturally transgressive, potentially revolutionary nature. So, for Dyer:

> Marriage is the social institution of the private of sexuality – the vampire violates it, tapping at new windows to get in, providing sexual scenes for the narrator to witness. Marriage contains female sexuality – hence the horror of the female vampire walking the streets at night in search of sex. Finally marriage restricts sexuality to heterosexuality – vampirism is the alternative, dreaded and desired in equal measure.[27]

Vampirism enacts sexual licence, and its social aftermath – dread, disgust, punishment and death. Dyer sees vampirism as a metaphor for homosexuality or lesbianism, emphasising its transgression. Because vampires engage with both traditional metaphors of boundary crossing and challenges to conventional constructions and representations of sexuality, the status quo, they are seized on by writers whose work seeks to challenge gender constructions and representations and to show that these are one of several constraints upon our nature as 'becoming'.

Liberating energies which merely turn the tables do not enable a fundamental demythologising and remythologising. They do nothing to expose and critique the way the world works. However, the figure of the vampire in women's writing by Poppy Z. Brite, Pat Califia, Katherine Forrest and others actually alters the meanings of vampire women, to radical and liberating effect. Desire, passion and sexual activities have, as Foucault points out, always been regulated and contained by law and language.[28] The figure of the vampire refuses this containment, liberating the explosive power these generate, breaking down boundaries, behaviours, taboos and regulatory practices, denying the constraints of our lives as they fulfil both the terrors (devouring and death) and the promises (undying love and life) of popular myths and fictions.

Contemporary lesbian Gothic horror writers deliberately reverse and trouble the forms and figures of the vampire genre, refusing the narrative trajectory which would condemn female and lesbian vampires to death as a punishment for their transgression. Lesbian Gothic vampire fiction by contemporary women writers rarely demonises or destroys the vampire herself, seeing relationships as mutually rewarding, based on compacts and companionship, regulating otherwise overwhelming desire and the highly charged eroticism of encounters without conventional taboos. Transgressive lesbian eroticism upsets reductive, binary, binding norms of self/Other, male/female.

The use of the erotic in women's horror is not only transgressive, however, it is also transgressive in order to suggest new ways of behaving and relating in both heterosexual and homosexual love/sex/erotic unions. A mutual recognition of the Other as a subject, however similar or different, is the basis of positive human relations. Women's lesbian and gay Gothic erotic horror can be used to explore the creative and celebratory potential of relationships of mutuality, where difference, becoming, metamorphosis, change are reasons for celebration.

In *Bonds of Love: Psychoanalysis, Feminism and the Problem of Domination* (1988), the psychoanalyst Jessica Benjamin argues that relationships and development demand 'mutual recognition, the necessity of recognising as well as being recognised by the other' as well as 'the reciprocity of self and other, the balance of assertion and recognition'.[29] Jane Donawerth suggests, however, that there is a separation in our constructions and projections in everyday society which militates against such mutuality and recognition of the validity, uniqueness and value of differentiated individuals. She notes that in our culture fathers tend to be idealised as figures representing differentiation and mothers as figures who represent symbiosis.[30] However, as Benjamin indicates, neither state of mind is a truth about gender, merely a dangerous ideal, leading to imbalance.[31] Lesbian vampire erotic horror combines the frissons of horror with the charged, eternal promise of fulfilled and constantly re-fulfilling desire.

In the 1970s, lesbianism began to be aligned with feminism, in what has been latterly seen as perhaps politically necessary (for the time) but in a somewhat homogenising, simplistic manner. Elyce Rae Helford, in *Fantasy Girls* (2000), notes that 'Dominant during this era was the belief that lesbianism offered the purest and highest ideal to which women could aspire in ridding themselves of patriarchal oppression and living an egalitarian life'.[32] Helford quotes Parkin and Prosser as labelling this 'the most clearly marked exit from the phallocracy'.[33] Ironically, for Parkin and Prosser such identification might not lead to liberation:

> However, this can be interpreted not as a vision of unification but of co-optation of lesbianism. Most individuals live their sexual identities in some relationship with the political, but desire is not always about doing what is deemed best for the movement. Butch/femme roles, s/m play, and other nonegalitarian sexual practices were deemed harmful to lesbian feminism, leaving some lesbians to wonder. What happens to the possibilities for sexual pleasure when we've been set up as 'good' feminists precisely because we're not supposed to be concerned with the excesses of sexual pleasure?[34]

Helford, Prosser and Parkin, and Roof question the necessity of constructing lesbian relationships as always nurturing, a notion built on the conventional gendered constructions of women as always feminine and maternal. Instead, they suggest that it is possible now to re-recognise and celebrate butch/femme and other lesbian relations.

The vampire in lesbian Gothic and lesbian Gothic erotic horror can be constructed and read in a variety of ways, sometimes as a figure of a nurturing sisterhood (for example as in Jewelle Gomez's *The Gilda Stories*, 1992).[35] In other lesbian vampire relationships, butch/femme and S&M (sadomasochism) predominate, validated and valorised. In many respects, the violence of the vampire is a best fit metaphorically for such relationships, and, as a figure of liberating and queering of all kinds of normative beliefs and practices, can be inclusive, refusing abjection.

Lesbian Gothic erotic horror often acts as a form of politicised expression, seizing identity and the creative power of love, and relationships with others, offering a personal and political freedom for women recognising their sexuality as woman-identified. In the terms of Adrienne Rich's lesbian continuum it enables a celebration of sexuality and eroticism which avoids debasing heterosexual power relations.[36]

Pam Keesey's edited collection of lesbian vampire tales *Daughters of Darkness* (1993) establishes a lesbian literary history where 'the lines between sexuality and violence become blurred' – an idea that is pivotal to Pat Califia's groundbreaking lesbian S&M, 'The Vampire'.[37] Waspwaisted, blonde Iduna, whose 'complexion was so pale it was luminous. In the dark she almost seemed to glow' (170), actively seeks out the leatherclad dominatrix, Kerry, who takes her male victims literally, beating them past endurance, but refusing the blood she needs. Iduna represents an alternative partner, no victim, freely offering her blood and enjoying the exchange, conditioned and 'well schooled' (183). Equally needy, Iduna actively hunts Kerry out, adapted to this new kind of vampire relationship of mutual exchange. At the height of vampire passion:

> The venom that had prevented her blood from clotting and closing the wound sang now in her veins, making her see colors behind her closed eyelids, making her warm inside, simultaneously relaxed, alert. No other drug could ever duplicate this ecstasy, this calm. She should know, she had had long enough to search for a substitute. (182)

Califia's tale reverses significant elements in the conventional vampire narrative, while retaining others. Iduna, the 'prey', seeks out her predator. In this contemporary lesbian feminist vampire tale, no punishment is necessary; the exchange between Kerry and Iduna is predicated upon each adapting to feed the needs of the other. Energy, self-determination, sexual choice and becoming predominate in their erotic engagement.

Kristeva's observation that blood represents 'a fascinating semantic cross-roads, the propitious place for abjection where death and femininity, murder and procreation, cessation of life and vitality all come together' provides entrance into discussion of ways in which radical lesbian vampire writers reappropriate vampire figures and vampire exchange, suggesting a positive interaction of mutual benefit, a becoming rather than a reining in, engagement and metamorphosis.[38] The conventional narrative trajectory that would condemn lesbian vampires to a permanent death as a punishment for their transgression is rejected in favour of new relationships sought and felt to be mutually rewarding, based on companionship, sisterhood, familial relationships and erotic, eternal exchanges regulated by mutual pleasure rather than invasive draining and destruction. Individuals are in a state of becoming, metamorphosis is creative, energised potential, not loss and death.

Lesbian Gothic horror is transgressive, acting out new ways of behaving and relating. Through its challenge to conventional gender role constructions and relations this offers models of becoming and new lesbian and/or heterosexual relations. Jane Donawerth argues that there is a separation in our constructions and projections in everyday society. She argues that the father is idealised as a symbol of differentiation, and subjectivity, and the mother as the symbol of symbiosis.[39] Jessica Benjamin argues that 'neither state of mind represents real relationships as the truth about gender – as merely an ideal' and 'Either extreme, pure symbiosis or sure self-sufficiency, is represented as loss of balance'.[40] This imbalance prevents mutuality, fair exchange and recognition of the validity, uniqueness and value of differentiated individuals.[41] A mutual recognition of the Other as a subject, however similar or different, is the basis of positive human relations. As noted earlier, Benjamin argues that successful relationships and development demand 'mutual recognition, the necessity of recognising as well as being recognised by the other' (23), and that they also depend on 'the reciprocity of self and other, the balance of assertion and recognition' (25). Some lesbian Gothic horror explores the creative and celebratory potential of relationships of mutuality, where difference is a reason for celebration not destruction, and transition, metamorphosis (into the vampire or otherwise monstrous creature) figure the positive potential of becoming.

Katherine Forrest's short story 'O Captain, My Captain' manages genre metamorphosis, merging science fiction, romance and horror, and blending the Gothic motif of the vampire with the science fiction motif of the alien Other. Space captain, female vampire Drake (Dracula and adventurer Sir Francis Drake), captain of the ship 'Scorpio IV', seduces her travelling companion, military lieutenant Harper (after Jonathan Harker in Stoker's *Dracula*) neither as prey nor as food but as her lover. In awakening Harper to bodily pleasures in a highly erotic union, Drake initiates a mutual, aware exchange which respects difference. These contemporary lesbian vampires, like Califia's and those of Amelia G in 'Wanting', do not need to drain their victims unto death. Instead their embrace is mutually chosen, an exchange that reaffirms both partners while refusing the traditional turning of one, as prey, into a member of the undead. Forrest, Califia, G and others use the transgressive power and the liberating eroticism of the vampire relationship to indicate new heights of mutual passion, a new kind of becoming relationship and developing self. No harm is done. Sensuality and self-awareness are released. Harper, stunned that Drake derives nourishment from sexual juices rather than blood, asks: 'Do you diet between women?' (225). But Drake gains her nurturance from her partner's sexual arousal in a mutually pleasurable, life-affirming relationship, once Harper, having experienced a vampire embrace but without the need to pass on the vampire curse, learns to replicate with later partners. Similarly in Amelia G's short story 'Wanting' (1994), the vampire exchange is sought, eroticised, not fatal – and a lasting relationship has begun based on passion, wanting, becoming:

> The images I had known were there. 'Are you going to drink my blood?' I asked. 'No, silly.' She threw her head back and her long heavy hair flew up into the air behind her and cascaded down over her shoulders into my breasts like a black waterfall. She laughed and it was the most beautiful music I had ever heard. 'What I need is your wanting, just your wanting'. (p. 32)

In many examples of women's erotic vampire writing, death is avoided, and conventional closure refused. In relationships of eroticised exchange and becoming, transcendence and mutual exchange are more likely endings.

Figures of werewolves and vampires are appropriated by contemporary women Gothic horror writers both to critique oppressive, limiting gendered behaviours and to enable the exploration of lesbian and gay identities and relationships. Challenges appear in Anne Rice (*Interview with the Vampire*, 1976), Poppy Z. Brite (*Lost Souls*), Jewelle Gomez (*The Gilda Stories*, 1992), Katherine Forrest ('O Captain, My Captain'), Melanie Tem ('Wilding'), Angela Carter ('The Company of Wolves'), Pat Califia's 'Vampire' and Amelia G's 'Wanting' and others.[42] These writers reinterpret the figures of the werewolf and vampire to their own radical ends, investing them with disruptive powers, troubling gender roles, questioning the stability of what is taken for granted as 'normal' cultural and social behaviours. Rewriting figures of sexualised conventional horror, the werewolf and, more popularly, the vampire, these contemporary women Gothic horror writers demolish established philosophical and cultural binary oppositions, that is, male/female, good/bad, day/night, normal/Other. Their queer Gothic horror fiction critiques society and its myths, which consistently configure the lesbian or gay as the desired or feared Other. Transformation and becoming are threshold concepts in this context. While Melanie Tem's Lydia is unable to transform into a new being, remaining stuck in the doubly abjected state of lesbian and werewolf or everyday person, the lesbian vampires in tales by Forrest and others survive and flourish because of their flexibility, transcendence, metamorphosis, in a positive reading of becoming.[43]

NOTES

1 Sue-Ellen Case, 'Tracking the Vampire', in Katie Conboy (ed.), *Writing on the Body: Female Embodiment and Feminist Theory* (New York: Columbia University Press, 1997), p. 4.
2 Katherine Forrest, 'O Captain, My Captain', in Pam Keesey (ed.), *Daughters of Darkness: Lesbian Vampire Stories* (San Francisco: Cleis Press, 1993), p. 225.
3 Anne Rice, on the film *Interview with the Vampire*, www.maths.tcd.ie/~forest/vampire/morecomments.html (accessed 30 July 2003).
4 Julia Kristeva, in Geraldine Meaney, *Unlike Subjects: Women, Theory, Fiction* (Oxford: Routledge, 1993), p. 154.
5 Melanie Tem, 'Wilding', in Pam Keesey (ed.), *Women Who Run with the Werewolves* (San Francisco: Cleis Press, 1996). All subsequent references are to this edition, and are given in parentheses in the text.
6 Judith Butler, 'Critically Queer', *GLQ: A Journal of Lesbian and Gay Studies*, 1/1 (1993), 17–32 at p. 19.
7 Gilles Deleuze and Félix Guattari, *A Thousand Plateaus*, trans. Brian Massumi (London: Athlone Press, 1988), p. 291.
8 Pat Califia, 'The Vampire' in Pam Keesey (ed.), *Daughters of Darkness* (San Francisco: Cleis Press, 1993), pp. 167–85.
9 John Hough, dir., *Twins of Evil*, Hammer Films, 1971.
10 Sheridan Le Fanu, 'Carmilla', in *In a Glass Darkly* (London: R. Bentley & Son, 1872) reprinted in Pam Keesey (ed.), *Daughters of Darkness* (San Francisco: Cleis Press, 1993), pp. 27–89. Bram Stoker, *Dracula* [1897] (Harmondsworth: Penguin, 1979). For an earlier lesbian vampire see Samuel Taylor Coleridge, 'Christabel' in *The Portable Coleridge*, ed. I. A. Richards (Harmondsworth: Penguin, 1980), pp. 106–27.
11 Kristeva in Meaney, *Unlike Subjects*, p. 219.
12 Julia Kristeva, *Strangers to Ourselves* (New York: Columbia University Press, 1988), p. 192.
13 Melanie Tem, 'Mama', in Lisa Tuttle (ed.), *Skin of the Soul* (Northampton MA: Interlink Publishing, 1990), pp. 78–93.
14 J.-P. Bourdon, A. Cournée and Y. Charpentier, *Dictionnaire normand-français* (Paris: Conseil International de la langue française/PUF 1993), p. 315.
15 Marina Warner, *Six Myths of Our Time: Little Angels, Little Monsters, Beautiful Beasts, and More* (New York: Vintage, 1995), p. 181.

16 Pam Keesey (ed.), *Women Who Run with the Werewolves: Tales of Blood, Lust and Metamorphosis* (San Francisco: Cleis Press, 1996).
17 Angela Carter, 'The Company of Wolves', in *The Bloody Chamber* (London: Virago, 1981), pp. 108-18.
18 Tem, 'Wilding', p. 162.
19 Poppy Z. Brite, *Lost Souls* (Harmondsworth: Penguin, 1992). Poppy Z. Brite (ed.), *Love in Vein* 1 (New York: Harper Prism, 1994), p. vii.
20 Richard Dyer, 'Children of the Night: Vampirism as Homosexuality, Homosexuality as Vampirism', in Susannah Radstone (ed.), *Sweet Dreams: Sexuality, Gender and Popular Fiction* (London: Lawrence and Wishart, 1986), p. 54.
21 Barbara Creed, *The Monstrous Feminine: Film, Feminism, Psychoanalysis* (London: Routledge, 1993), p. 121.
22 Terence Fisher, dir., *Brides of Dracula*, Hammer, 1960.
23 See Gina Wisker, 'Women's Horror as Erotic Transgression', *Femspec*, 3/1 (2001).
24 Amelia G, 'Wanting', in Cecilia Tan (ed.), *Blood Kiss* (Cambridge, MA: Circlet Press, 1994), pp. 24-32.
25 Rosemary Jackson, *Fantasy: The Literature of Subversion* (London: Routledge, 1981), p. 120.
26 Dyer, 'Children of the Night', p. 54.
27 Ibid., p. 54.
28 Michel Foucault, *The History of Sexuality, Volume 1: An Introduction*, trans. Robert Hurley (London: Penguin, 1998).
29 Jessica Benjamin, *Bonds of Love: Psychoanalysis, Feminism and the Problem of Domination* (New York: Pantheon, 1988), pp. 23, 25. All subsequent references are to this edition, and are given in parentheses in the text.
30 Jane Donawerth, *Frankenstein's Daughters: Women Writing Science Fiction* (New York: Syracuse University Press, 1997), p. 46.
31 Benjamin, *Bonds of Love*, p. 158.
32 Elyce Rae Helford, *Fantasy Girls* (Lanham, MD: Rowman & Littlefield, 2000), p. 147.
33 J. Parkin and A. Prosser, 'An Academic Affair: The Politics of Butch-Femme Pleasures', in Joan Nestle (ed.), *The Persistent Desire: A Femme-Butch Reader* (Boston: Alyson 1992), pp. 442-50 at p. 447.
34 Parkin and Prosser, 'An Academic Affair', p. 448. Quoted in Helford, *Fantasy Girls*, p. 147.
35 Jewelle Gomez, *The Gilda Stories* (London: Sheba, 1992).
36 Adrienne Rich, 'Compulsory Heterosexuality and Lesbian Existence', *Signs*, 5/4 (1980), 631-60.
37 Pam Keesey (ed.), *Daughters of Darkness: Lesbian Vampire Stories* (San Francisco: Cleis Press, 1993), p. 16.

38 Julia Kristeva, *Powers of Horror: An Essay on Abjection*, trans. S. Roudiez (New York: Columbia University Press, 1982), p. 96. All subsequent references are to this edition, and are given in parentheses in the text.
39 Donawerth, *Frankenstein's Daughters*, pp. 105, 109, 123 and 158.
40 Ibid., p. 46, quoting Benjamin, *Bonds of Love*, p. 158.
41 See Donawerth, *Frankenstein's Daughters*, p. 46.
42 Anne Rice, *Interview with the Vampire* (St Ives: Futura, 1976).
43 See Deleuze and Guattari, *A Thousand Plateaus*.

9
'The taste of blood meant the end of aloneness': vampires and gay men in Poppy Z. Brite's Lost Souls

William Hughes

In the Gothic of the later twentieth and early twenty-first centuries, the male vampire has progressively become associated both with the physicality of homosexual practices and with the expression of a specifically gay identity. This association, which finds its adherents within the ranks of critics as often as those of authors, is somewhat problematic, however. On the one hand, it is a pointed assertion of identity, of difference, of a consciousness of dogged persistence within a world that is characteristically intolerant and persecutory. The vampire is a figure whose existence (whether derived from the precedent of folklore or of fiction) is apparently ideally suited for appropriation by writers expressing the pleasures, frustrations and, indeed, dangers of the gay lifestyle. The vampire is as adept at conveying oral and penetrative gratification as it is of demonising queer-bashing or of lamenting the debilitations of AIDS.

On the other hand, though, the application of the vampire persona to the male homosexual perversely confirms much of the heterosexist prejudice directed against the gay lifestyle. Within the assumptions of such prejudice, gay men, like literary vampires, characteristically hunt alone and at night, often ensnaring unwilling or unwitting victims into their milieu. They may infect those they encounter with a subtle, blood-borne poison as much as through the inculcation of unspeakable desire. They are seemingly promiscuous by nature, and the modern literary development of the narrating, as opposed to the narrated, vampire often suggests an at-best ambiguous, and at worst guilty, reflection upon one's own identity and inclinations. Little wonder, therefore, that, for some, the coffin has now become as shameful a place of simultaneous retreat and safety as the closet.[1]

The banality of the modern vampire – his ability to co-exist with the heterosexual world, to slip imperceptibly from his distinctive nocturnal identity into the conformity and anonymity of a working-day persona – is his strongest armour and his greatest shame. It is his compromise with the world, a condition of his safe existence which none the less makes his encounter with the community of humans less than ideal in a liberal, modern world. Gone, in postmodernism, is the grand disdain of a Count Dracula who may display his sanguine credentials to his opponents with the same bravado with which he proclaims a lineage derived from Attila the Hun.[2] The contemporary vampire takes his predominant tone not from Stoker's Count, nor indeed from Stephen King's imperious Barlow, arguably Dracula's final avatar, but from Anne Rice's 'utterly confused' and ambivalent Louis de Pointe du Lac.[3] Louis, in his vampire state, is as conscious of what he has been as much as he is aware of what he has become. He continually gazes back towards a halcyon existence from which he seemed, in *Interview with the Vampire* (1976), all too willing to depart.[4] He is perplexed by desire, confused by the relationships thrown up by that desire, and mystified as to what his status now is in the culture and identity he has left behind.[5] Yet Louis, for all his talk of closets and coffins, for all his physical intimacies with Lestat and Armand, is a vampire in his perplexity rather than a gay man who is also a vampire, struggling to come to terms with his homosexuality. The ambivalence of Rice's novel is such that homosexuality is an implication or an association of Louis's indwelling reflection, not its true and singular focus. Louis, after all, is bitten by Lestat but is never buggered.

Vampire fiction with an explicit – rather than symbolic – gay content, where sexual acts are depicted and where discretely same-sex relationships are embedded within same-species alliances, however, takes full advantage of this introspection, and extends it somewhat beyond the limiting association with self-conscious guilt or perplexity. To be alone is in a sense to be heteronormative in a world whose standard is community at the most broad level, and the reproductive family at the most intimate. Yet the homosexual is never truly alone: he will know always that there are others of his kind, others who exist in an underground network which, though disparate, may still preserve the flexibility to allow a sporadic remodelling along the paradigm of the heterosexual family as much as the broader concept of community. This is not necessarily the somewhat overstated family that Lestat constructs between himself, Louis and the child-vampire Claudia in *Interview with the Vampire*, in part as a patronising concession for Louis's nostalgia for mortal life.[6] Rather, it is centred upon the couple as a unit rather than as the matrix for offspring – though the partnership envisaged may well be enabled through a reproductive, though not sexual, act: vampirism.

For the modern vampire, therefore, the desire to consume blood escalates from the need to seek not simply another meal, a temporary relief from corporeal hunger, and becomes instead a drive towards absorbing another being into a more sustaining companionship, making a meal of a mate and a mate of a meal. This is, it might be argued, an implicit rejoinder to the common heterosexist disdain for the promiscuous gay, and the equally promiscuous vampire. It admits to an element of choice, and, indeed, the assertion of a certain discretion as to who may – or may not – be admitted to the ranks of the un-dead. To those within its purlieu, it is an all-consuming way of life, to be celebrated as such, rather than a deviant departure from the life lived before, the life lived by others not called to the coterie. To be outcast may thus be rescheduled as to be chosen. The act of choice and conversion may be a matter of economic necessity – as is demonstrated in the alternately frustrating and elevating relationship between Lestat and Louis – but it may equally be a matter of personal taste and sexual attraction, these being the very things that allegedly structure the long-lasting, idealised relationships beloved of the heterosexual romance and of domestic fiction.

The gay vampire lifestyle, though, is rarely scripted with the comforting closures and concluding contentments that characteristically distinguish the domestic novel. The experience of the gay vampire protagonist in his encounters with, variously, vampires and homosexuals, and humans and heterosexuals, remain for the most part problematic and fraught with danger. If there is a centrifugal drive in modern vampire fiction, gay or otherwise, towards community, then there is, for gay fiction at least, an opposing centripetal force which proclaims solitariness as the safest course through which to preserve a relatively untroubled and innocuous existence. This solitariness is maintained by a variety of fictional strategies, from abstinence to the transience of the traditional one-night-stand, and though it may not be explicitly present in every gay vampire fiction it enjoys an implicit and covert existence as a fall-back position, a closeted place of safety and anonymity.

The tension between the ability to enact desire and the corresponding ability to express or own to that desire is thus imbricated within the sexual plots of modern gay vampire fiction. Writings of this type do more than merely fictionalise the relationship between a homosexual consciousness and a prototypically hostile heterosexual world: they embody also the tensions within the homosexual identity, the rationalisation of issues within the alternative community. They are, in a sense, an index of competing and divergent versions of a discrete sexual politics, marking the faltering common ground between those gays who advocate, in particular, a degree of cultural separation from the heterosexual world and those who embrace co-existence.

One of the most striking commentaries upon this debate may be found in Poppy Z. Brite's *Lost Souls* (1992), a novel short-listed for the Lambda Literary Award for Gay Men's Science Fiction/Fantasy.[7] Ostensibly a conventional vampire fiction, embodying a traditional conflict between mortal heroes and un-dead villains over the body of a compromised heroine, *Lost Souls* advances a striking revision not merely of the vampire species' relationship to humanity but also of the decadence and degeneration that, criticism insists, divides the one from the other.[8] Brite's central innovation in the novel is to envisage a world in which vampires are created not by some occult transformation of the living but through a wholly sexual – indeed, specifically heterosexual – process analogous to mortal reproduction. Vampires, in Brite's novel, are thus not un-dead but conventionally alive – though they retain the distinction of enhanced longevity and a rapid biological recuperation after any physical trauma.[9] As Arkady Raventon, keeper of a New Orleans shop specialising in dubious charms and potions, notes: 'They are not undead. They have never died. Some of them never do, or not for hundreds upon hundreds of years' (275). These distinctions, though, are scripted as being matters of biology rather than of theology: vampires are a parallel to, rather than a deviation from, the known human paradigm.

In *Lost Souls*, therefore, vampires cannot be regarded as degenerate, in the way that they are in *Dracula* (1897), as they have no infection or disease to transmit to mortal humanity, no imperative to convert others to simulacra of their own state.[10] As Christian, the eldest of the vampires depicted in *Lost Souls*, reflects, following his draining of a willing victim, who has explicitly sought conversion to the un-dead state:

He could not turn the boy into one of his kind any more than the boy could have bitten him and turned him human. They were of separate races, races that were close enough to mate but still as far away from each other as dusk and dawn (68)

This mating, though, invariably results in the death of the mother. Not surprisingly, female vampires appear characteristically reluctant to engage in unprotected or reproductive coitus: as Richelle, the only female vampire mentioned in the novel, tells Raventon,

> *Our babies are born without teeth ... but even so they manage to chew their way out. Perhaps they have a set of womb teeth. Perhaps they claw their way out with their tiny fingers. But they kill, always they kill. Just as I ripped my mother apart.* (277, original italics)[11]

For this reason, Zillah, Twig and Molochai, the trio of young vampires whose sexual exploits underpin the plot of *Lost Souls*, can accurately be depicted as, in Christian's words, 'the fire of a dying race' (247). Because of the unavoidable mortality associated with childbirth, the integrity of the vampire bloodline, the purity or exclusivity of the species, will always be compromised through the presence of conventional humans such as Jessy and Ann, the two women made pregnant by the vampire, Zillah.

The major consequence of this is a dilution of distinctive vampire qualities. In a rather teasing echo of Stoker, in these vampire–human hybrids one sees not 'the characteristics of the vampire coming' in the victim, but rather the characteristics of the human modifying the vampire.[12] Where, for Stoker's Mina, 'Her teeth are some sharper' following contact with the Count, Brite's twentieth-century vampires illustrate that the reverse may be true.[13] The narrator notes in passing that Zillah, Twig and Molochai 'wished they had fangs but had to make do with teeth they filed sharp, and they could walk in sunlight as their great grandfathers could not' (5), though Christian, who exhibits a violent reaction to alcohol and a sensitivity to sunlight (334-5, 151) is somewhat more explicit:

> The others – Molochai, Twig and Zillah – drank incessantly, even *ate*; they drowned their true natures in gluttony. But they were young. They were of a newer generation. Their chemistry was subtly different; they were hardier, their organs perhaps more thick-walled, less delicate. (59)

It would be simplistic to suggest that Christian is being nostalgic for a mortal life he has never known, though he may envy the greater freedom of modern youth, ironically scripted here as a form of biological evolution. What *is* noteworthy here, though, is the elder vampire's reflection upon the passing of a true nature, of an essential distinction that encodes vampirism.

The purity of a discrete vampire existence can be maintained only by separation from mortal humanity, and thus – assuming an unwillingness to reproduce to be common amongst female vampires – by participation in non-reproductive sexuality. Brite's male vampires are, without exception, bisexual, and the only extended relationships they maintain – perhaps inevitably, given their physical longevity – are with their own kind. There is a suggestion in the novel that vampires have historically organised themselves somewhat in the manner of a secret society – Molochai introduces himself to Christian by presenting him with an ancient doubloon bearing a vampiric visage, which initiates a ritual exchange: 'How – how do you come?' … 'In peace' (7). The implication is that the past has been one of sporadic relationships, of temporary and fluid alliances amongst those who travel.

Zillah, Twig and Molochai, however, are explicitly depicted as being 'as much a family as anyone could be, anywhere, ever' (83). They travel as such, maintaining a semblance of relationship despite the fact that, until the arrival of Nothing, Zillah's son by Jessy (223), there is no blood tie between them. All that links them, indeed, is a common species. Yet that tie, which is more of a tie of common interest, is enduring and, for all its violence, affectionate.

Lost Souls is unequivocal regarding the dysfunctional nature of human families. Nothing's troubled relationship with his adoptive parents might well be inevitable, given his then-unknown vampire origins, though his youthful human associates are also scripted as being characteristically at odds with their parents and guardians. Rebellion is almost institutionalised in this bourgeois mortal world, a form of controlled aberration, a *rite-de-passage* even, through which one must pass in order to reach college (33) and an ultimately respectable adulthood. Youth forms a surrogate family, though one which Nothing (in his non-vampiric incarnation of Jason) feels inadequate to express his own angst:

> He looked around the room. Several of the kids were groping each other ineptly, kissing each other with sloppy wet mouths. Veronica Aston had pulled Lily Hartung's skirt up and had two fingers inside the elastic of Lily's panties. Nothing stared at this for several minutes, dully interested. Bisexuality was much in vogue among this crowd. It was one of the few ways they could feel daring. Nothing himself had made out with several of these kids, but though he had tasted their mouths and touched their most tender parts, none of

them really interested him. The thought made him sad, though he wasn't sure why. (32)

It is through chance that Nothing meets up with Zillah, Twig and Molochai, his eventual and 'real' family. Though they are 'a wilder crowd than he was used to' (139), their initial approach to him appears to be a mere continuation of the regime of bisexuality, drugs and alcohol into which he has already been inducted. However, the thin veneer of resemblance is disturbed when they offer him blood, mixed with alcohol. His reaction is, ironically, somewhat jaded and humanly worldly: 'I don't think drinking blood is so weird', he said (141). The narrator, too, concludes on Nothing's behalf, 'Anyone who wanted to *play* vampire was all right by him' (142, my italics).

Ironically, of course, they – and he – are not 'playing' at being vampires in the manner in which Veronica Aston and Lily Hartung are voguishly 'playing' at being lesbians. As the narrator observes:

> Most hitchhikers were glad enough to party with them, to share a pipe or a tab of acid or a tumble on the mattress. Then – always after these pleasures, for it made their blood sweeter – the wine bottle was brought out. Or the whiskey bottle, or whatever they had put the latest batch in. This was Molochai and Twig's favourite part: the hitchhiker, already drunk or high or fried on acid, would swig eagerly from the bottle. Then his eyes – or her eyes – would grow big and frightened, and his mouth – or her mouth – would twist in terror and disgust as the blood drooled back out of it, and Molochai, Twig, and Zillah would be upon him. Or her. (142-3)

Nothing's essential and enduring identity, hitherto scripted as a quite conventional youthful rebellion (70), is vested in his unfeigned response to the proffered blood. His easy assimilation to their practices, given the novel's conflation of male homosexuality and vampirism, should come as no surprise to the reader: semen, as Nothing's friend Laine has previously informed him, *has almost exactly the same chemical makeup as human blood* (124, original italics). Notably, Nothing 'had drunk from the bottle of blood without choking, without spitting or gagging. To the contrary – the blood had seemed to revive him, freshen his skin, brighten his eyes' (142). Because he swallows and does not spit, Nothing is simultaneously both a copybook vampire and a willing (and apparently instinctual) participant in gay, oral sexuality. His vampire nature, it would appear, has rested dormant because he has never considered it other than through fiction, though he has licked his own blood (76), and even experienced inchoate desires regarding 'other children in his class, imagining how it would be to hold them, taste them, feel their flesh between his teeth' (71). His gay identity, though, has been developed through youthful experimentation consequent upon inclination (71). The narrator recalls, following Nothing's first sexual encounter after leaving home to seek both his 'true' family and his identity, that 'Nothing had never minded swallowing come. Something about it settled his stomach and made his whole body feel good' (123). Even the adulterated, bottled blood, mixed as it is 'with some kind of liquor – vodka or gin, something oily and stinging', having a taste which is 'dark and sweet and a little decayed', seems reassuringly 'Familiar' (141) to him. It is only when these remarks are read in the context of Laine's chemical equation between the sanguine and seminal fluids that the close connection between vampirism and homosexuality in *Lost Souls*, a connection not wholly dependent upon a conventional script of persecution and associated symbolism, becomes glaringly apparent.

In effect, Brite's novel redefines the family as a relational concept by noting the inadequacies and shallowness of the human, heterosexual familial grouping, vested as it is in blood ties and the inheritance not merely of genes but also of qualities, aspirations and property (70). With the imbrication of vampire and gay identities in *Lost Souls*, the alternative and fulfilling family, as sought and found by Nothing, becomes defined, for much of the novel at least, not through the duties of descent and lineage but by pleasure. Identity is vested in what sensations can be given and what received, making the family an erotic and recreational rather than an administrative and reproductive unit. The taboos which restrict unbridled pleasure in the human family – most notably those against orality, homosexuality and, specifically, incest – have no real function in a world in which spontaneous practice rather than legalistic lineage qualifies one for membership. Nothing's momentary distaste when he learns that he has fellated his own father –

> For a week now you have been fucking your own father. His tongue has been in your mouth more times than you could count. You've sucked him off ... you've swallowed stuff that could have been your brothers and sisters! (232, original italics)

– is a residual expression of the morality he has learned within the human family in which he was reared. Its equivalent, surely, is Louis's similar reluctance to take human prey in *Interview with the Vampire* – though Nothing is quicker to discard his uncongenial, guilty self than Rice's reflective vampire. The narrator qualifies Nothing's last stirrings of his human conscience thus:

But he could not disgust himself. He could not make himself ashamed. He knew these were things he was supposed to feel, things the rational daylight world would expect him to feel. But he could not force himself to feel them. (232)

Brite's narrator moves quickly to conflate these reflections upon homosexuality and incest (which *Nothing* further elaborates through imagining how his human school friends might themselves participate in such incestuous activities) with the conventionally fatal activity of the vampire: 'Were members of his race born with some sort of amoral instinct that shielded them from the guilt of killing to stay alive?' (232). This sudden (and, it has to be said, short) shift from homosexuality to haemosexuality, though, is not wholly convincing.[14]

Despite the precedent for reflective vampirism provided by *Interview with the Vampire*, *Lost Souls* resolutely refuses to allow vampirism *as* vampirism to function as the central issue of its exploration into the troubled nature of identity within the alternative family. The act of killing, admittedly, physically sustains a vampire, but it does not uniquely structure his accession into the group of like-minded individuals, banded together by common identity, that is the supportive vampire family. Instead, it is vampirism *as* homosexuality or, more precisely, vampirism *which routinely embodies* homosexual practice as one of its regular accoutrements, that constitutes the pivot around which the troubled lives of Christian, Zillah, Twig, Molochai and Nothing revolve.

Difficulties thus characteristically arise when vampires step outside of the supportive framework of the family for sexual or sensual pleasures rather than simply to feed. To toy with one's food, to sleep with it or to mutilate it, is acceptable in the context of a *collective* action – this happens to Nothing's friend Laine (160), as it might well have happened to Nothing himself, had he not demonstrated his common identity with the family. But Nothing realises the fragility of his own position as an associate of Laine, whom he describes as 'my friend ... From back home': 'Surely Zillah wouldn't make Twig stop the van and put Laine out in the chill September night just because Nothing knew him from back home' (156). The rules are quite clear: the new life does not carry over a residual content from the old, even if the neglectful mentor-father does not vouchsafe that vital information to the neophyte-son:

> no one had sat him down and told him how quickly and inexorably the other world – the day world, he supposed – would begin to slip away. Zillah hadn't said to him, *We are your whole world now; we and others of our kind. We are the only friends you can have now.* (188-9, original italics)

It is a departure, a bringing of the self into a family or a species whose rules are adapted not merely to protect the individual but also to provide identity for a community, to emphasise that, without the identity, one is truly alone, unprotected, unfulfilled. 'The taste of blood meant the end of aloneness' (160), as Nothing soon realises:

> Nothing twisted to look at Zillah. Zillah smiled a dark smile and said, 'Come and be one of us', and Nothing knew he was being told to make his choice. Come and be one of us – or suffer the consequences of your refusal: die, or be alone, and never drink from the bottle of life again. *For the blood was the life* – (160, original italics)

Nothing, who from this point never undertakes a sexual act other than with a male vampire, becomes no longer bisexual, no longer a compromise between two alternative ways of life. To be 'one of us' recalls – and beautifully inverts –the anti-gay slang phrase, 'one of them': the irony is, however, that it is Zillah rather than Nothing who undermines the sustaining, all-male community into which he has just unknowingly inducted his biological son. Zillah, perversely, is a closet heterosexual.

If one leaves aside the fatal case of the female vampire Richelle, whose pregnancy was a consequence of her rape at the hands of a non-vampire (277), there are only two incidences of heterosexual, cross-species sexuality in *Lost Souls*. In both cases, Zillah is the male perpetrator, though it is the second – with its complex extra- and infra-familial motivations and consequences – that underpins both the final, pivotal phase of the novel and the reflection provided by the concluding Epilogue, depicting events 'Fifty Years Later' (355). *Lost Souls* opens with the first of these two heterosexual interruptions to Zillah's longstanding homosexual attachment to Twig and Molochai. The Mardi Gras encounter with Jessy in Christian's New Orleans bar is opportunist, unsought and unanticipated, at least by Zillah. Jessy is a wannabe vampire who, in a striking prefiguring of her son's later relationship with Zillah, has committed incest with her father in her quest to become a vampire.[15] She awaits 'The vampires' (4), which she assumes will convert her to the un-dead state, at Christian's bar, though the novel never makes it clear how she becomes certain that they will one day arrive there. Certainly, Christian fails to perceive their vampiric qualities upon their arrival, and does not appear to even anticipate their advent (7). Their interest, significantly, is focused solely upon Christian, and not upon Jessy.

Jessy's subsequent attempt to disrupt the vampiric bonding between

Christian, Twig and Molochai produces a response on the vampires' part that is, predictably, both sexual and sanguine, simultaneously signifying lust and blood-lust. The narrator recalls how:

> Jessy stood up very quietly, and then the bloodlust she had wanted so badly was upon her. She leapt, tore Molochai's arm away from Twig, and tried to fasten her lips on the gash. But Molochai turned furiously on her and batted her away, hard across the face, and she felt the pain in her lip before she tasted the blood there, her own dull blood in her mouth. Molochai and Twig and even kind Christian stood staring at her, bloodied and wild-eyed, like dogs startled at a kill, *like interrupted lovers*. (8, my italics)

One of the vampires, though, stands aloof, not caught up in the gay, sado-masochistic orgy enacted in the name of vampirism. Zillah, certainly, does appear to have been 'interrupted' by her actions, and appears to have been a voyeur rather than a participant within an encounter which Molochai has initiated (7). The account continues:

> But as she backed away from them, a pair of warm arms went round her from behind and a pair of large strong hands caressed her through the silk dress, and a voice whispered, 'His blood is sticky-sweet anyway, my dear – I can give you something nicer.' (8)

Zillah's 'nicer' here is equivocal. He is offering the semen of the sexual encounter rather than the blood of the vampiric, though his love-making does appear to involve an element of sanguine ingestion, given that 'her blood was smeared across his face' (8). That semen, though, is taken vaginally rather than orally (anal intercourse, curiously, does not seem to figure in the vampires' regime of sexual activity), and its effect on the family unit is noteworthy enough to require acknowledgement by the narrator:

> It was one of the rare nights that Molochai, Twig, and Zillah spent apart. Zillah slept on the blanket with Jessy, hidden between cases of whiskey, cupping her breasts in his hands. Molochai slept in Christian's room above the bar with Christian and Twig cuddled close to him, their mouths still working sleepily at his wrists. (9)

Once the night is completed, and Mardi Gras over, the incident is seemingly forgotten: 'Molochai, Twig, and Zillah left town the next evening after the sun went down, so they never knew that Jessy was pregnant' (9).

Zillah's sexual encounter with Ann, some fifteen years later, though, is a far less dismissible matter, even where it retains the suggestion of opportunism. By this stage of the novel, Zillah's gay-vampiric family has expanded to incorporate Nothing, and a possessive and increasingly exclusive relationship has become forged between the eldest and the youngest vampire, though both still remain ignorant of their biological relationship. Zillah's possessive attitude towards Nothing is amply demonstrated before the encounter with Ann, not merely through the disposal of Laine, Nothing's final sexual link with his mortal Maryland childhood but also in the attacks which the elder vampire leads against Ghost and Steve, the two rock musicians whom the younger vampire was seeking when he first encountered his 'family'. Having met his rock heroes, and witnessed Zillah's intolerance of any commitment, sexual or otherwise, outside of the vampires' van, Nothing is keen to move on, realising that 'There was no place for him here, not with his new family' (212).

Though Zillah suggests explicitly that Nothing has 'learned [his] lesson' (194) regarding consorting with non-vampires, and has thus gained his mentor's forgiveness, it is apparent that the elder vampire is exhibiting behaviours more immediately associated with the human world. Zillah sulks – 'When Nothing had tried to hug him, Zillah pulled away' – and, as the narrator observes, 'Nothing had seen his friends back home use such behavior on one another' (191). Indeed, Zillah's mood seems to be infectious: as Nothing observes, 'He had thought them older and more sophisticated than he, but right now they were acting like a bunch of teenagers who are mad at each other but aren't sure why' (192). Zillah is duplicitous. Nothing's lesson, even if it has been learned through this one incident, has only just begun.

Zillah's manipulation and humiliation of Nothing is enacted through the body of Ann, the former girlfriend of Steve, the young vampire's guitar-hero. Ann is no stranger to such games: she has herself been the focus of Steve's jealous violence, and has not failed to play her own sexual activities off against her estranged lover's alternating frustration and desire (108). An invitation to smoke opium with Zillah, extended to Ann after she has yet again been verbally abused by Steve (207), accelerates into a sexual encounter from which Nothing is excluded. Ghost and Nothing, both seeing with a supernatural sentience denied to the other characters in *Lost Souls*, witness not just the sexual act but anticipate its true meaning, its function in the relationship between the vampires themselves, and between the vampires and humanity. The clash of interests is registered simply and strikingly in two assessments, rendered almost as a couplet:

> 'That's Steve's girlfriend in the van there', said Ghost.
> 'That's my lover in there with her', Nothing said. (217)

Indeed, the whole encounter is punctuated with the (human) rhetoric of exclusive sexual ownership. First, Ann rejects Steve when he comes either to claim or abuse her –

> Steve looked from Zillah to Ann. His eyes gleamed; his mouth worked soundlessly. 'Ann?' he managed at last. 'You didn' … you cou'n …'
> Ann walked right up to Steve. She held her head high and her back very straight, smiled sweetly into his stricken face. 'I could and I did', she said, 'and you don't have a goddamn thing to say about it.' (218)

Then Zillah rejects Ann, brutally and unequivocally:

> Ann reached Zillah and tried to link her arm with his. For a moment it seemed that he would embrace her. But then Zillah's hands closed on her shoulders, and he gave her a hard shove away from him … Zillah gazed at Steve. His eyes were triumphant. 'So sorry', he said, 'I didn't know the slut belonged to you'. (219)

The real issue of ownership, though, concerns not Anne but Nothing, and it is the latter who voices the focus of the whole sordid and violent incident: 'Nothing looked at Ann. His expression was pitying, a little disdainful. "Go away", he told her. "Go find somebody else. *I* belong here – not you"' (221, original italics).

The familial dynamic of the vampire circle, though, has changed as a consequence of Zillah's behaviour. Zillah's encounter with the human, enacted as it is on this occasion for revenge and power rather than to physically exhaust a mere passing lust, has compromised the exclusivity of the alternative family. Zillah's actions and motivations have interposed the heterosexual and reproductive into the vampire culture, creating a new rhetoric of ownership and, potentially, a drive towards monogamy to challenge the pre-existent and freer vampire culture of collective co-existence and polygamy. This compromise is further compounded, a moment or so after Ann has been spurned by Zillah, by Christian's revelation that Nothing is the vampire's son (223). The subsequent rhetoric, again, reflects a human conception of identity and responsibility rather than the more fluid and open relationships vested in species and sexual taste:

> His bond to Zillah was now also his bond to this world of blood and night. He knew now that Zillah would not leave him, would not abandon him … Zillah had wanted him from the beginning. There must have been some biological

pull between them. The seed returning to the sower. But Zillah hadn't known why. The sentiment might still have been revocable … But when Christian spoke those words outside the club – those terrifying, magical words, *You're Zillah's son* – the bond had become flesh. (233, original italics)

Family lineage, the mutual duties that link a parent and an offspring, have now become important, and with them comes a new sort of exclusivity: a more human jealousy that aggressively regards discarded lovers as rivals, to be challenged, fended off, humiliated. The vampires' van, as it were, has been too long parked in one space, and they have become too closely associated with the human culture around them, even going so far as to take up regular employment (Christian is not merely a bar-tender but sells flowers also) and rent a dwelling place amongst the trailer trash at the edge of town (245-6). The glamour of fluid relationships, the spontaneity of promiscuity, it would appear, is rapidly disappearing from the vampire lifestyle. Even if a gay exclusivity is maintained, the spectre of a monogamous respectability lurks in the prototypical aspirations that, in the American Dream, ought to take one eventually from the rented trailer to the purchased house.

The novel's troubled homosexual script is resolved only with the death of Zillah at the hands of Steve and Ghost, an act of revenge whose origins explicitly lie in that vampire's interference in the proprietary power structures of heterosexual relationships (343). Though Nothing immediately experiences sorrow at the prospect of 'never feeling those strong veined hands on him again, of never kissing that lush mouth' (347), he fails to register any anger or regret that recalls Zillah as his father. Indeed, 'He thought of never again having anyone tell him what to do' (347). Nothing's sorrow and regret are focused upon a sexual rather than a familial loss. Zillah's death marks the true beginning of Nothing's vampiric identity, his utter incorporation into a morality that has rejected not merely routine heterosexuality but also its institutionalised and limiting relationships.

The vampire relationship outlined in the Epilogue to *Lost Souls* represents not so much a return to the culture of Zillah's bisexual community as its realisation as a truly separatist gay life. Set fifty years after Nothing has reassured Ghost by postcard that '*You are safe … You will be safe as long as I live: forever, or nearly so*' (353-4, original italics), the Epilogue visits Nothing, Twig and Molochai in their guise as members of a New Orleans snuff-rock band (358). Twig and Molochai remain, explicitly, 'his family', though they take their blood, still mixed with alcohol, not directly from the body but more discreetly, through a hypodermic needle (358).

There is anonymity, or rather, incongruity here – the vampires look no different from the humans who make up their audience. Nobody seeks them as vampires. Yet, despite this close proximity to the human world, there is no sense in the Epilogue that the family has been exceeded, no suggestion that the trio are ever tempted to look outside of the enclosing yet liberating sexual circle of their own sex and species for anything other than blood. They have returned, as it were, to a legendary time before Jessy, before Zillah even, and their continuity has seemingly been assured by their polygamous commitment to each other and their rejection of those beyond the bounds of the common identity.

Lost Souls thus arguably represents the culmination of gay vampire fiction, in its twentieth-century incarnation at least. The novel rejects the persecution ethic in favour of an assertive, if not aggressive, expression of self-sustaining difference. To compromise this difference is to become culturally involved in a system of values and morality based upon inheritances and lineages which quite simply do not function satisfactorily in either vampire or gay culture. The gay vampire exists, even prospers, within the heterosexual human world, but is ultimately not committed to it. Indeed, in the Epilogue, the sexual has become separated from the sanguine, the family from the food. With the rejection of heterosexual promiscuity comes the promise of homosexual integrity, of a decline that has been stopped at a late moment, so that the essential self of the species may no longer be diluted, through sex and birth, with the blood of the Other. 'Blood', as Ghost realises, 'calls to blood' (241): and blood and sex, whatever academic criticism may say, are not exactly the same thing in gay vampire fiction.

NOTES

1 The analogy between these two tense spaces was first explicated in fiction by Anne Rice: see *Interview with the Vampire* (London: Futura, [1976] 1988), p. 28. Rice's lead has been taken up by, among others, gay activist Jeff Flaster who heads 'a vampire fan organization for gay and lesbian people who have an interest in vampires and vampirism' known as the Bite Me in the Coffin Not in the Closet Fan Club, active since the 1990s. See: J. Gordon Melton, *The Vampire Book* (Detroit: Visible Ink, 1994), pp. 47-8.
2 Bram Stoker, *Dracula* (Oxford: Oxford University Press, [1897] 1982), pp. 28–9, 306.
3 Stephen King, *Salem's Lot* (London: New English Library, [1975] 1976), p. 158; Rice, *Interview with the Vampire*, p. 29.

4 Rice, *Interview with the Vampire*, p. 91.
5 Ibid., p. 90.
6 Ibid., p. 103.
7 The 1992 Lambda Award for Gay Men's Science Fiction/Fantasy went to *China Mountain Zhang* by Maureen F. McHugh. See www.lambdaliterary.org/awards/previous_winners/paw_1992_1995.html (accessed 12 June 2007).
8 See, for example, Daniel Pick, *Faces of Degeneration: A European Disorder, c.1848–c.1918* (Cambridge: Cambridge University Press, 1996), pp. 172-5.
9 Poppy Z. Brite, *Lost Souls* (London: Penguin, 1994), pp. 36, 90-1, 193, 357. Subsequent references are taken from this edition, and appear in parentheses in the text.
10 Stoker, *Dracula*, p. 51.
11 *Lost Souls*, indeed, opens with just such an incident, the vampire father in question leaving before the mortal mother discovers her pregnancy. See Brite, *Lost Souls*, pp. 9-10.
12 Stoker, *Dracula*, p. 323.
13 Ibid.
14 Christopher Frayling, *Vampyres: Lord Byron to Count Dracula* (London: Faber and Faber, 1991), p. 388.
15 Jessy is, explicitly, a reader of Stoker's *Dracula*, and her seduction of her father, with its emphatic 'Come to me', reads rather like a clumsy paraphrase of Lucy Westenra's attempted predation of her fiancé, Arthur Holmwood. See Stoker, *Dracula*, p. 211; Brite, *Lost Souls*, pp. 71, 79.

10

Michael Jackson's queer funk

~

Steven Bruhm

Can there be a queer Michael Jackson? In some ways the question is naive: Michael Jackson *can be nothing but queer*, if we take 'queer' to mean sexually ambiguous, protean, corporally illegible. Yet critically speaking, there is no queer Michael Jackson: the MLA on-line bibliography gives me no hits for Michael+Jackson+queer (or '+gay' or '+homosexual' or even '+sexuality'). Of course there *is* academic writing on Jackson – mostly having to do with race[1] – and there *is* some consideration of him in the context of sexuality: academic analyses of him at their most sympathetic see him as a scapegoat for a larger culture of childhood sexualising[2] and at their most damning present us with a figure who exploits his reputation as a child-lover to bolster his career.[3] But childhood sexualisation and child-loving are precisely the rub here: they produce a queer pop star whom both the academic and the popular press continually talk about as sexual yet never talk about *as queer*, if by 'queer' we mean politically resistant to hetero-normative, sanctioned versions of sexual performance.[4] Even more profoundly, childhood sexuality subtends the readings of a man who remains interesting more for the postmodern indeterminacy of his face and race than for any 'meanings' – any interventions into normative sexuality – produced by his 'art'. If we speak of Jackson and transgressive sexuality, we must be sure to code it as *scandal*, and to offer no sophisticated or engaged reading of the actual performance art, for such engagement may be to condone the child-loving, to participate in it or at least to deny its importance.

Our attraction or repulsion to Michael Jackson has nevertheless produced a number of 'truths' about his career. They are:

MICHAEL JACKSON'S QUEER FUNK

- Since Michael Jackson by his own admission never had a childhood (whatever 'having a childhood' might mean), he continually tries to recapture it in his adult life.
- The most effective way for him to recapture that childhood is by continued association with children, and with young boys in particular.
- His videos – and specifically the videos dealing with violence (the Gothic and the mafia) – are expressions of his angers and his fears. They offer direct access to something we can call 'Michael Jackson's psyche'.
- The perpetual surgical alterations to his face are Jackson's pathetic attempt to remain forever young, and/or to remain totally ambiguous in terms of race and gender. Through them, we can posit a direct link between his transformations of identity in his videos.

While there may be some validity in any of these assumptions, I think we need to get past the questionable (and boring) stabilisings that they enact – the 'this-equals-that' mentality that we bring to our analysis of Jackson the celebrity. I propose instead to read Jackson's Gothic – the mode that catapulted him to superstardom with the release of *Thriller* – for what it can tell us about queer sexual performance and its shifting terrain in the thirteen years between 1984 (the release date of the *Thriller* video) and 1997 (with his return to the Gothic in *Michael Jackson's Ghosts*, his response to the first round of criminal charges against him).[5] And time here really is of the essence, for these thirteen years were to have seen Jackson 'grow up', to 'develop' as a singer, a dancer and a black heterosexual, to put childish things aside and perfect a stable maturity that was future-looking only in its effects. It is in this futurism, and its vexed relation to children, that Jackson's Gothic modalities find their most complex significations.

QUEERING THE DANCE

Time fascinates Michael Jackson. I say this not in order to launch the usual scandal-mongering about Peter Pan fixations, hyperbaric chambers, and anthems to lost childhood, although they clearly matter to the figure Jackson has cut in the world. Rather, I want to argue that Jackson's movement, his style as a dancer, repeatedly engages with issues of the temporal both in the stories his dances tell and in the choreographic gestures that embody those stories. Specifically Jackson's passion for the *danse macabre* or dance of the dead, can tell us something about what he is up to. A primarily medieval phenomenon, the *danse macabre* takes its name from the Arabic *kabr*, meaning 'grave', and *maqbara*, meaning 'graveyard'. In its earliest (twelfth-century) forms, the dance was performed in graveyards by dancers who would swoon to the ground as if in a trance, then leap up in frenzy, pointing at others to accuse them of the sins they had committed. In the fourteenth century this dance crossed over into visual art, beginning with an image (now lost) over the gates of the Cemetery of the Innocents outside Paris and finding its most famous iconography in the woodcuts of Hans Holbein. Here the dancers became skeletons, figures of mobile death who escort the living – mortals from all the different classes of society – to their graves. What interests me for theorising Michael Jackson's temporal Gothic in this tradition is the way the skeletons – the dead, the desubjectified, the dis-spirited – are joyous, playful and limber. Only the dead dance; only those on the far side of the living display life, as if the energies of human embodiment, expression and physical signification belonged properly to those ostensibly unable to signify in any active or purposeful way. And while these dead dance, the living, including those of the highest stations with (presumably) the healthiest bodies, are lumpen, stolid and lifeless. Any energy they express is merely for the purpose of fighting off Death. Given this paradigm, it would seem that dancing into death means finding new life, but not in some conventional Christian afterworld of heavenly angels. This afterworld, rather, is a life-in-death. In the *danse macabre*, only the dead body is the animated body; and the living body, if we can call it that, is already dead in spirit if not in tissue and organ. But with the death of those tissues and organs, the body – in the form of the dancing skeleton – takes on a new and sensual life.

So, how might we begin to theorise the rich contradiction of Gothic choreography, where one must die in order to dance? What rubric can we find to explain our fascination with the un-dead, most alive because they are least alive? And what might all of this have to do with a specifically queer Michael Jackson? The tension between the quick and the dead as a mode of our desire inevitably takes us to Freud, whose speculations on the death instinct begin to explain how death may generate bodily movement. In *Beyond the Pleasure Principle* (1920), Freud explores the 'daemonic' quality of the repetition compulsion where what gets compulsively repeated is an unpleasant experience, like the child's loss of the mother re-enacted in the famous *fort–da* game with the spool. For Freud, this repetition of unpleasure takes us to something beyond the pleasure principle, by which he means 'before' it, prior to it, that actually structures the search for pleasure. That something, Freud suggests, is a fundamental instinct, whose purpose, he says, is *'to restore an earlier state of things'*, to reduce the amount of stimulation the developed organism experiences as it encounters the demands of the outside world.[6] Freud then pushes his point one step further: because *'inanimate things existed before living ones'*, our first instinct is 'to return to the inanimate state' (311-12); thus, *'the aim of all life is death'* (311). This death instinct is not a moralising check on the pleasure principle, as the medieval dances of death might suggest, but rather that which initiates the pleasure principle and dictates its function. Freud suggests that the search for pleasure – through what he calls the life-serving or sexual instincts – is really a way of ensuring that the organism prolongs the search for death until it can die 'in its own fashion' (312). '[T]he living organism', he says, 'struggles most energetically against events (dangers, in fact) which might help it to attain its life's aim rapidly – by a kind of short-circuit' (312). Thus, Freud concludes,

> It is as though the life of the organism moved with a vacillating rhythm. One group of instincts [the death instincts] rushes forward so as to reach the final aim of life as quickly as possible; but when a particular stage in the advance has been reached, the other group jerks back to a certain point to make a fresh start and so prolong the journey. (313)

Freud's positing of a 'rhythm' returns us to the world of dance and its relation to death. For is not the medieval *danse macabre* uncannily suggestive of Freud's death instinct? The human subjects live, yet their entire lives are oriented toward death, to which they are being ushered with all possible speed. And as we see in Jackson's appropriation of the medieval dance, the dancers are dead – death is their nature, their identifying principle – yet they sport and play with pleasure, the pleasure of the dance, the pleasure of mastery over the weaker subjects, in a way that testifies to their non-deaths. In Holbein's woodcuts and frescos, as in Jackson's choreography, no subject ever really reaches his or her destination – no one wholly inhabits the site of pure life or pure death. This, I think, is precisely Freud's point, and the point of the dance of death as we have seen it so far. Gothic choreography seems to imagine some ontological place where death generates life forces, the movements of pleasure, and the pleasures of movement. These choreographic performances are founded upon forces that would otherwise render them impossible. That's why, in Michael Jackson's Gothic choreography, it is primarily the dead who dance.

To the degree that Freud's project in *Beyond the Pleasure Principle* was to theorise the way *drive* underscores and unravels pleasure, it is, intuitively speaking, a counter-queer project – if 'queer' in *this* sense means a politicised liberation of non-hegemonic sexual pleasures. However, recent thinking about drive, and its relation to pleasure, death and temporality, takes us closer to a queer affect in Jackson's Gothic dance. In particular, Lee Edelman sees in Freud's death drive the human being's inexorable subjection to the pulsion that remains beyond desire and the negotiations of the ego. This pulsion or forward movement toward death destroys the humanistic subject and any sure politics on which this subject can be founded, asserting instead what Edelman calls, after Lacan, the *sinthome*, a repeated symptom of the death drive's presence that continually deflects itself into a compulsive Otherness. Edelman writes:

> As the name for a force of mechanistic compulsion whose formal excess supersedes any end toward which it might seem to be aimed, the death drive refuses identity or the absolute privilege of any goal. Such a goal, such an end, could never be 'it'; achieved, it could never satisfy. For the drive as such can only insist, and every end toward which we mistakenly interpret its insistence to pertain is a sort of grammatical placeholder, one that tempts us to read as transitive a pulsion that attains through insistence alone the satisfaction no end ever holds. Engaged in circulation around an object never adequate to fulfil it, the drive enacts the repetition that characterises what Judith Butler has called 'the repetitive propulsionality of sexuality'.[7]

While Edelman emphasises an ontological instability most handily imagined as a 'pulsion' or a 'circulation' around a death-centre, this pulsion can, I think, be readily made to frame – or even allegorise – what the *danse macabre* might do for an artist like Michael Jackson. That transitive pulsion, that engagement in physical circulation around a meaning, that insistence upon an ontology that can never be inhabited or embodied, is the rich paradoxical status of the macabre dancer, for this dancer signifies through choreography the impossibility of the subject whose teleology is to signify. Jackson's dance, like the medieval one, revels in the expressive impossibilities of the non-subject.

There is a rich schism between Michael Jackson's child-centred agenda and his Gothic dance of death, a dance we can best understand through Edelman's arguments on the Freudian drive. For Edelman, the death drive, that radical compulsion to repeat, signifies a queer intervention into a culture of the future, what he calls 'reproductive futurism' that uses the Child as its central image and call to arms. (And who more than Michael Jackson has treated us to the endless call to exalt children as our future, not to mention our glorified past?) For Edelman, '*queerness* names the side of those *not* "fighting for the children"', as Jackson at his most sentimental, and as the rhetoric of American politico-religious conservatism continually asserts that we must do. Rather, queerness names 'the side outside the consensus by which all politics confirms the absolute value of reproductive futurism[;] ... *queerness* figures, outside and beyond its political symptoms, the place of the social order's death drive' (3). Elsewhere:

> queerness exposes sexuality's inevitable coloration by the drive: its insistence on repetition, its stubborn denial of teleology, its resistance to determinations of meaning (except insofar as it means this refusal to admit such determinations of meaning), and, above all, its rejection of spiritualization through marriage to reproductive futurism. (27)

This 'haunting excess' of the death drive upon futurity and its narratives offers us purchase on the seeming disconnection between the ostentatious child-centrism and teleological futurity of Jackson's late videos and the thoroughgoing repetitiveness of the *danse macabre*, itself a repetition of the death drive symptomised on the human body. This very disconnection, a version of what Edelman will theorise under the neologism '*sinthom*osexuality', not only contradicts Jackson's ostensible project of saving the world through loving the Child; it also sketches the central paradoxes of Jackson's queer Gothic. For, in *sinthom*osexuality:

> the structuring fantasy undergirding and sustaining the subject's desire, and with it the subject's reality [in this case, Michael Jackson's 'child-loving' in all of its discursive regimes], confronts its beyond in the pulsions of the drive whose insistent circulation undoes it, derealizing the collective logic of fantasy by means of which subjects mean, and giving access, instead, to the jouissance, particularised and irreducible, that registers the unmasterable contingency at the core of every subject as such. (73)

By turning directly to Jackson's two Gothic videos, I want now to tease out the way the child-centrism of those videos intersects with their treatment of Gothic dance. The effect of this intersection is, I think, less of a smokescreen for whatever futurity Jackson would like to (re)produce than it is a symptom of Gothic dance's queer derealisations of futurity.

THRILLER: THE FUNK OF FORTY THOUSAND YEARS

The pulsions of death's drive underlie the constant sense of transformation in Jackson's Gothic, the ubiquity of what Deleuze and Guattari would call 'becomings'.[8] In *Thriller*, for example, Michael becomes something else more than once. In the first part of the video, Jackson and his girlfriend (played by Ola Ray) enact roles from a stock 1950s horror movie, in which our hero, a connoisseur of the obvious, tells her that he is not like other guys, that he is, well, different. We see the nature of this difference when he suddenly becomes a teenage werewolf and chases his hapless lady through a dark wood. In this transformation he becomes much more Michael than he was before: hands and fingernails elongate, facial and body hair grow, teeth and cheeks bulge, and his previously relaxed, laconic body performs the manic gesticulations of a hormone-high teenager (see Figure 1). Yet, if this transformation bespeaks a forward-pulsion

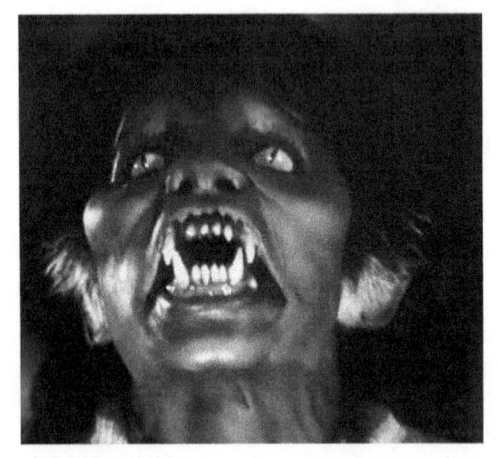

Figure 1

of bodily growth and hormonal maturity in heterosexual frenzy, it also points to its opposite, a devolution or reversal of the human into its more bestial or animal origins. Jackson's bodily movements are frenetic and shapeless, B-movie clichés of an atavistic physicality beyond the control of a civilising, 'mature', culturally determined superego. The video thus plays with contradictory ideas of temporal development that underpin the Gothic fantasy in a number of ways: as the adolescent body pushes forward into sexual plenitude, it collapses anti-phylogenetically into drive; and as a character named Michael, whom we recognise as the contemporary pop star, recedes in time to (the narrative conventions of) the 1950s, he does so in a video that was meant to change the *future* of pop video generally (in terms of its sheer length, but also its narrative sophistication, dance sequences and special effects). This future orientation, moreover, is the joke that places the whole teenage thriller scene in an actual movie theatre where the 'real' Michael, clad in futuristic red leather, and his ever-so-1980s girlfriend are watching it in 'real' time. In its entire concept, then, *Thriller* satirises the linearity of male sexual development – both biological and filmic – demonstrating instead the *sinthom*ic drive that shatters the subject into incoherent gravitations toward (and retreats from) a 'mature' death.

If the first half of the video imagines a masculine future continually mitigated by the drives of the past, the second half of the video reverses the temporal axis. Sensitive thing that she is, the Ola Ray character insists she and Michael leave the theatre and walk home, at which point he meets up with the ghouls who will provide the *corps de ballet*, with an emphasis on '*corps*(e)'. He becomes one of them, and terrorises her a second time. In this second transformation, the becoming of the video's first half is reversed: Jackson's cheeks cave in, his eyes burn into his head, his haute-couture clothing rots from his torso (see Figure 2).

Figure 2

Whereas the becoming-werewolf saw Michael's body develop and grow into a devolved animal, becoming-zombie witnesses a body in decay, a future orientation to a death-state characterised by a body that has become less than it already was: development as decomposition, the Freudian body rushing forward toward death. As with the skeletons of the medieval *danse macabre*, this is the un-dead body that will dance, that will enact the pulsions of death and signification, and, most importantly, that will terrorise the regimes of heterosexual normalcy upon which the

∽ 165

video's narrative is based. For Kobena Mercer, the zombie sequence is at one with Jackson's attraction to sexual indeterminacy:

> Unlike the werewolf, the figure of the zombie, the un-dead corpse, does not represent sexuality so much as asexuality or anti-sexuality, suggesting the sense of *neutral eroticism* in Jackson's style as dancer ... The dance sequence can be read as cryptic writing on this 'sexual vagueness' of Jackson's body in movement, in counterpoint to the androgyny of his image.[9]

I am not so sure. Asexuality and anti-sexuality are not the same thing, especially when the ante of 'anti' is the heterosexual fulfilment that *Thriller*'s teen narrative plays with, and with which some readers of Jackson have so brutally demanded he comply. More to the point, what Mercer calls '*neutral eroticism*' is, in my reading, an eroticism of a driving *fort-da*, a choreographic allegory of *sinthom*osexuality's pulsions that refuse linear temporality – and its own allegorisations of normal sexual development. This drive enacts instead a temporal jumble that sacrifices heterosexual desire to the terrorising pleasures of Gothic dance. If *Thriller* is the inaugural moment in Michael Jackson's Gothic HIStory, it renders the normalising trajectories of history as a mere symptom of the (anti-) sexuality that refuses sexuality's story.

Furthermore, the death drive's pulsions – a choreographic move toward the future that can always and only return to the past of the body's d/evolution – actually exceed the confines of *Thriller* and take us to one of its earlier inspirations, John Landis's 1981 film *American Werewolf in London*.[10] It is no accident that Jackson wanted Landis to direct *Thriller*, since *American Werewolf* was one of Jackson's favourite films, and it is that film's fascination with issues of sexuality and temporality that frame much of what Jackson's queer Gothic is doing.[11] Like *Thriller*, *American Werewolf* divides victims of terror into two categories: werewolves and the walking un-dead. True to folkloric tradition, Landis's werewolf is produced by a sort of vampiric bite: the lycanthrope, embodied by David Kessler (David Naughton) in the film, emerges from the human being who is bitten but not killed by another werewolf. Like Michael Jackson at the beginning of *Thriller*, Kessler's future seems to be a compulsive drive to the past, an inexorable degeneration into a former state of being. Contrasting this degeneration is the zombie, embodied in the film by Jack Goodman (Griffin Dunne), who dies in the initial attack that turns Kessler into a werewolf. Jack's state seems to be nothing but future-orientation: in each successive appearance throughout the film his body is more decayed. Each scene shows us less Jack, as his face starts to rot off, his eye falls out, his skin becomes putrid and fetid. And that the film should open by emphasising the boys' differing relations to heterosexual desire is significant, in that Landis uses the difference to play a joke on each of them: Jack, who as a living boy can think of nothing but his girlfriend's perfectly sexy body, is rendered sexless and frustrated by his un-dead body, while David, who can only critique Jack's desire for said girlfriend, is overcome by wolflike sexual lust following his lycanthropic bite. Thus *Thriller* not merely incorporates the (parodic) fascination with werewolves and zombies, it mirrors the questions of developmental temporality that Landis made central to his film.

But *Thriller* mirrors with a difference. While the two sex/dead entities remain separate in *American Werewolf*, *Thriller* brings them together. Michael *first* becomes a werewolf and *then* becomes un-dead. The video makes linear and contiguous what is separate and contrasted in the movie; it collapses the film's sex/death temporality into a singular being we call Michael Jackson. And that contiguity is exactly what the *choreography* – and not just the narrative – of *Thriller* is doing as well. *Thriller*'s central dance sequence begins with zombies rising from their graves or emerging from their tombs and sewers, from which they trudge slowly along the street. Creatures of earth and shit vomit their decayed insides over their decayed outsides, creating a scene marked by enervation and degeneration. But then, signalled by an ominous close-up on Michael, the dancers merge into his co-choreography. They begin the ensemble section with heavy, gravity-conscious stomps but quickly switch to a light, gliding, almost ethereal choreography, drawn heavily from Bob Fosse and James Brown. What gives this choreography its power (indeed, what may give all choreography its power) is the way the bodies translate the temporal into the spatial, they way they enact in the dance space the workings of time. In *Thriller* in particular, this spatial working of time plays itself out along the axis of life and death: the dance remains intensely centred and earthy, using a lot of deep knee-bends (pliés), keeping the dancers' heels on the floor – as we see in the sweeping overhead hand-clap and in Jackson's famous turns on the heel rather than elevated on the ball of the foot; it deploys low jazzy leg-crossings, and mitigates its vertical movements by collapsing the head to the shoulder and pushing the arm out to the side of the body rather than high into the air (see Figure 3).

Yet this zombie dance is performed with lightening speed and coverage of space: pelvises twitch, feet skip, bodies gallop forward and back as if

STEVEN BRUHM

Figure 3

to enact allegorically the *fort–da* pulsion. If the *narrative* of *Thriller* sends up developmental time to parody male sexual development, its *choreography* writes on the body the symptoms of the death drive that render such clean linearity impossible. The dancing body simultaneously rushes forward and jerks back (to echo Freud); it travels up in space but is pulled back down by its attractions to the earth and grave. Death dances not simply to express the pleasures of movement but to enact the *sinthom*ic refusals of normalised space-time, and to deconstruct the logics of spatial and temporal linearity.

Indeed, Michael Jackson's dance in *Thriller* is a Gothic *funk*, in all senses of that word. When a rapping Vincent Price tells us that the *mis-en-scène* is shrouded in 'the funk of forty thousand years', he encapsulates in a phrase Jackson's queer performance of time. The funk in question is primarily musical, a rhythmic pattern that dislodges time through heavy syncopation and by driving a 3/4 beat over the framing, regularised 'common time' beat of 4/4. 'Funk' is also cowardly fear, a shrinking away in agitation as the body – a Freudian body – seeks escape from disturbance in the pleasures of quiescence. But 'funk' is also sex, the smell of fucking and of bodily fluids – which is precisely the sense African-American musicians since the 1950s wanted to capitalise on when they call their music 'funky'.[12] Sex, death, fear, and deconstructions of time – Jackson's funk of forty thousand years celebrates a sex that death constantly interrupts and fulfils, and that has no little scorn for the heteronormalcy that frames teenage romance. Little wonder, then, that the 1950s segment of *Thriller* ends with the bloody soundbite, 'See you next Wednesday': this is not just the promise of macabre Gothic repetition, the taunting realisation that we all come back for more of the pleasures of terror; nor is it merely a deferred gratification until a future time, the promise that pleasure/death awaits us (*da*), but only in a week's time (*fort*); it is also the name of the pornographic movie that the lycanthropic David and un-dead Jack watch together in *American Werewolf* as they discuss the necessity of David's eventual suicide. The porn title signifies the boys' own sex, their own funk, the cohabitation of sexual fulfilment, delay and death, a funk that Jackson slyly imports into the texture of *Thriller* as we see teenage girl and teenage boy rent apart by the Gothic. Given these terms of *sinthomo*-sexuality, it should also not surprise us that the contemporary section of *Thriller*, and the video proper, ends as it does: Michael escorts Ola out of her dream and back home, but turns to us with demonic eyes. The future *is* the past here, the video continues to generate the degenerate, the *sinthome* does its work.

MICHAEL JACKSON'S *GHOSTS*: FUNK THE CHILD

It is difficult to imagine a less likely candidate for the critique of reproductive futurism than *Michael Jackson's Ghosts*, his 1997 epic video responding to the first set of child-molestation charges and the public frenzy that ensued. The video tells the story of a group of angry townspeople and their puritanical mayor – all inhabitants of 'Normal Valley' – who march to the house of a local 'freak' who has gained a reputation for scaring children by telling them stories. The mayor wants to run 'the Maestro' (Jackson's Gothic persona) out of town because his acts of wanton storytelling are somehow corrupting the children, not least because these children (all boys) seem committed to keeping the stories secret from their parents. The mayor and the Maestro get into a pissing contest over who can scare the other more effectively, and of course Michael wins by mounting a huge song and dance number, enlisting a huge cast of ghoulish dancers and, through the use of blue-screen technology, transforming himself into a skeleton at some points and a monstrously large ogre at others. The video concludes with a touching tableau where the parents admit to being scared but that they 'had a good time', that they too have been able to join in childhood fun and to be won over by the perennially different Michael Jackson. The children themselves adopt Michaelesque scare techniques – dressing in his skeletal clothes, embodying the magic of his special effects – but all in good fun. Child's culture is not merely harmless, it is salubrious, and we would all do well, the video argues, to relax into the scary games we play with/as children. Children *are* our future in this video because they enable us as adults to reach into our own pasts and discover the pleasures of imaginative, bodily excitation. We all live happily ever after.

While the child-centrism of *Ghosts* is painfully heavy-handed, the Gothic milieu that conveys it is as problematic as it was in *Thriller*. And as in *Thriller*, Jackson enacts these problems through use of the *danse macabre*. When we first see him in *Ghosts*, he is hiding behind a skeletal mask, a joke he plays on the townspeople in an attempt to scare them. However, as the video progresses the skeletal image takes on a far more ominous meaning. When the Maestro comes to understand that he must truly scare the mayor if he is to protect himself, he pulls off the face that he had been presenting to us up to this point to reveal that he is nothing but skeleton underneath (see Figure 4). This is accurate enough physiology,

Figure 4

I suppose, but following the presentation of this skeletal face he then smashes its bones with his hands, so that the familiar face of Michael Jackson can once again break through. The argument here is clear enough – you cannot know which is the real me; given my constantly shifting face, you cannot pin me down to one stable identity that you can then condemn – but, given Jackson's concern with temporality, the moment also suggests a confusion between his orientation toward youth and his orientation toward death. This moment of skeletal death will lead to a huge dance sequence in which the Maestro has removed not just his facial flesh but *all* flesh, and dances as a skeleton in the medieval tradition, hoping among other things to heap shame upon the corpulent mayor for his hypocrisy and moral short-sightedness (see Figure 5). In its orgy of special effects,

Figure 5

the video ultimately depicts that same fucking with temporality that we saw in *Thriller*, but here the stakes have been raised: Jackson combines the charges of paedophilia – itself a crime of fucking with the temporal – with the vortexes of the death drive, so that what gets facilely called 'fun' in *Ghosts* is something much closer to a Freudian 'pleasure' that signals its own beyond, the workings of the *sinthome* that underlie and undo it.

I argued earlier that the choreography of *Thriller* capitalises upon a parallel between the vertical and horizontal movement axes and the orientation toward spiritual or ghostly ethereality and grave-oriented, earthy embodiment. The Gothic aesthetic of *Michael Jackson's Ghosts* does much the same thing. Throughout the *corps de ballet* Michael does to death (as it were) heavy foot-stomping, pounding upon the floor, and foot-dragging. More than any other Jackson choreography I know, this one holds its bodies in continual flex at the waist to emphasise the dancers' groundedness, and his uncanny use of the skeletal – emphasising knee, hip and elbow joints in flexion, all opened to the audience/camera for maximum effect – ensures that joint flexions propel the body

Figure 6

downward, into its own weight, into the floor, into the earth (see Figure 6). At one particularly manipulative moment, Michael slams his head on to the tile floor; the head crumbles into dust and returns to the elements from which it presumably came. But at the same time the choreography exploits special effects to have dancers walk up walls, dance on ceilings (doubtless an homage to Jackson's hero, Fred Astaire, who dances on the ceiling in *Royal Wedding* [1951]), and completely defy gravity in lots of other ways – including transforming the ghouls into angels at one point as they descend slowly from the ceiling to the dance floor. As in *Thriller*, the dancing body reminds us here of its pulsations toward death. The future it predicts is at best a paradoxical one where death subtends physical movement and life – the feeling of pleasure, the having of 'fun' – in a series of choreographed moments whose temporal promises can never be kept. Explosions of a dance spectacle in Michael Jackson's Gothic are actually explosions of the *sinthom*ic drive where the present – not just the future – is made the stuff of death.

Exercises in weight and gravity go deeper into the dancer's sinews in *Ghosts*: they indeed seem to connote an energy that comes from the core of the body itself. Jackson's choreography repeatedly deploys circular movements to present the feeling of a movement that paradoxically goes nowhere: the head circles on the shoulders, the upper body, through contracted abdominals and constricted shoulders, circles around itself, and travel patterns continually form circles, taking dancers back to the point from which they came. A well-established break-dancing tradition places dancers on the spot where they perform rippling movements as if energy were running up one limb, through the torso and down the other (a choreography Jackson employed at the end of *Thriller* as well). And most notably, given Jackson's own dance career, *Ghosts* repeatedly uses a move that seems to be the reverse of his famous moonwalk (which itself appears numerous times in the video). If the moonwalk is a method of walking backward so as to give the illusion of moving forward (shades of Freud's vacillating rhythm), an illusion achieved by a sleight-of-foot, Jackson uses in *Ghosts* a forward walk that actually takes him nowhere – as if moving toward a space or condition that he will never reach. And the effects of these choreographic techniques are ultimately the same as in *Thriller*: the choreography achieves its enchantment through the impossible juxtapositions of movements toward life and movements toward death. In each case, the death movements exude embodied energy and lightness while the life movements are always shrouded by death. Bodies incorporate and telegraph the *sinthome* of death's drive, its constant reminder that our sexual choreographies end in quiescence, and that the temporal development toward normal sexual maturity is mere humanist illusion.

As Maestro of the castle, Jackson is also its choreographer, the 'father' of a 'family' (his word) of un-dead ghouls in which he, paradoxically, is the youngest and most 'alive'. Yet another temporal dislocation in a Gothic aesthetic that is full of such dislocations, this move makes of Jackson a kind of living death, one that extends beyond the *corps de ballet* and into the body of the living mayor. Sporting the grotesquely large body of an ogre (a tumescence that harks back to the becoming-werewolf of *Thriller*), Maestro comes into the mayor's mouth (pun intended) and inhabits his body – a Freudian Gothic scene of demonic possession if there ever was one. From here the incorporated queer forces the mayor to dance the dance that Maestro himself had just performed as a skeleton, the dance whose vocabulary works the axes of space and time as I described them above. This is a visual joke to be sure: the mayor, a visual allusion to Prosecuting Attorney Thomas Sneddon, only younger and fatter, is forced to pervert his body into the death-ridden, sexually explicit choreography that has served as a metonym for what he has been attempting to eradicate. But this metonymic re-enactment turns the visual joke into the performance of *sinthom*osexuality: the drive, as Edelman defines it, is that which is totally out of the control of the conscious self, that which reveals and destroys the moralising centre by which forbidden sexualities are condemned, that which vilifies a body dedicated to purity. And that the visual performance of death's drive should be inaugurated by the oral incorporation of *another man* brings Michael Jackson's queer choreography to completion: it is not kids he has been fucking with (whether this is 'true' or not), it is adults. If there is a future-orientation in this video at all, it has as much to do with the destruction of normative adulthood in ways that surpass the cliché of embracing the inner child. Jackson wants less to embrace than to destroy – destroy the self-righteous (super) ego that orchestrates the normal into the temporal.

If the mayor can dance the *danse macabre* convincingly, it is little wonder: his character is played by a heavily padded, heavily made-up Michael Jackson himself. Given this, the coming into the mayor's mouth is not only homoerotic but homo-narcissistic – as we see in a scene where, from inside the mayor's body Maestro forces him to confront his image in a mirror. To the degree that the mayor's 'insides' are Maestro/Michael Jackson himself, Jackson is depicting the site of death within life, or life as Normal Valley USA likes to imagine it. Put another way, Jackson does not simply allegorise the *danse macabre* as a critique of heteronormativity, he elevates himself to the status of the *sinthome*. While videos like *You Are Not Alone* and the famous televised plea from Neverland were stage-managed to make Jackson look like a sacrificial Christ or Angel of Goodness, his Gothic produces a gleefully embodied death drive, a physical, dancing force that guts the pious, future-oriented, homo-violent culture that, as Edelman points out, deploys the signifier 'child' to suspend or invalidate the rights of any other group (3). And if we can follow Edelman's chorus to 'Fuck the ... Child in whose name we're collectively terrorised' (29), we can also follow Michael Jackson's Gothic choreography and Fuck (or is it Funk?) the Child Within, that alleged centre of innocence and goodness that, with the proper care, can develop over time into the responsible, loving, heteronormative adult. We would do well in the end not to view Michael Jackson as the instigator or destroyer of a certain kind of subjective agency but to see him as *agency itself*, the pop-cultural embodiment of a *sinthome* that puts us in an ineluctable – and queer – *pas de deux* with death.

NOTES

1 See especially Ron Alcalay, 'Morphing Out of Identity Politics: *Black or White* and *Terminator 2*', in The Bad Subjects Production Team (eds), *Bad Subjects: Political Education for Everyday Life* (New York: New York University Press, 1998), pp. 136–42; and Kobena Mercer, 'Monster Metaphors: Notes on Michael Jackson's Thriller', in Andrew Goodwin, Lawrence Grossberg and Simon Firth (eds), *Sound and Vision: The Music Video Reader* (New York: Routledge, 1993), pp. 93–108. The closest thing I can find to a queer reading of Jackson's work is Cynthia Fuchs, but, like the other work I cite here, Fuchs is interested in Jackson's racially coded body and its malleability in the context of media hype. She has little to say about video or dance performances as discrete objects for analysis. See Cynthia J. Fuchs, 'Michael Jackson's Penis', in Sue-Ellen Case, Philip Brett and Susan Leigh Foster (eds), *Cruising the Performative: Interventions into the Representation of Ethnicity, Nationality, and Sexuality* (Bloomington: Indiana University Press, 1995), pp. 13–33.
2 James Kincaid, *Erotic Innocence: The Culture of Child Molesting* (Durham, NC: Duke University Press, 1998).
3 Richard D. Mohr, 'The Pedophilia of Everyday Life', in Steven Bruhm and Natasha Hurley (eds), *Curiouser: On the Queerness of Children* (Minneapolis, MN: University of Minnesota Press, 2004), pp. 17–30.
4 One exception to this is Jerrold Hogle's brief discussion of Jackson in *The Undergrounds of the Phantom of the Opera: Sublimation and the Gothic in Leroux's Novel and Its Progeny* (New York: Palgrave, 2002). I owe much to Hogle's work here.
5 John Landis, dir., *Michael Jackson's Thriller* (USA: MJJ Ventures, Inc., 1984); Stan Winston, dir., *Michael Jackson's Ghosts* (USA: Heliopolis and MJJ Productions, 1997). All subsequent references to the videos will be taken from these productions.
6 Sigmund Freud, *Beyond the Pleasure Principle*, in *The Penguin Freud Library, Vol. 11, On Metapsychology*, trans. James Strachey, ed. Angela Richard (New York: Penguin, 1991), p. 308. All subsequent references are to this edition, and are given in parentheses in the text.
7 Lee Edelman, *No Future: Queer Theory and the Death Drive* (Durham, NC: Duke University Press, 2004), p. 22. All subsequent references are to this edition, and are given in parentheses in the text.
8 Gilles Deleuze and Félix Guattari, *A Thousand Plateaus: Capitalism and Schizophrenia*, trans. Brian Massumi (Minneapolis: University of Minnesota Press, 1987); see especially chapter 10.
9 Mercer, 'Monster Metaphors', p. 104.
10 John Landis, dir. *American Werewolf in London* (USA: Universal Studios, 1981). All subsequent references to this film will be taken from this production.

11 Michael Jackson, *Moonwalk* (London: William Heinemann Ltd, 1988), p. 222.
12 Don Michael Randel, *The Harvard Dictionary of Music*, fourth edition (Cambridge, MA: Belknap Press, 2003), p. 339.

11

Death, art, and bodies: queering the queer Gothic in Will Self's Dorian

∼

Andrew Smith

Anxieties about death or the return of the dead have underpinned some of the more canonical theoretical discourses that concern the Gothic. In Burke's *Philosophical Enquiry* (1757) and Freud's 'The Uncanny' (1919), death can be identified as a self-evidently key Gothic register. However, the picture is more complex than this for in both Burke and Freud death is not simply about visceral fears of non-existence, because death functions as the point at which meaning, or analysis, disappears. Neither Burke nor Freud is ultimately able to account in any systematic way for Terror or uncanniness because such experience seems to elude representation and so frustrates attempts at interpreting the radical absence of meaning that death implies. Terry Castle covertly develops this view in her exploration of spectrality in Ann Radcliffe's *The Mysteries of Udolpho* (1794). Castle argues that the novel represents characters as ghosted by others, and subject to anxieties about whether the living are dead. For Castle, following the work of Philippe Ariès, this indicates the presence of a reconceptualisation of death in the eighteenth century in which the ghost projectively gives meaning to non-absence in a new mode of seeing; so that 'The successful denial of mortality ... requires a new spectralized mode of perception, in which one sees through the real person, as it were, towards a perfect and unchanging spiritual essence'.[1] The dead thus never really die, but merely evoke some quasi-Platonic ideal spiritual identity, an identity that, for Freud, asserts itself at moments of uncanniness, which is felt 'in the highest degree in relation to death and dead bodies, to the return of the dead, and to spirits and ghosts'.[2] The projective figure of the ghost also raises questions about the kind of meaning that is being

∼ 177

restored. At one level the answer appears to imply a banality because the ghost seems to provide solace for loss in an increasingly secularised age (in which the ghost more often attracts pseudo-scientific monitoring, rather than theological explanation). However, it is the issue of projection which complicates this. What is projected and how that projection of meaning is constructed generates insight into how death and its cultural configurations are formulated.

This chapter explores Will Self's *Dorian* (2002). The novel is an updated version of Wilde's *The Picture of Dorian Gray* (1891) set in the 1980s and 1990s which revolves around a gay culture which has been affected by AIDS. The modern-day Henry Wotton is an aristocratic figure who, with Baz Hallwood (a conceptual artist), vies for the affections of Dorian Gray who is, at the beginning, a somewhat naive recent Oxford graduate living in London. Dorian is seemingly immortalised in Hallwood's video installation titled *Cathode Narcissus*, which frees Dorian to indulge in all kinds of supposed sexual depravities and, as in Wilde's novel, he is responsible for the death of Hallwood, amongst others. However, ultimately this narrative is revealed to be an imaginary account of Dorian written by Wotton, who dies of AIDS. In reality, so the Epilogue suggests, Dorian is a self-centred amoral entrepreneur but he is not an updated version of Wilde's dangerous, corrupted hedonist. The novel's reconstruction of Wilde's narrative through Wotton indicates an engagement with postmodern ideas, which are also represented in the novel through numerous references to contemporary art. The novel focuses also on the dead and the dying, and reworks the problem of meaning and absence that characterise a peculiarly Gothic metaphysic. These ideas are established through an ostensible queer Gothic mode, but one in which queerness becomes increasingly associated with absence (as an aspect of the postmodern) as the novel projectively represents the AIDS crisis as an exercise in abjection. Approaching *Dorian* in this way indicates how this projection harbours within it an unresolved homophobia which identifies death as the self-generated preserve of particular communities, even whilst such an abjected placing of death reworks the type of cultural anxieties identified by Castle. The dead, dying and ghosts are not just part of an ongoing grand metaphysical script, as Castle suggests, but rather are involved in a complex process of cultural displacement that implicates homophobia in a strategy of keeping the mortal, perverse, corruptible, body at bay. The initial starting point for this enquiry involves an exploration of how the novel is inflected by issues about postmodernism.

David Alderson has examined the ideological work conducted by *Dorian* in the name of an ostensible anti-essentialist postmodernism. However, although Alderson also wants to avoid an essentialist argument, he claims that Self's 'identification as straight' colours how gay culture is represented in the novel.[3] For Alderson, Self perceives the attempt to establish a gay identity politics as 'delusional' (327) because it is imbricated by a consumerist ideology which renders it complicit with Thatcherite economics. This means that seemingly anti-establishment figures, such as Henry Wotton, are ultimately challenged by narratives which consistently undermine their potential for rebellion. Wotton's subversive Wildean *bon mots*, for example, suggest his intellectually superior 'social domination' but this is ultimately compromised by his 'determining feminine masochism' (319). For Alderson it is this 'reification of gender' (324) which collapses the novel's seemingly self-conscious postmodern queering of identity.

Dorian, however is an exercise in the postmodern as well as a commentary upon it. Stylistically this is suggested in the revelation that the main narrative is the memoir of Henry Wotton, which represents Dorian as a self-destructive narcissist. Indeed, it is Wotton who appears to represent, and focalise, a discourse of postmodern play that is rendered in queer terms to the degree that it is sexualised and implies an ambivalent tension between surfaces and desires, as noted in the contention that 'For much of the time Henry Wotton wasn't altogether sure which human gender he preferred, or even if he liked sex with his own species at all. Pudenda? Pricks? Petals? What now?'[4] This represents an openness to experience that is captured in Wotton's refrain that 'the chameleon is the most significant of modern types' (39). However, Wotton's protean desires are implicitly mapped on to an incoherent notion of history, to the point that he is unable to reflect on his past in any meaningful way, 'In Henry Wotton's childhood the years were inseparable and their events were confused. JFK stood trial in a glass booth in Tel Aviv and was sentenced to orbit the moon' (53). The end of one era – Adolf Eichmann's trial for Nazi war crimes – becomes confused with the emergence of another – the space race – and this is in keeping with the novel's presentation of an explicitly Baudrillardian discourse of history when, at a dinner party, Dorian states 'Of course, the Gulf War never *really* happened' (143), which glosses an earlier claim made in the novel that television is 'so much *realer* than reality' (66). Dorian's, and Wotton's, implied amorality is articulated as an historical dislocation which means that they place themselves beyond, and above, political events. This is demonstrated during the dinner party when Wotton's wife, an academic historian nicknamed Batface, a government minister, and others, discuss politics: 'Their talk was earnest, full of the names of people not personally known to them – Yeltsin, Gorbachev and Rajiv Gandhi' (147). Simultaneously, another group congregates at the end of the table consisting of Wotton and Dorian, amongst others, who form an alternative gathering in which 'The chatter ... was perverse, cynical and brittle, incorporating the names of people they knew only too intimately' (147). These two groups are separate because they 'had repelled each other' (147), but nevertheless the novel locates Wotton within a history which works upon him and so mutes his attempts at ironic agency. For Batface what is Gothic about the world is the crisis in the Balkans and the state of the Cold War, whereas what specifically ghosts the lives of Wotton, Dorian and their friends is the AIDS crisis.

Wotton is amongst those who become infected by HIV, whereas Dorian appears to be immune to disease because his 'body' has been effectively transformed into Baz Hallwood's art installation, *Cathode Narcissus*. The novel describes the ravages of the disease in a language which reworks the implicit images of Nazism which were referred to in Wotton's confused, partial recollection of the Eichmann trial. The description of an AIDS ward, for example, conflates images of the perpetrators and victims of war, to create a somewhat inconsistent image that dwells on appearances which seem to slide over each other:

> in the Broderip Ward on that day in 1991, there were whole squadrons of young men with Bomber Command moustaches who had been targeted with the incendiary disease. Their radiator-grille ribcages and concentration-camp eyes telegraphed the dispatch that this was less a place for the mending of civilian injuries and quotidian wounds than a casualty station near the front line with Death. (78)

Later it is noted that such victims 'found themselves transported to the cellular Auschwitz of AIDS' (252). Wotton, commenting on his health, refers to the cathedral at Cologne, which famously was one of the few historical buildings that survived the Allied bombing of the city: he notes 'I feel gothic with disease – as if Cologne Cathedral were being shoved up my fundament' (236). This claim also brings back into focus the reference to the patients with their 'Bomber Command moustaches' in which a surviving cathedral from a heavily bombed city phallically represents not the possibility of survival but an image of pain and infection that is in keeping with the blurring of images of victims and perpetrators (because the infection is innocently transmitted). These references to war are not simply a conceit for an AIDS culture in the 1980s and 1990s; they also represent the inescapability of historical narratives despite Wotton's studied attempts to divorce himself from all kinds of political, or politicisable, issues.

Wotton's binding to history is represented through his associations with the jiggling man, who seems to be a mentally disturbed neighbour whom Wotton can see rocking backwards and forwards from his house. For Wotton 'he was a sibylline metronome prophesying the day' when they would all die (136). The jiggling man's progressively aged and ravaged appearance provides a gloss on Wotton's battle with AIDS. However when Wotton 'dies' (according to his narrative) he is confronted by the jiggling man who tells him 'I ... was meting out the seconds, minutes and hours. But I was meting them out solely for you' (255). Time and its inescapability are thus emphasised in relation to Wotton whereas Dorian appears to be able, because of *Cathode Narcissus*, to transcend it.

History is not, however, merely a matter of one's personal history, and the novel develops connections to demonstrably public histories through the dream world of Wotton's ageing and dying friend Fergus, who is known as 'the Ferret'. The Ferret's subconscious refracts political dramas through a queer reading of them which mockingly sexualises the macho posturing of a certain type of political leadership, in what becomes an alternative version of world affairs:

> In the Ferret's cerebral cockpit, penis-nosed premiers – Rabin and Arafat, Mandela and de Klerk, Major and Reynolds – were for ever jousting. They warily circled the rose garden of the White House under the simple gaze of Bouffant Bill, their cheeks spattered with the jism of peace. (198)

The Ferret is represented as the historical consciousness in the novel, even if he does turn world politics into an orgy. He becomes 'a sort of god' because his dreams 'incorporated world events that were likely to occur as well as those that already had', meaning that 'he would become aware of things currently occurring – massacres in Rwanda, coup in Moscow, earthquake in Los Angeles – that he had already foreseen (albeit incorporating a cast of multicoloured centaurs and singing seahorses) in his dreams' (199). The point is that Wotton and the Ferret are unable to transcend the political forces which contextualise their lives. The explicit postmodernism of the novel is thus purposively challenged by the grand narratives of history (war, and public politics), which indicate that the novel's self-conscious use of postmodernist tactics is articulated in order to challenge a version of postmodern amorality. In other words the novel attempts to develop some notion of a shared 'humanity' (or 'politics') which enables a critique of the postmodern moment. That Self has this in mind is suggested by his attack on what seems to be a specifically postmodern version of art, although one which through its reference to Narcissus seems to implicate a combination of artistic egotism and postmodern surface.

Dorian's manifestation as *Cathode Narcissus* stands in for Wilde's portrait. As in *The Picture of Dorian Gray*, Dorian assimilates many of Wotton's ideas and is described as having become 'a social chameleon' (107). Initially in the novel he is characterised as easily influenced and corruptible, but he becomes increasingly violent as the novel progresses (according to Wotton's narrative). He is also represented as a narcissist and Steven Bruhm has noted that one consistent feature of the myth of Narcissus is its inherent queerness, because: 'Narcissus comes to figure stably as an emblem of instability; he occupies both sides of those familiar binaries structuring our culture: self/other, surface/depth, active/passive, masculine/feminine, soul/body, inside/outside, sanity/psychosis'.[5] For these reasons Narcissus 'comes to look like the rather predictable product of another historically specific intellectual moment: the postmodern' (174). According to Bruhm the myth possesses a radical ambiguity because it is ambiguity which subverts unified notions of subjectivity. As he notes, 'The Gothicism of our culture is terrifying because it threatens to destroy certain constructions of the self. The narcissism of our culture is promising for exactly the same reason' (173). To a significant extent the roots of this radical ambiguity can be found within camp. In *Dorian*, Wotton's association with camp and a patrician disposition suggest the presence of what Susan Sontag has referred to as the 'snob taste' that characterises camp.[6] Thomas A. King's exploration of the history of camp argues that camp was ascribed to the aristocracy by a middle-class culture which came to view them as economically unproductive. The roots of this are to be found in the seventeenth century, but its associated class antagonisms provide a way of accounting for how aristocratic figures such as Wotton attempt to depoliticise their experience of the world. King notes:

> In light of the development of 'real' or substantive political issues, the bourgeoisie interpreted the continued promulgation of aristocratic legitimacy

through spectacular self-display and conspicuous consumption as empty gesturing, mere appearance with no underlying being.[7]

Such a view supports Alderson's argument that *Dorian* suggests that gay identity politics have been tarnished by embracing consumerism. King further argues that the perception of camp as an essentially empty form was a device intended to make homosexuality invisible, as it implicates a strategy of denying the homosexual a 'social being' (26). However, camp is also radically ambivalent (echoing Bruhm's analysis of Narcissus) because it suggests that models of the self are performative and thus provide a reassertion of 'the primacy of performance beyond the epistemological prejudice of identity' (46). Narcissus can thus be related to camp because both function as forms of repudiation. Camp repudiates the idea of presence, but at a more complex level it also subtly repudiates any attempt to designate it as superficial because it contains within it the possibility of generating alternative (subversive) identities. In *Dorian* this is manifested at a level where the postmodern is conflated with a queerness that indicates that identity is protean and so undoes any ideology of human essence which could help support a heteronormative culture. However, *Dorian* is also *about* the postmodern moment and is therefore a critique of it. This means that whilst *Dorian* ostensibly appears to Gothically subvert norms, ultimately, because of its meta-analytical approach, it effects a repudiation of repudiation. This complex attitude towards queering subjectivity is related to the novel's generalised discussion of art, and to its specific critique of conceptual artists.

It is significant that Dorian is aware of the complicated set of self-conscious gazes that are suggested in *Cathode Narcissus*. The installation consists of nine monitors showing Dorian dancing nude. This multiple, and so overdetermined, model of Narcissus is mocked when Baz asks Dorian what he thinks of the installation, 'To tell you the truth, Baz, looking at myself looking at myself looking at myself isn't exactly my idea of a turn-on, even if it's yours' (51). To which Baz replies that Dorian has missed the point because it is about 'transcendence', but then admits that perhaps its not quite an unalloyed, or depoliticised transcendence, 'but I did try and say a true thing in all this ... 'bout you, me, 'bout bein' gay, 'bout ... stuff' (51). And *Cathode Narcissus* does seem to provide Dorian with a form of transcendence; later 'Baz sensed that Dorian had not only escaped the clutches of the virus, he had also freed himself from all the dreary claims of the body' (141). Paradoxically this is also a feeling that Baz has when Dorian murders him: 'it was with acute relief that Baz realised he was dead, and stepped away from the lolling gargoyle of his corpse' (166), which represents, in part, a mistrust of the body that runs throughout the novel.

The novel's representation of the art scene is related to this issue of the body. There are a number of references made to contemporary art. Wotton makes a specific reference to Baz's art which incorporates wider reference to British art, when he states that 'his work remains that bizarre mixture of stupid execution and clever intentions that always entitles someone to be called a representative British artist' (202). Earlier Dorian had playfully suggested that he belonged to a group which could preserve his body after death, which elicits the response from Gavin (one of the Ferret's associates), 'You should come back to London with me, get Hirst to preserve your corpse in formaldehyde' (196). Baz effectively represents the type of abstractions which characterise Hirst's work, because he too in *Cathode Narcissus* attempts to preserve the body. Art seems in Baz's terms to grant immortality, or transcendence, because it replaces the 'real' body with an abstract representation of it. It is therefore telling that Wotton's attack on contemporary art focuses on how abstractions have replaced the body. Wotton states:

> I loathe the so-called 'art' of the twentieth century with a particularly rare and hearty passion. Would that all that paint, canvas, plaster, stone and bronze could be balled up and tossed into that fraud Duchamp's *pissoir*. With a few notable exceptions – Balthus, Bacon, Modigliani – the artists of this era have been in headlong flight from beauty or any meaningful representation of the human form. (220)

In the Epilogue the focus is on Dorian's activities as an entrepreneur, which include attending a meeting at the Royal Academy to discuss arranging the publicity for an 'audacious exhibition of the most controversial contemporary British artists' (267). Dorian becomes haunted by the voice of Wotton which enters into his mind in order to provoke the thought that:

> Conceptual art has degenerated to the level of crude autobiography, a global-village sale of shoddy, personal memorabilia for which video installations are the TV adverts ... I wonder if the Royal Academy gift shop is doing special offers on bottled piss, canned shit and vacuum-packed blood. (267)

Such a view also suggests that abstract art can, however, also be read in terms of Kristeva's conception of abjection as it indicates what a culture needs to expel. Significantly abjection requires a necessary casting off that keeps death at bay, Kristeva notes that:

> These body fluids, this defilement, this shit are what withstands, hardly and with difficultly, on the part of death. There, I am at the border of my condition as a living being. My body extricates itself, as being alive, from that border.[8]

Kristeva's focus on the liminality of abjection suggests that it is this blurring between the living and the dead which is the principal source of the abject; so that the most abjected figure is 'the corpse' because death ultimately 'has encroached upon everything' (3). In other words Wotton's parody of conceptual art ironically (and unconsciously) conceives of the body, and its by-products, within an aesthetic context that identifies such art as the site of projected anxieties. This projection represents the mortality of the body as necessarily culturally excluded, as beyond forms of coherent representation (but nevertheless manifested as fragments, waste, blood). Images of the abject in *Dorian* suggest this but they are also implied (in an alternative way) through how the specific image of Narcissus functions as a queer being upon whom a heteronormative culture abjects (casts off as projection) that which it wishes to expel. The irony is, as Bruhm has noted, that 'the suspicion of narcissus as delimiting, self-delusive, and potentially dangerous can be used to represent straight culture to itself' (9). The mirror which is Narcissus in the guise of abstract art (*Cathode Narcissus*) thus represents what a heteronormative culture needs to abject: a fear of death and dying which is symptomatically 'Othered' as part of the AIDS crisis. To that degree *Dorian* articulates an ontological ambition in its striving for an immortality which conceals the reality of death. The model of a camp identity therefore provides the surface which harbours beneath it cultural anxieties about death. A clue to Self's interests in such matters can be found in an interview he conducted with Damien Hirst in 1994.

Whilst waiting for Hirst to arrive for the interview Self reflects on 'the Hirst anti-aesthetic – a quotidian elision between the surreal and the banal'.[9] However, when Hirst arrives Self is struck by his 'genuine charisma' and he associates this with Hirst's fascination with how to command space in which 'Like many spatial artists he is concerned with the interplay between individuals' senses of embodiment and their capacity for extroception' (287). Self also develops a view of Hirst's art which is relevant to a reading of the duality of *Cathode Narcissus* (both abstract art *and* a record of decay) when he says to Hirst that 'Your art is very kinaesthetic, it's about the internal sensibility of the body' (289), a view that Hirst agrees with in a Gothic image of entombment within one's body: 'I remember once getting really terrified that I could only see out of my eyes ... I got really terrified by it. I'm kind of trapped inside with these two little things' (289). This suggests that abstract art enables a transcendence of the body by relocating the body into an alternative form (sculpture, painting and so on) which enables one to escape from this troubling 'internal sensibility' by objectifying the body. Hirst, however, also wanted to explore an explicit conjunction between sex and death, which bears relevance to a reading of physical decline in *Dorian*. He describes his installation *Couple Fucking Dead Twice* as:

> Just two tanks, with no formaldehyde in them, and there are four cows – two in one tank, two in the other – and they're just these peeled cows. One's just stood upright, and the other one goes on its back, giving it a really tragic, slow fuck. They're both cows, so it doesn't matter. And they'll just rot. By the end there'll just be a mess of putrid flesh and bones. I just want to find out about rotting. (291-2)

This conjunction of sex and death becomes recorded on *Cathode Narcissus* which comes to represent 'an anguished figure, his face, neck and hands covered with Kaposi's, his mouth wet with bile, his eyes tortured by death and madness, his bald pate erupting with some vile fungus' (163).

The novel's superficial references to postmodernism are compromised by this aesthetic of bodily decline. At one level Hirst seems to be toying with Self when he plays a game with him in which Self has to make choices based on certain questions. One of Hirst's questions incisively addresses concerns about the body which are articulated in the novel, 'Which do you hate more, serial killers or flab?' (292). The novel also emphasises an insistent presence of the flesh, which is represented as the site of trauma because it eludes figuration and is touched by mortality. Before discussing this representation of the body it is worthwhile briefly exploring the image of Dorian as a psychopath through whom the flesh becomes mortified.

George E. Haggerty sees the image of the homosexual predator as a central figure in the queer Gothic. Haggerty notes, in a discussion of Anne Rice's vampire Lestat, that 'The homosexual, cunning and lethal, figures as a kind of symptom of everything that is most thrilling but also most deadly about contemporary culture'.[10] In Haggerty's terms Dorian would represent a mainstream culture's vicarious, and projectively queered, pleasure in destroying cultural norms. This implicit level is at odds with the explicit representations of Dorian as unambiguously malevolent, as a character whose depravities are secretly recorded by *Cathode Narcissus*. For Haggerty:

> Culture wants its young heroes to defy convention; to escape demands on health, family, and sobriety; and to move with the freedom of the night. At the same time culture must condemn such movement as unhealthy, immoral, and deadly. (191)

In *Dorian* it is the deliberate transmission of AIDS which indicates that Dorian is 'unhealthy, immoral, and deadly', in what appears to be a highly conservative critique of queer (one which is linked to the rebuttal of the postmodern). There is a perception that Dorian is 'the AIDS Mary' who is immune to the disease and who is a 'malevolent and intentional transmitter of the virus' (112), and indeed Dorian becomes a serial killer who has made 'in excess of a thousand thousand HIV impregnations' (231).

Wotton explicitly lampoons conceptual art, but implicitly it is a Hirstian vision of sex and decay which runs throughout the novel and which informs a series of moments where the flesh is emphasised. Early reference is made to Wotton's 'disconcertingly fleshly and spatulate fingers' (4). The young Dorian is represented in *Cathode Narcissus* as 'like a fleshy bonbon, or titillating titbit, wholly unaware of the ravening mouth of the camera' (12). Later Octavia, whom Wotton accuses Dorian of having infected with HIV, asks the Hirstian question, 'Are we all simply skin suits stuffed with meat?' (104). Dorian is described as looking for victims in places where there is a 'variety of flesh on offer' (227). Later, Dorian seduces Helen, an old university friend, and is repelled by her fleshiness, 'Her underwear was flesh-coloured, but alas, it wasn't the same colour as her flesh, which, he noted fastidiously, had the alarming, greasy hue of uncooked veal, to go with the kitchen smell of her favours' (231). However, this disgust with the flesh is subsequently transferred to Dorian and begins the process of his decline. Helen says to him, 'you have the body of a young lad' which initially she had found attractive but now it gives her 'the creeps ... In part it's because I know you're putting it about everywhere you can, but I also find your baby body revolting in itself' (246). Dorian is stung by such a view and becomes reclusive, left only with the one working tape of the final *Cathode Narcissus* for company:

> he sat and stared, sinking down deeper and deeper into the mineshaft of his own insanity, where flesh slapped against flesh and the cloacal air was rent by

the groans of the abandoned. He was left alone with the last of the Narcissi whose magical lives had guaranteed his charmed one. (252)

This new, increasingly re-embodied Dorian destroys the final tape, and the firemen and the police who discover his decomposing body 'dealt with the naked bloated body on the floor in a straightforward way' (252-3).

Read in these terms *Dorian* appears to harbour a grand, metaphysically considered, anxiety about mortality, which Castle sees as inaugurated by the late eighteenth-century Gothic. This is a complex issue in the novel because the novel's archness appears to function as a strategy to forestall analysis of it, so that to critically evaluate this narrative about mortality requires an analysis of a textually unconscious complexity that the novel's explicit handling of its issues seems to deny the presence of. The novelist, Devenish, for example, attempts a contextual discussion of homosexuality by stating that 'After all, homosexuality was only defined as a pathology in response to the alleged healthiness of heterosexuality' (212), a view that Wotton regards as academic given the presence of AIDS. Devenish apologises for 'being tactless', but Wotton says that Devenish was not being tactless but was 'merely a plagiarist' because 'not everyone knows fuck all about Foucault' (213). This type of explicitness is also emphasised when Baz, following a comment by William Buckley Junior, refers to gay men as 'the sex that will not shut up' (86), which is in calculated contrast with, as Alderson has noted, Alfred Douglas's 'the love that dare not speak its name' and the covert Queer identities developed in Wilde's *Dorian Gray*.[11]

This representation of explicit or implicit sexualities cannot be separated from the discussion of art. The focus on this chapter has been on Self's novel rather than on how it rewrites Wilde's *Dorian Gray*, because the emphasis of the enquiry is on the late twentieth century. However, it is useful at this juncture to bring Wilde into the argument briefly because his interest in aesthetics provides another context for reading art in *Dorian*. Michael Foldy has explored how Wilde's aesthetics were indebted to classical concepts relating to how Platonic ideas contrasted with an Aristotelian notion of inherent form.[12] Wilde rejects Platonic ideas because the notion of an Ideal form which ghosts all artistic endeavours implies that the artist is imposed upon, rather than actively searching for, new forms of artistic expression. An Aristotelian concept of art helps to support the Wildean metaphysic which challenged conventional ideas about art and asserted the fundamentally creative, because ultimately transgressive, status of the artist. The idea of an inherent form also enabled Wilde to imply a discrete homosexual presence which he could simply conceal, as he did during his trials, by stating that *Dorian Gray* was 'just' about art (such as Shakespeare's sonnets).[13] Wilde could thus be strategically ambiguous about such matters, in which a non-Platonic notion of art became the vehicle through which to challenge convention *and* conceal an inherent queer identity politics that he could deny the presence of through asserting a proto-postmodernist 'Art for Art's Sake' attitude that suggested that it was, in reality, all about surfaces. Wilde might be regarded as thus making a virtue of necessity in which the prosecution's pursuit of 'depth' is repelled by giving primacy to the 'surface'. For Bruhm this means that Wilde's writing 'closes off the possibility of a Neo-Platonic surface-depth dichotomy, it presents surfaces in a way that implicates them in the notion of depth' (64-5). Bruhm's more general commentary on Narcissus also suggests ways in which Self's novel can be explored, in a myth which subjects 'male cultural hierarchy' or 'his phallic oneness' to an act of 'division, multiplication, and a melancholia that is always homoerotic' (19), and this illustrates how, as discussed earlier, 'straight culture' of a certain kind comes to project anxieties about death on to a model of an allegedly moribund gay culture.[14] Narcissus thus becomes a conceit for loss. However, as outlined at the beginning of this chapter, this is not straightforwardly about death as a form of loss, it is also about a loss of meaning that is suggested in Self's particular view of postmodern art. Narcissus thus, paradoxically, represents at another level a desire for self-presence in a world conditioned by postmodern absence even whilst Narcissus (rendered in postmodern terms) suggests the impossibility of such presence. Such tensions between presence and absence become repeated throughout the novel as an unresolvable dialectic.

In *Dorian* it is, however, the very explicitness about debates on art which attempt to negate any hidden, subversive, narrative. Dorian, for example, at one point joins a beach party, described as a 'colloquy of modern Platonists' (110), and he can join them because he, too, represents an Ideal form. *Dorian* is thus a novel which explores the idea of surface within a *milieu* that is explicit about issues of identity so that, paradoxically, there are no obviously hidden depths because everything is in the open. Wotton, however, represents the insistent presence of the past, and the body. These are the hidden narratives of *Dorian* and *Cathode Narcissus* as both attempt, problematically and unsuccessfully, to depoliticise a metaphorics of death that is represented by an AIDS culture, but which nevertheless transcends that culture.[15]

These issues about death are also addressed in the Epilogue, which suggests that Wotton has correctly, if symbolically, identified an amorality which defines Dorian. Wotton's voice repeatedly enters into Dorian's consciousness and at one point tells him to look up the German word for uncanny. Freud's idea that the uncanny concerns a 'return of the dead' (364), is literalised when Dorian sees Wotton and they go for a walk, only for Wotton to turn into Ginger, who in Wotton's narrative held Dorian accountable for the death of his friend Herman. Ginger becomes Freud's 'uncanny harbinger of death' (357) as he slits Dorian's throat in a public toilet.

Dorian is not so much a queer Gothic novel as an ideological reading of the queer Gothic. Self's version of queer Gothic asserts the presence of an identity politics which, in its insistence on a grand (if implicit) debate about life and death, tends to obscure (because it redirects) the politics of the queer Gothic. Ultimately, the central anxiety in *Dorian* concerns a fear of death in a secular culture. This is not a fear which asserts Burke's sublime Terror, but one which indicates that such anxieties can only appear obliquely within a narrative form which wants to abject such fears. The body, its passing pleasures and susceptibility to decay, and how to represent that in a postmodern age, constitute its main preoccupation, even whilst its displacement of these anxieties on to gay culture enacts a homophobia that reveals that Self speaks from an introjected cultural centre which is both heteronormative and fearful of its possible passing.

NOTES

1 Terry Castle, 'The Spectralization of the Other in *The Mysteries of Udolpho*', in *The Female Thermometer: Eighteenth-Century Culture and the Invention of the Uncanny* (Oxford: Oxford University Press, 1995), pp. 120–39 at p. 136. See also Philippe Ariès, *The Hour of Our Death*, trans. Helen Weaver (New York: Alfred A. Knopf, 1981).

2 Sigmund Freud, 'The "Uncanny"', in *Art and Literature: Jensen's Gradiva, Leonardo Da Vinci and other works*, in *The Penguin Freud Library*, vol. 14, trans James Strachey, ed. Albert Dickson (Harmondsworth: Penguin, 1985), p. 364. All subsequent references are to this edition, and are given in parentheses in the text.

3 David Alderson, '"Not Everyone Knows Fuck All about Foucault": Will Self's *Dorian* and Post-Gay Culture', *Textual Practice*, 19/3 (2005), 309–10 at p. 310. All subsequent references are to this edition, and are given in parentheses in the text.

4 Will Self, *Dorian* (London: Viking/Penguin, 2002), p. 39. All subsequent references are to this edition, and are given in parentheses in the text.
5 Steven Bruhm, *Reflecting Narcissus: A Queer Aesthetic* (Minneapolis: University of Minnesota Press, 2000), p. 174. All subsequent references are to this edition, and are given in parentheses in the text.
6 Susan Sontag, 'Notes on Camp', in *A Susan Sontag Reader* (New York: Vintage Books, 1983), pp. 105–19 at p. 117.
7 Thomas A. King, 'Performing "Akimbo": Queer Pride And Epistemological Prejudice', in Moe Meyer (ed.), *The Politics and Poetics of Camp* (London: Routledge, 1994), pp. 23–50 at p. 24. All subsequent references are to this edition, and are given in parentheses in the text.
8 Julia Kristeva, *Powers of Horror: An Essay on Abjection* (New York: Columbia University Press, 1982), p. 3. All subsequent references are to this edition and are given in parentheses in the text.
9 Will Self, 'Damien Hirst: A Steady Iron-Hard Jet', first published in *Modern Painters*, Summer 1994, reprinted in *Junk Mail*, (Harmondsworth: Penguin, 1995), pp. 285–94 at p. 286. All subsequent references are to this edition, and are given in parentheses in the text.
10 George E. Haggerty, *Queer Gothic* (Urbana and Chicago: University of Illinois Press, 2006), p. 196. All subsequent references are to this edition, and are given in parentheses in the text.
11 See Alderson, 'Not Everyone Knows …', p. 310.
12 Michael Foldy, *The Trials of Oscar Wilde: Deviance, Morality, and Late-Victorian Society* (New Haven: Yale University Press, 1997), pp. 110–16. See also Oscar Wilde, 'The Critic as Artist', in *The Complete Works of Oscar Wilde*, ed. G. F. Maine (London: Collins, 1992), pp. 948–98.
13 See the quotation from the relevant trial transcript in Richard Ellmann, *Oscar Wilde* (Harmondsworth: Penguin, 1987), p. 422.
14 Bruhm, *Reflecting Narcissus*, p. 9.
15 Issues about mortality had earlier concerned Self in 'The North London Book of the Dead' from *The Quantity Theory of Insanity* (Harmondsworth: Penguin, 1991), and his novel *How the Dead Live* (New York, Grove Press: 2000). 'The North London Book of the Dead' focuses on the death of the narrator's mother from cancer, accounting for it in such a way that it suggests the type of transformation in identity that Dorian is also subject to. The narrator notes that 'Her self-consciousness, sentience, identity, what you will, was cornered, forced back by the cloud [the cancer] into a confined space' (1). However, the dead simply move to Crouch End (a somewhat unfashionable part of London – in *How the Dead Live* they move to 'Dulston' a fictitious area in north London), and resume their lives. At one level this is obviously meant to be comedic, but it does suggest a strange immortality in which 'There are lots of dead people in London and quite a few dead businesses … Most dead people

have jobs, some work for live companies' (11). A tale in the same collection, 'Waiting', suggests that, in a televisual age, people have become immune to concerns about death: 'In the past, the ending of an era, of even a century, was viewed with great fear ... The end of this current era will ... be met at worst with indifference and at best with some quite good television retrospectives' (186). Death and responses to it thus constitute a strand in Self's writing that in *Dorian* is developed both in the main narrative (Wotton's tale) and in the Epilogue.

Index

abjection 123-4, 126, 129, 131, 135, 136, 167, 184-5
AIDS 69, 142, 178, 180-1, 185, 187, 188, 189
Alderson, David 179, 183
androgyny 17
anti-Semitism 59, 69

Beckford, William 2, 15, 21, 22, 27, 30, 31
   Vathek, 14, 15, 24, 27, 29, 30, 32
bestiality 19, 23
bisexuality 83, 102, 147-8, 151
blackmail 57, 58
Botting, Fred 39, 46
Brite, Poppy Z. 2, 3, 124, 134
   Lost Souls 132, 138, 145-56
   Love in Vein 132
Bruhm, Stephen 12, 182, 185, 189
Byron, Lord 49

Califia, Pat 124, 134, 137
   'The Vampire' 133, 136, 138
camp 2-3, 37, 183, 185
Carter, Angela
   'The Company of Wolves' 129, 138
   The Passion of the New Eve 13
Castle, Terry 57, 177, 178, 188
childhood 147-8, 153, 158-9, 169-70, 174
closet homosexuality 2, 143, 144, 151, 156n.1

Coleridge, S. T.
   'Christabel' 12-13
Collins, Wilkie, 67
   The Woman in White 65, 68
'coming out' 66
cross-dressing 16, 17, 18, 19, 26, 27, 30, 119, 128

danse macabre 159-60, 161, 163, 165, 169, 171, 174
Davison, Carol Margaret 59
Dean, Tim 31
degeneration 59, 75, 145
Douglas, Lord Alfred 22, 23, 188
   'Two Loves' 21-2, 188
du Maurier, George
   Trilby 74, 77, 79

Edelman, Lee 162-3, 173, 174
effeminacy 75
Eliot, George 57, 60, 64, 67, 69
   Adam Bede 68
   Daniel Deronda 55-70 *passim*
   Middlemarch 57-8, 64, 68
   The Mill on the Floss 57-8
   'The Lifted Veil' 57

Feher-Gurewich, Judith 31
female Gothic 107, 108, 113, 120, 145
Forrest, Katherine 134, 139
   'O Captain, My Captain' 133, 137-8
Forster, E. M. 89, 90, 91, 96, 100, 101
   Alexandria 89

INDEX

Maurice 91
A Passage to India 89–102 *passim*
Foucault, Michel 23, 32, 39, 106, 114, 188
   The History of Sexuality: An Introduction 14, 22, 29–30, 36, 37, 43–4, 134
   'What is Enlightenment?' 31
Freud, Sigmund
   Beyond the Pleasure Principle 160–2, 167–9, 171
   Three Essays 22
   Totem and Taboo 19, 20–1
   'The Uncanny' 177, 190
   'The Wolf Man' 129

G, Amelia 124
   'Wanting' 133, 137–8
Gomez, Jewelle 2, 135, 138
Goth 3
Greven, David 38
Gubar, Susan 5

Haggerty, George E. 16, 29, 186–7
Hall, Donald E. 4
Hall, Lesley 74–5
Hammer Films 125
Hinduism 92, 93, 94
Hirst, Damien 184, 185–6, 187
Hogle, Jerrold E. 28
homophobia 37, 42, 43, 51, 69, 102, 105, 106, 142, 145, 178

incest, 16, 17, 19, 23–4, 25, 27, 49, 149, 150, 151
Ireland, W. H.
   The Abbess 24
Islam 92, 96, 99

Jackson, Michael 158–74 *passim*
   Michael Jackson's Ghosts 159, 169–74
   Thriller 159, 163–9, 170, 173
   You Are Not Alone 174
Jackson, Rosemary 49, 133
'Jewdar' 63

Judaism 55–70 *passim*

Keesey, Pam 2,
   Dark Angels 12
   Daughters of Darkness 136
   Women Who Run with the Werewolves 129
King, Stephen
   Salem's Lot 143
Kristeva, Julia 123–4, 127, 132, 136, 184–5

Lacan, Jacques 19, 28, 61, 115
   Écrits 19–20
   'Kant with Sade' 29
   Seminar 1 21–2
Landis, John
   American Werewolf in London 166–7
   Thriller 159, 163–9, 170, 173
Le Fanu, Joseph Sheridan 59,
   'Carmilla' 12, 125–6
   In A Glass Darkly 73
lesbian Gothic 105, 107, 123–39 *passim*
lesbianism 26, 57, 100, 102, 105–20 *passim*, 126, 135–6, 147–8
   and feminism 135
Lewis, Matthew 21, 22, 24, 27–8, 31
   The Monk 14, 16–17, 18, 23, 24, 25, 26, 27, 28, 29, 30, 32, 108

masturbation 60, 74–5, 79–80, 101, 109
Maturin, Charles
   Melmoth the Wanderer 17–19, 24, 26, 27, 29, 48, 55, 56, 64, 112
Meyer, Moe 31
Miles, Robert 13, 16
Miller, D. A. 44

necrophilia 23
Norton, Rictor 13

O'Brien, Richard,
   The Rocky Horror Picture Show 11

INDEX

perversion 21, 23, 29, 37, 41
pornography 73, 77, 169
Protestantism 21, 28, 113, 114
psychoanalysis 19–22, 28, 61, 109, 123–4, 128, 161–3, 167–9, 171, 173, 177, 190

queer cinema 12
queer theory 4, 123, 124–5, 127

Radcliffe, Ann 107
   The Italian 13, 14
   The Mysteries of Udolpho 13, 14, 113, 177
   The Romance of the Forest 13
   A Sicilian Romance 13, 14
Rice, Anne 2, 124
   Interview with the Vampire 12, 143–4, 149, 150
Roche, Regina
   The Children of the Abbey 24
Roman Catholicism, 17, 21, 24–5, 26, 28, 105–6, 107–8, 109, 113, 114, 115, 118, 119
   clerical celibacy 17, 18–19, 25–6

sadomasochism 118, 135, 136, 152
scientia sexualis 22, 30, 32, 73–7 *passim*, 82, 84, 99–100, 188
Sedgwick, Eve Kosofsky 14, 27–8, 37, 38, 42, 55–6, 58, 61, 69, 112, 113, 116
Self, Will
   Dorian 12, 177–90 *passim*
semen 148, 149, 152, 181
sensation fiction 59, 65
sexology
   see scientia sexualis
Shelley, Mary 50
   adaptations of *Frankenstein* 50–1
   Frankenstein 36–51 *passim*
Sinfield, Alan 73
sodomy 23, 24, 25, 30, 42, 44, 45, 51, 74, 75, 77, 143, 152

Stenbock, Eric, Count
   'The True Story of a Vampire', 74, 77–8, 79, 81, 83, 84
Stevenson, Robert Louis 22
   Dr Jekyll and Mr Hyde 32, 43, 94
Stoker, Bram 2, 22
   Dracula 11, 59, 94, 125, 137, 143, 145, 146, 157n.15
Stryker, Susan 4
Sublime, the 46–7, 177

teenagers 147–8, 153, 164, 165, 166
   see also childhood
Tem, Melanie 127–8
   'Mama' 128
   'Wilding' 128, 129–31, 138, 139
transvestism
   see cross-dressing
Tuite, Clara 27

vampire cinema 12, 125
vampires 12, 58–9, 63, 66, 67, 78, 81, 123, 125–6, 127, 132–4, 135, 136–7, 139, 142–56 *passim*

Walpole, Horace 2, 3, 21, 22, 28
   The Castle of Otranto, 15–16, 28, 31
   The Mysterious Mother 14, 16
Warner, Marina 128–9
Weeks, Jeffrey 23
werewolves 127, 128–32, 138, 164, 165, 166–7, 173
Whale, James 11
   Bride of Frankenstein 11
   Frankenstein 11, 45, 46
Wilde, Oscar 3, 22, 23, 48–9, 73, 117, 188
   Dorian Gray 32, 43, 178, 182, 188–9
   Teleny 73, 85
Williams, Anne 13
Winterson, Jeanette
   Sexing the Cherry 13

Žižek, Slavoj 19, 20, 28–9